FAILED TIMES and TWISTED FOLLIES
True Adventures of a Princes Boy

John E. Carr

Published by DolmanScott in 2022

Copyright©Frank Carr 2022

This edition edited by Margaret Bowden, Em Bee's Editing Services

All rights reserved. No part of this publication may be reproduced, stored in a retrieval system, or transmitted in any form or by any means, electronic, mechanical, photocopy, recording or otherwise, without prior written permission of the copyright owner. Nor can it be circulated in any form of binding or cover other than that in which it is published and without similar condition including this condition being imposed on a subsequent purchaser.

ISBN: 978-1-190-55535-8

Published by
DolmanScott
www.dolmanscott.com

PREAMBLE

This book is intended for my son Francis (Frank), my daughter-in-law Brigid and my granddaughter Caitlin, born in New Zealand on October 1st 2013.

I arrived on Earth on March 8th 1934, the day before the birth of the first orbiting man in space, the pioneering Russian cosmonaut Yuri Gagarin. Hiding somewhere within me lives my whole lifetime's experience of "Failed Times and Twisted Follies", mercilessly waiting to be told. Before it's too late, I share what I can remember here.

****

My son, Francis Louis Carr, was born in New Zealand on January 14th 1966. We only met the first time when he was 21, and from then until the present we have been together a grand total of maybe 10 weeks, so you can see we still hardly know each other. Nor did Francis know his many Australian relations. Until our first meeting, Francis had not even seen photos of other past or present Welch or Carr family members still hanging on in "OZ".[1] In 2013, when I began updating my original scribbled "Follies" from 2010, my son Francis was still a young 47. Frank married Brigid Slykerman, 40, in Auckland New Zealand on November 27th 2010, and I was there for their Antipodean wedding "Down Under". Welcome aboard Brigid! I turned 80 in March 2014 and have just celebrated my 87th birthday (8th March, 2021).

---

[1] The terms "OZ" and "Down Under" are generally slang terms for Australia. But here, "Down Under" refers to New Zealand

Failed Times and Twisted Follies

Brigid Slykerman & Francis Carr united in 2010

My Granddaughter Caitlin and Me

Brigid, Caitlin and Frank

To fill in some of the blank spaces about my rather obscure haphazard life and times before I get the final call, I thought it may be of interest to Francis and his descendants if I put down on paper a few descriptions, mainly for him, of some of the off-the-beaten-track odd places and strange situations in which I have occasionally been involved.

These are mostly short, toilet-visit length true stories – otherwise you may never have a time, place or inclination to read them quietly! – plus a few longer episodes. They are descriptions of real events and stuff-ups.

Peter and Rosemary Cooper in Adelaide, and Richard and Rosemary Chalmers in France, who suggested I was unwittingly in possession of a "font of knowledge" about Africa, as Richard put it, all happened to be interested in seeing the stories I was writing for Francis in New Zealand, presuming these stories would eventually see the light of day. Julie Engel, ensconced in Adelaide, having mistakenly read some of my earlier accounts, also encouraged me to keep scribbling on regardless as a sort of time-consuming, brainless mental therapy. These friends collectively thought my stories may in fact be of a more general interest to a possibly wider global community

– or, at least as far as South Australia is concerned, a much smaller "Princes" (Prince Alfred College/P.A.C.) and/ or "Saints" (St. Peters College/S.P.S.C.) local community

– so they initially encouraged me to keep writing as best I could, completely unedited, ink spots, warts and all. Peter Cooper wrote me a note that I have taken the liberty of using as his unwitting, unintended introduction.

Friends from times and places other than school who live in my memories and appear in my book include my longest-standing old friend John Oliver Brook, as well as "The Sunshine Kid" Ian Murray,

Preamble

Ian "Perce" Campbell, Frank, Geraldine, Ray and Peter Hannan, John and Judy Watts, Peg and Jack Playford Conquest, Geoff, Jessie and Donald Holt on Delmore Downs Station via Alice Springs, and Jack Absalom, who was still hanging on and painting landscapes as good as ever in Broken Hill when I wrote my original version. Jack died, aged 91, in March 2019.

It dawned on me that a lot of my stories were earlier connected to Adelaide's Rose Park Primary school scholars, and later to P.A.C and Saints students, now unfortunately more past than present. I wondered whether the title "Adventures of a Princes Boy", in the case of P.A.C., would be more to the point, so Peter Cooper said he would talk to the Headmaster of P.A.C., Mr. Tutt, to find out. Having absentmindedly read some of the stories, Mr. Tutt mistakenly said without thinking he was not against the idea, and as long as there was nothing suspect, said, "Go ahead".

The stories, in roughly chronological order, are of generally odd-ball topics, set mainly in Australia, Africa, New Zealand[2] and one only in England, and are sadly true accounts of true events. They were first published by my English drinking mate Richard Maxwell Chalmers (and his surprisingly tolerant wife Rosemary), ex the cosmopolitan "Cockatoo Bar" of the Balalaika Hotel in affluent Sandton, a northern suburb of Johannesburg, South Africa. That is the transposed English Chalmers family, now relocated across the English Channel, publishing these "Anglais" stories in France, salivating on frogs' legs and snails, scoffing champagne by the bucket and living in idle luxury. I think. I hope!

****

---

[2] The terms "OZ" and "Down Under" are generally slang terms for Australia. But here, "Down Under" refers to New Zealand

Author's notes: Some of the language reflects terms and concepts used in earlier times. I mean no disrespect to any Indigenous peoples or people who have become accustomed to the use of gender-neutral and politically and culturally correct usage. The language is a true reflection of its time, and my usage and that of my workmates, friends and other characters featured in the stories (including swearing and slang). Verbal exchanges are as I remember them. I talk of measurements and temperatures in miles, yards, feet, inches, tons, pounds (lb), ounces (oz) and degrees Fahrenheit, as well as in decimal system terms (e.g. kilometres), and in some places I talk about money in terms of pounds (£) and shillings (s), as well as dollars ($). Australia changed to a decimal system in 1966.

People in some of the images used to illustrate the stories have died. Their relatives have given me permission to continue to use the images. All photos belong to me unless I have noted otherwise.

Editor's notes: The rough copy updated version of this manuscript was littered with instances of what seemed initially to be strange capitalisations. I realised that John had used capitalisation to emphasise the importance to him of certain people, animals, places and events, and joyous exaggerated descriptions of twisted-beyond- belief follies. These have been left in to add to the impact of the stories, provide insight into John's character and to keep his voice. Hopefully you won't find this use of capitalisation disconcerting. There were other odd capitalisations for which I could detect no reason. These have been edited out to avoid confusion.

Different terms are used interchangeably to denote the same person, thing or place, for example Francis/ Frank, Aborigine/ Aboriginal/ Native, crocodile/ croc, Johannesburg/ Jo'burg, Grandmother/ Grannie/ Nana, in keeping with John's storytelling.

Similarly, strictly grammatical editing would remove the authentic voice, particularly in the retold verbal exchanges, so it has not been applied where it would detract from John's storytelling. Similarly, colourful vernacular remains as spoken.

In relation to language, instances where common expressions of the time would have been very offensive to certain groups of people, and most certainly are now, have been changed to proper terminology or a different description entirely, but denoting the same meaning. I hope this does not detract from the reading.

CONTENTS

ILLUSTRATIONS xiv

INTRODUCTION 1
  1.   MY UNQUALIFIED BACKGROUND 5
  2.   SCHOOL DAZE 8

SOUTH AFRICAN STORIES 1969-1972 13
  3.   MAGALIESBURG 14
  4.   BLUEBIRD FARM 18
  5.   MISS SOUTH AFRICA 20
  6.   SYD JAMES 21
  7.   GREEN AND GOLD 22
  8.   AS CLOSE AS CLOSE COULD BE 26
  9.   BOOMERANG BY STARLIGHT 28
  10. AN UNCANNY COINCIDENCE 31

RHODESIAN STORIES 1972-1977 35
  11. MATEBELELAND 36
  12. ROOFING GUTTERS 40
  13. JOHN MASEKO 44
  14. IRENE MARY NIGHTINGALE 48
  15. AFRICAN DUNG BEETLES 50
  16. ENTEBBE 53
  17. DEVIL'S DICE 57

AN ENGLISH STORY 61
  18. EL-SHERANA PITCHBLENDE 62

BOTSWANA STORIES (FORMERLY THE BRITISH BECHUANALAND PROTECTORATE OR B.P.) 69
  19. A SHOWER OF SPARKS 70

20.	THE SHINAMBA HILLS TRACK	74
21.	LIONS: IT HAPPENS	76
22.	SIESTA INTERRUPTUS	78
23.	CATTLE COUNTRY LIONS OF NATA	80

EVENTS IN 'OZ' 89

24.	GERMS AND OTHER ADULT "CRAP"	90
25.	DAISY BATES 1941	94
26.	DIAMOND JIM 1943	96
27.	JOHNNIE SNOWBALL 1946	97
28.	HOME AGAIN 1947	99
29.	KLEINEBOOFYHAUSEN 1948	101
30.	THE ROCKET'S RED GLARE 1948	106
31.	KYM BONYTHON AND THE YELLOW SUBMARINE	109
32.	THE SUPERGUN 1950	111
33.	DELMORE DOWNS 1950	113
34.	THE GHAN 1950	118
35.	ALICE SPRINGS AND DARWIN 1950	122
36.	A MEANS TO AN END: DARWIN 1950	127
37.	GROUND LEVEL 1951	129
38.	COLT 45 1951	135
39.	T. S. PEARCE 1951	137
40.	HAND SIGNALS 1952	140
41.	A MATTER OF MANNERS	143
42.	GHAN AGAIN, MINING AND EL-SHERANA DISCOVERY 1954	145
43.	MONTY O'SULLIVAN: THE FULL STORY 1954	156
44.	URANIUM WAR OF '54	159
45.	FRUIT SALAD 1955	164
46.	WHISTLECOCK 1955	176
47.	CAVENAGH WATERS 1955	179
48.	A STALKING LESSON 1955	181
49.	YATUNGKA AND WARRI 1955	189
50.	BANYAN BILLABONG 1955	201
51.	CARRICKALINGA 1960	207

52.	THE ALMANDA MINE 1960	209
53.	ROBBIE CHAPMAN 1960	212
54.	GREAT WHITES CEDUNA 1960	215
55.	THE VESPER CELESTE	223
56.	THE BUTCHERS' PICNIC 1960	232
57.	GREAT WHITES, SUBURBAN ADELAIDE 1962	235
58.	NOTORYCTES TYPHLOPS 1962	240
59.	TUMBLING TURDS 1962	244
60.	POEPEL'S PEG 1962	251
61.	DONALD CAMPBELL 1962	254
62.	BILBIES 1966	258
63.	A GOOD BIG BLOKE 1966	262
64.	MARBLE BAR 1966	264
65.	GOLD TO BE GOT	265
66.	CIRCUMCISIONS AND A DESERT CHOPPER 1966	269
67.	METEORITES	275
68.	LASSETER'S REEF 1968	278
69.	STAN BRIDGMAN 1968	282
70.	DISSUASION 1968	286
71.	TASMANIAN BUSH 1977	290
72.	ECHIDNA VENGEANCE 1978	294
73.	THE SUNSHINE KID 1981	296
74.	THE SAME QUESTION 1981	302
75.	THE MUTT (CIRCA 2000)	304
76.	VAN DE MERWE 2010	305
77.	WHIMSICAL: A POEM OF SORTS FOR DREAMERS 2010	307
78.	THE "CARR-B-Q" BUSH BARBECUE APPARATUS: BACKGROUND OF THE ALMOST ENDED STORY	311

THE ABSOLUTE END! 341

79.	MEMORIES OF MY FATHER, JOHN EDWIN CARR	342
80.	JOHN CARR: EULOGY	346
81.	ROGER KLOBE *(by Frank Carr)*	350

ILLUSTRATIONS

BRIGID SLYKERMAN & FRANCIS CARR UNITED IN 2010 iv

MY GRANDDAUGHTER CAITLIN AND ME v

BRIGID, CAITLIN AND FRANK v

AN INQUISITIVE VISITOR IN THE TREE OUTSIDE
THE WINDOW OF MY CARAVAN AT GWABEGAR NEW
SOUTH WALES, 2010 3

ME, ROBERT TEMME, SANDRA RICHARDSON,
ROSEMARY COOPER AND PETER COOPER AT COOPERS
NEW BREWERY 4

PETER AND ROSEMARY COOPER AND ME AT A LOCAL
BURNSIDE RESTAURANT 4

ME, MY MOTHER DOROTHY AND MY SISTER PAMELA, 1937 .. 5

IN THE HALLWAY OF OUR OLD HOUSE AT
BURNSIDE IN 1948 6

ME WITH A KUDU SHOT AT JOHN BAWDEN'S INSIZA
RANCH IN RHODESIA, FOR CONVERSION TO "BILTONG"
IN THE KITCHEN 17

ELEPHANT DUNG WAITING FOR DUNG BEETLES 52

RICHARD CHALMERS AND DAUGHTER SOPHIE 63

TREENA ENGEL'S MOUNTED LION CLAW BROOCH 77

ME ON ROBIN	100
CONNELLAN AIRWAYS BAGGAGE LABEL	132
OUTBACK ADVENTURE FLYING CONNELLAN AIRWAYS	132
CONNELLAN AIRWAYS NORTHERN TERRITORY ROUTE MAP, 1955	133
MOUNT ISA MINES – ME, STAN TRCKA AND LOTHA TISCHMAN IN 1954	147
EARTHEN TERMITE MOUND AND ME, ARNHEM LAND, 1954	155
FRUIT SALAD EXPLOSION	172
BAREFOOT HUGHIE, THE UNFORTUNATE DINGO AND ME, 1955	188
YATUNGKA WITH CHILD, ME, WARRI WITH BANDAGED FINGER	194
WARRI HUNTING WITH A SPEAR AND WOOMERA	195
ME WITH MY PRIZED CROCODILE, BANYAN BILLABONG 1955	206
A GREAT WHITE "SMILING" SHARK	208
ME, MY RUBBER-POWERED SPEARGUN AND AN UNFORTUNATE EAGLE RAY, MINUS TAIL. SNAPPER POINT, SOUTH AUSTRALIA	236

NOTORYCTES TYPHLOPS AND ITS ZIG-ZAG TAIL-MARKED TRAIL IN THE RED DESERT SAND 243

KEN WARBY SETTING A NEW WORLD RECORD ON BLOWERING DAM, 1978 257

ME HOLDING THE ELUSIVE YEEDARRADOO (BILBY/ RABBIT EARED BANDICOOT) 261

IAN MURRAY IN FRONT OF A BOAB TREE AT TIMBER CREEK, ON THE VICTORIA RIVER, NORTHERN TERRITORY 1981 300

IAN BURNING RUBBISH IN HIS GARDEN AT MITTAGONG ABOUT 2005 301

ME WITH MY PAINTING OF OZ 306

BUTCHERING FOR MEAT; A CULLED ELEPHANT IN THE WANKIE GAME RESERVE 315

ARTHUR WARD AND ME AT LAKE PEDDER TASMANIA, ABOUT 1980 325

ARTHUR WARD, JOHN CARR, AND ARTHUR'S DAUGHTERS AT REAR, AND JUNE AND ROB, WHO ACTUALLY NAMED MY B.B.Q. THE CARR-B-Q. (I OWE YOU ONE ROB) 326

ARTHUR WARD USING A CARR-B-Q AT AIRLIE BEACH QLD IN 1981 326

MOUNT WELLINGTON BEHIND HOBART, A VIEW FROM MY HOUSE AT BLACKMANS BAY 328

HOBART MERCURY PHOTO OF THE CARR-B-Q AND
ME IN 1979..329

SQUASHED FLAT CARR-B-QS ON ARRIVAL IN ALICE
SPRINGS, 1981 338

DR DALLAS CLARK, OF NORWOOD USING THE ORIGINAL
MODEL CARR-B-Q AT HIS HOLIDAY SHACK SOMEWHERE
NEAR THE MURRAY RIVER 340

INTRODUCTION

It was that phone call and the unknown voice saying, "Hello Tig", that threw my mind back over 50 years.

****

Only close relations still called me by my nickname, but I knew this was no relation. After a few words (and in-depth thinking) I said, "Is that John?" The amazed caller said, "Yes it is". More amazed was myself, as I had not seen John since our departing from school days at Prince Alfred College (P.A.C.) in 1950.

One thing led to another and he ended up visiting us from Gwabegar in outback New South Wales. We chatted a while and went out to dinner. John was staying at another friend's place for a few days, so for old times' sake we arranged a trip to oversee "Coopers NEW Brewery", as John used to live opposite Fernilee Lodge (a Cooper family home) on Greenhill Road in Adelaide, and his family had many ties with our Cooper family. It was a great afternoon, and reminiscing was the topic of conversation until we began to hear some of John's adventures.

John was always a wild one; always doing unusual things like taking reptiles to school in his kitbag. Later in life he was to travel Australia, New Zealand, England and Africa, not as a tourist but as an adventurer, travelling the wild outback of those countries and working in situations that can only now be described as dangerous.

This man is now retired but holds a magnificent vocabulary of English diction. When our meeting came to an end I said to John, "You have an excellent way of expressing yourself, why don't you write a book?" He then told me he had actually started with a couple of episodes, and would I like to look at them to see if they were presentable? Time passed and a few weeks later I received a large envelope in the post, enclosing John's notes; just a few short stories that stunned me with the awe of how I knew John could describe things. Imagine his descriptions of the rest of the world he has so-far explored!

I lost my father when I was only 17, with only one year remaining at school, then out into the world of hard knocks to survive; that was hard for me. John lost his father much earlier[3] and was determined to find out "the hard way" what made this big world tick. John still has a sister Pamela who went to P.G.C. (Seymour) with my sister Boronia, in Adelaide.

We wish John well and hope he can keep the stories initially entitled "FAILED TIMES and TWISTED FOLLIES" coming forth.

Regards and best wishes,
Peter and Rosemary Cooper
November 18th 2009.

---

[3] John had never met his father until after 1979 and his father died in 1987

Introduction

An inquisitive visitor in the tree outside the window of my caravan at Gwabegar New South Wales, 2010

Me, Robert Temme, Sandra Richardson, Rosemary Cooper and Peter Cooper at Coopers New Brewery

Peter and Rosemary Cooper and Me at a local Burnside restaurant

1.
MY UNQUALIFIED BACKGROUND

I grew up in an all-female household without the benefit of any experienced male advice or guidance readily at hand relating to my forthcoming irresponsible life and times ahead.

Me, my mother Dorothy and my sister Pamela, 1937

Halfway through my Intermediate year in 1950, I was enticed to leave school by Gary Wight (P.A.C.) and join News Ltd. as a copy boy at £2 a week. This was the year before young Rupert Murdoch, about a year or two older than me, was installed by his father at the News to begin clawing his way up the long ladder to success. RUPERT, I am sure, WOULD HAVE BEEN PAID a bit MORE THAN £2 a WEEK!

Over the years I have been a commercial traveller for Kodak and Bleakly Photographics (Canon Cameras, Aldis 35 mm projectors etc.), Chubb Safes, Polaroid Sunglasses and Knoll Laboratories, and managed Hannan Brothers Marine, the South Australian Evinrude Outboard Motor dealers in 1949/ 50.

In the hallway of our old house at Burnside in 1948

I found myself increasingly involved in mineral mining and/or exploration activities in Australia, New Zealand, Botswana and Rhodesia, interspersed with selling Toyotas in South Africa. I worked for Northern Uranium Development (later to become part of Uranium Mines N.L.) when we discovered the rich El-Sherana Uranium Mine in 1954.

The next year, 1955, I was with Geosurveys of Australia in the extreme North-West corner of South Australia and adjoining Western Australia.

Introduction

Later I joined the Western Mining Corporation, mainly for activities in the Warburton Ranges area of Western Australia, and at Mt Camel, not far, surprisingly, from Melbourne in Victoria. I worked underground on the Lake Manapouri hydro-electric project in New Zealand, Peko Gold Mines at Tennant Creek in the Northern Territory, Mt Isa Mines in Queensland, and for six months under contract underground at the large mines at Shabani in Rhodesia, Africa, operated by African Associated Asbestos. This dangerous occupation, on reflection, has understandably concerned me somewhat ever since.

I suppose the good thing is I have a good retentive memory and although I stuffed around a fair bit in other ways, these events and diverse occupations at least qualify me to write a book or two of sorts, in this my 80th year,[4] so here goes!

---
[4] This refers to the manuscript updated in 2013

2.
SCHOOL DAZE

Presbyterian Girls College (P.G.C.), where my older sister was a boarder in 1938. John Brook (Scots College) and Don Brown (P.A.C.).

Rose Park Primary school 1939-47, from where many fellow students went on to either P.A.C. ("Princes") or Saint Peters College ("Saints"). For me it was form 4B at P.A.C. in 1948.

John "Pug" Keeves was a well-liked teacher and it was a good year. I did well at English, History, Geography and Drawing; minor science moments after adding carbide to the ink wells; Chemistry under "Chops" Cleland; moments of confusion in Physics – "for every action" etc. – and hopelessness at Maths.

Because I was twice as fast as the rest of the class at climbing the rope in Claude Bennett's gym (of Alaskan Klondike Gold Rush fame) – I didn't use my feet … they were a hindrance to a Monkey – my classmates showed me their undeniable respect by calling me "THE APE" from that moment on.

"Yarra Brae" Wonga Park, on the River Yarra near the Dandenong Ranges in Victoria – the 1948 World Scout Jamboree, led by "Pug" Keeves, the P.A.C. Scout Master. A boy scout tragically drowned in the River Yarra during the jamboree. A visit to the State Theatre in Melbourne to see "Paleface" starring Bob Hope and sexy Jane Russell.

Rowing on the Torrens. I was stroke of a "four"; Frank Froelich (ex-Hungary) as coach, Warren Litchfield as a cox and a rower a couple of years later. Rowing camps at Murray Bridge. Frank Beauchamp and his aunt's café. Aquaplaning on the Murray. Peter Tanner failing badly when trying to pick up a threepenny piece from the top of an upturned dry, powdery, loose-moulded flour cake with his teeth; as it seems, his face somehow detached and fell in!

The school chaplain "Redleg" Perry asking at morning assembly if anyone was interested in nursing a Kookaburra with a damaged wing, followed by a unanimous exclamation from the seated assembly of "Carr, Sir!"

Another day I had a small brown snake in a coin bag in my satchel. I had shown it to a few of the other students and was now sitting quietly in class when Kerry Griff from Broken Hill suddenly called out to the teacher "Tagger" Luke, "Sir! CARR'S GOT A SNAKE IN HIS BAG".

Tagger said, "Shut up Griff", then turned to me and said, "CARR, HAVE YOU GOT A SNAKE IN YOUR BAG?" I said, "Yes sir", and Tagger said, "GET OUT and don't come back until you've got rid of it!" So I simply went home early. (It was NOT a hard act to follow).

School holidays. Bruce Greenslade, Urania, York Peninsula, his father Fred and his very large Aussie stamp collection. Bird's egg collecting and especially a visit to the very last of the magnificent steel hulled three- and four-masted sailing ships; the great windjammers the "Pamir" and the "Passat". The great ships, almost the last of their breed, moored for loading in deep water well away from the shallow jetty; loading hand-sewn, manual-humped, bag-hook grabbed and handled bagged wheat from small boats or "lighters" at Port Victoria on South Australia's rich, grain-endowed York Peninsula. The great sailing ships later raising anchor manually by windlass, four strong men to four great wooden spokes of a hand-turned capstan and setting sail by compass with a hopeful breeze in harness off the quarter.

South into the Roaring Forties and further South again below Tasmania and the latitude of our sister country New Zealand. Then South of South again below the regular Howling Winds, below 50- and 60-degrees

Failed Times and Twisted Follies

South latitude and the seemingly perpetual whitecaps, strongly under sail with the kindly caring ghosts of the "Ancient Mariner" and his "Wandering Albatross" looking on from somewhere strategic high above the highest yardarm.

This was but a few years before the sad demise of our present contemporary, rapidly- declining albatross population, not at the hands of the Ancient Mariner and his crossbow, but on one of hundreds of miles of long lines of barbed, baited, stainless- steel, everlasting fish hooks, forever drifting, many lost and unattended, left enticingly in the great, lumpy, heaving, frigid waters of crowded fragile planet Earth's one and only globe-encircling Great Southern Ocean.

Sailing on across the great width of the South Pacific, West to East, below and around Tierra Del Fuego and the treacherous tip of Cape Horn, below the cold southern tip of South America and up the full length of the South Atlantic Ocean; perhaps becalmed hauntingly somewhere in Samuel Coleridge's "Painted Ship Upon its Painted Ocean" in the solitude of the equatorial doldrums; and finally over the imaginary equatorial hump and the illusory, sometimes weed-entangled Sargasso Sea before again picking up the freshening winds of the North Atlantic, then all being well, breezing back to overcrowded Europe – its many tongues, its many flags and its many choked, crowded and polluted international waters.

Meanwhile, still at home, Walter Brown senior, Don and Wally Brown junior, Beachport, South-East. Rabbit shooting. Lake George. "Jack" Salmon, Mick Peters, the matter of the disappearing sweetened condensed milk and Mick's unusual Lake George, fully-immersed, lifeless "rabbit" Jack Salmon "berley",[5] with UNUSUAL BLACK FEATHERS, A LONG NECK AND A RED BEAK NOT SEEN BY ME ON A RABBIT BEFORE OR SINCE!

---

[5] Fishing attracting bait released steadily into the water

The crunch came at Christmas 1949, just after we had strained our hearts out at rowing training at Murray Bridge. At the very last instant, the forthcoming annual "Head of the River" rowing race between "Princes" and "Saints" was abruptly cancelled due to possible health reasons. There was a perceived risk of increasing our chances of contracting highly contagious "poliomyelitis" from the current outbreak. As far as we were concerned, having already trained our guts out, it was like closing the door long after the horse had bolted.

Another P.A.C. schoolteacher, "Tex" Dillon. A surviving prisoner of brutal treatment at the heavy hands of his Japanese captors at Changi prisoner of war camp in Singapore in World War 2.

The later inevitable and well-deserved unfortunate meeting of the seat of my pants with the large, size 12 sole of a sandshoe in the quiet and peaceful solitude of his study for being cheeky.

"Pass the book!" (Don Brown was there and witnessed at close hand this isolated episode. He may still retain somewhere indelible memories of this long forgettable event).

Teacher "Tich" Allen; his love of music and his ongoing fascination with the crystal clear, haunting "Trumpet Serenade". Or was it the "Trumpet Voluntary" whose crystal- clear notes still linger on, tantalising in my slowly-slipping, sliding, downhill memory?

Student names like Donnel Shepley, Brian Dalton, Gary Wight, Neville Thomas, Don and Wally Brown, Bill and Carl Menz, Malcolm and Peter Cooper, John and Stan Schofield, Warren Litchfield, Peter Fisher, Ben Smith, Ian Burridge, Bruce and John Greenslade, Brenton Wandke, James "Tweedy" Wilson, Frank Beauchamp, Dean Smoker, Mick Perry, Bob Hamilton (tragically drowned in the normally dry Todd River in Alice Springs), Michael Faraday and Sam Humble, most of whom I haven't seen for more than 63 years, for some unknown innate reason still come to mind.

P.A.C school master "Tinny" Steele, his son Des and his souped up "racing" B.S.A. Bantam motorbike, and his sister, my very dear friend Patricia ("Tric"), who I introduced to my close friend John Brook of Scots College, and whom she married, much later divorced, married another and sadly passed away shortly after in 1983, aged 49.

Some of these brief memories may still strike a chord with my RAPIDLY- DIMINISHING, TENUOUSLY-SURVIVING, AGING CONTEMPORARIES; even the still-outstanding Trumpet Voluntary/Trumpet Serenade puzzle. One of you older, still- standing, waffling-on old codgers may even yet provide the answer.

I still remember a few Rose Park Primary school students and others who, mainly by their parents' thoughtless mistake, went on to Saints but still turned out OK. Names such as the four or five Allnut brothers, including Ian Allnut, my contemporary. Also Robbie Chapman, Ian Inwood, Don Young, Malcolm Hodge, Ian Lovegrove, Geoff McCrae, Tony and Guy Mathews, Doug Sabey, Colin and Innes McLeod at Silverton N.S.W., and Tony McIlvride, David and John Engel, David Keenan, Barry Waterman ("Wartz"), Michael "Rajah" Imray, John Faraday (whose twin brother Michael went to Princes), John Padfield, Ron Waxman, and Robert, Ian and Dr Paul Temme. These are but a few Saints' names who, after 63 vanished years, sometimes aimlessly come to mind.

SOUTH AFRICAN STORIES 1969-1972

3.
MAGALIESBURG

It was late 1969. I had only been in Johannesburg South Africa a couple of weeks and had no idea about the layout of the surrounding countryside.

I looked at various tourist maps and guides, and it seemed the tourist attractions were all more-or-less well to the East of "Jo'burg". The Drakensberg Mountains, the Kruger Game Park etc. were all in the direction of the morning sun. There was nothing of interest in the West, which was farmland and the language spoken was mainly Afrikaans, the language of the Boer farmers. If I went there I wouldn't understand a single word spoken. I was also told there was still a bit of resentment lingering against the British following the ANGLO/BOER WAR which had ceased back in 1902. And so, being naturally inquisitive, I WENT THE WRONG WAY – DUE WEST – towards the setting sun on the road towards Mafeking, the scene of Lord Baden Powell's famous "siege" during the war. All this was related somehow to Baden Powell's subsequent worldwide founding of the Boy Scouts and Girl Guides movement of which I had earlier been a member (Linden Park and P.A.C. scout groups) back home in Adelaide.

On the way West I called in on a small town, or "Dorp", called Magaliesburg, where I entered the local pub. It was a Saturday afternoon and I couldn't hear a single word of spoken English. I drank with the "flies" for a while when the guy on my left said something to me in Afrikaans. I answered in English saying, "I'm sorry, I can't speak Afrikaans. I'm Australian, I've only been here a couple of weeks". This instantly opened a Pandora's Box. All of a sudden, most of the Afrikaners around wanted to talk to me in good to perfect English.

The suntanned guy on my left said, "I didn't think you were a 'ROOI-NECK'. Your neck's not red enough. Australia hey!" "What's a ROOI-NECK?" I said. "Ah", he said, "if my grandfather laid eyes on a white-skinned, sun-starved man with a pillar box red neck in or out of uniform, he said he was 'MAUSER FODDER'. He was shot on sight. He was without a doubt English. A 'Limey' probably just arrived off the troop ship in Capetown with his giveaway red neck 'trademark' for all to see, telling us exactly who or what he was. Rooi is red in Afrikaans". I was suddenly GLAD IT WAS NOT PRE- 1902! "How do you think you'll go against the Springboks, eh?" I didn't realise the Australian Wallabies Rugby Union team were in South Africa and about to play their first test match against the well-fancied locals. I said, "I honestly don't know, I come from South Australia where we don't play either Rugby Union or Rugby League. We only play Australian Rules football, 18 men a side. It's a very different game".

One thing led to another, and a number of Cane and Cokes and Castle beers later Johnnie Van Rensburg and Frikkie Otto asked if I would like to go to a "BRAAI" on a local farm that night. I asked, "What's a BRAAI?" "Och mon, it's what you would call a BARBECUE". "I'd love to", I answered. I then followed my new-found host to his farm about 10 miles past "Milanis Eye", formerly owned by a man called Pratt. Mr Pratt's chief claim to fame happened the day he tried to stab the South African Prime Minister to death in Cape Town's Parliament House. He was still serving his life sentence in jail.

****

Continuing on to the braai, I had glimpses of African wildlife, mainly impala, a civet cat, a couple of ostriches and a beautiful, spiral-horned greater kudu antelope.

All the farm buildings, called "rondavels", were round in plan, whitewashed, large and small. They were beautifully thatched with natural straw, and decorated with African animal skulls and horns, including a recent Leopard's skull, and the remains of a lion's skull. The lion had been shot nearby at the time of the Anglo/Boer War. The farm garden and lawns were extensive, beautifully kept and well maintained by an overabundance of African gardeners, thanks to inexpensive farm labour readily available at the time.

Through the evening there must have been 40 or 50 guests at the braai. Most of those present seemed to talk English to some extent and I found myself being the odd man out; a minor centre of attention, which wasn't all that hard to take. I FOUND MYSELF ATTRACTED TO A MYSTERIOUS, SHAPELY, LONG BLACK-HAIRED

LADY draped in diamonds and gold who I will always wistfully remember in my imagination as a BARE-BREASTED QUEEN OF SHEBA paying court at the Temple of King Solomon.

Meanwhile, back on earth at the braai, I slowly started on lots of strange and unusual delicacies; Afrikaans sausages, meats and biltong (jerky in the U.S.A.), sosaties (skewered meats) and other unknown-by-me animal products. Not to mention a great selection of South African quality wines, including Nederberg "Hocheimer" and "Late Harvest". Also, a sort of sugar cane-based white rum called "Cane", usually mixed with Coke. And of course, South African-brewed Castle and Rogue beer. But sadly, NOT A DROP OF AUSTRALIAN COOPERS ANYWHERE IN SIGHT.

****

As the red-hot coals of the braai slowly turned to ashes and numbers dwindled, my new-found host suggested that since I had had a bit to drink it would be dangerous driving back 50 miles to Jo'burg late at night. He said I could sleep in one of his many furnished rondavels and drive back safely in the light of day. This made sense to me and

I gratefully accepted his offer, hit the sack and slept like a log. That was my very first African overnighter outside of Johannesburg and my very first, though rather late, experience in a foreign multi-language-speaking community.

I had, by the way, instantly learnt the meaning of a very common Afrikaans expression, "VOETSAK" (piss off!), pronounced "FOOTSAK" in English, which was on everyone's lips and ready for immediate utterance at the drop of a hat. It mainly seemed to be used at the time when addressing layabouts, certain Africans and nuisance dogs in the street.

Me with a kudu shot at John Bawdens Insiza ranch in Rhodesia, for conversion to biltong in the kitchen

4.
BLUEBIRD FARM

I was twisting my way along the winding road near Hekpoort, about 45 miles N.W. of Johannesburg in 1970, and passing by a number of large open fields, one of which contained a large dam, more like a lake, about half a mile wide. From the road, my fisherman's eye was pleased to see a number of fish rising in the very inviting shallows. There was not a house to be seen, nor a soul to ask, and I had in my immediate possession an "Abu" spinning reel and rod ready, hungry and absolutely trembling for action.

Over the fence I went and cast an Abu Sonette lure out 40 yards and hooked a good- sized fish, first cast. It fought hard. It was an American Large Mouth Bass, which I had never seen before, weighing about two pounds. I landed three or four Bass in the next few minutes but was startled by someone calling to me from the road. It was the driver of a large model ROLLS ROYCE limousine, which had quietly crept to a halt beside my Toyota.

Discretion being the better part of valour, I thought "Uh-huh" and guiltily walked up to the driver of the Rolls with my incriminating rod, reel and fish in hand to await my expected verbal execution. He said, "My name is Patterson, I'm the manager of this property, "Bluebird Farm". Lady Oppenheimer the owner is in the car. She requests you desist and move on immediately".

On hearing my answering accent for the first time, he said, "Oh, you're Australian, are you?" I said, "Yes, I've only been here a few weeks. I saw the inviting lake but couldn't see a house anywhere to enquire about getting permission to fish ". At this he said, "Look, if you would like to fish here some time, ring me at Bluebird Farm, it's in the book.

Lady Oppenheimer only comes here occasionally and you can fish in the main lake right in the centre of the farm".

A few weeks later I phoned and he said, "Next Sunday morning will be fine". Bluebird is not a farm; it's a village with its own church, cemetery, a general store, a bakery, a kindergarten, a junior school, a football oval, 20 or 30 house-sized, thatch-roofed rondavels, tennis courts, a hall etc. Two lakes take up a large portion of the "village". The bad news is I only caught one fish in the village. The previous lake, in the isolated paddock, was much better. I didn't fish there again.

About two years later, Lady Ina Oppenheimer was involved in a car accident driving her camper van through the Kruger National Park. Sadly she died from her injuries after a few weeks. Mr Patterson was very fortunate. He inherited the whole of Bluebird Farm, worth millions. Unfortunately, I haven't been back in South Africa since that time to, literally, test the waters!

5.
MISS SOUTH AFRICA

It was EASTER 1970. I was representing the Toyota car company at the Rand Easter Show in the evening and selling Toyotas during the day in the showroom for the Johannesburg distributors, Lawson Motors. Toyota Corona Mark 11 sedans, HI-ACE vans and HI-LUX "bakkies" (utes) were current models being unveiled at the time.

The Rand Easter show was similar to Sydney's Easter extravaganza; a wide marketplace, and anyone and everyone was there. The reigning Miss South Africa was on hand each night of the show wearing her Miss South Africa and Toyota sash. She was Mitzi Standter, a lovely young Afrikaans girl, and we were loosely thrown together on the Toyota stand each night for about ten days. During our breaks we usually had coffee or a sandwich, and I found her very switched on and good to talk to. I was then able to truthfully tell my friends and relations back in Australia that I had coffee with the current Miss South Africa, JUST THE TWO OF US, on a daily basis.

They didn't believe me! A few years later she married, but not much longer after her marriage she was tragically killed in a car accident.

6.
SYD JAMES

About 1970, I popped into the Hyde Park Hotel in Johannesburg's northern reaches in search of a throat-cleansing Castle Ale to tide me over until I got back home to the "SUMMIT CLUB" in up-town Hillbrow. At the time I was selling cars for Danny Alderton at his nearby Craighall Park main showrooms and had just finished my "day at the office".

There was only one guy in the saloon at the time, whose face stuck out like a sore thumb. He was Syd James, partner of Hetti Jaques in the long-running British T.V. "Carry On" series. At the time, we were both on our own and naturally entered into a

casual conversation at the bar. I said I was surprised to see him in South Africa. Even more surprisingly he told me he was actually born here – South African by birth – but had been away a long time in the U.K. and his accent nowadays was 99 percent cockney English. We shared a plate of mixed sandwiches and a couple more drinks at the bar, then I said, "Goodbye Syd". Pleased to have met him and taking a different direction, I headed for home.

7.
GREEN AND GOLD

I grew up in South Australia where "Rugby Union" and "Rugby League" are foreign words. Years later I found myself in South Africa where no one had ever heard of the main Australian football game, AUSSIE RULES. It was readily apparent that Australia and South Africa were worlds apart.

On one occasion in 1970, I heard the Queensland and New South Wales Rugby Union sides, who when united and representing Australia overseas called themselves the "Wallabies," were in Johannesburg and about to play the South African "Springboks" in a test match at Ellis Park. Since I was luckily there, it gave me my first opportunity to see a game of either rugby code.

Rugby seems to be an unusual game in which to unaccustomed eyes the main aim is to steal the ball from your opponent by any means within the rules if you possibly can, or if you can get away with it deceitfully by any other foul, under-hand means short of actual murder. If in a split second the opportunity arises and the umpire is otherwise occupied, KNEE THE OPPOSING PLAYER IN THE BALLS AND IF POSSIBLE TRY

TO GOUGE HIS EYES OUT! This is before you innocently push his face in the mud for a quick underwater drowning if you are somehow submerged under a HEAVY SCRUM of HAIRY, SWEATY ARMS AND GIANT LEGS, while hopefully out of sight of the umpire in an OOZY SEA OF MUD. All this while rubbing sand and grass clippings innocently into his eyes, while punching the opposing captain in the mouth and kidneys at the same time if you suddenly see a fortuitous chance, and he is, by his own stupid mistake, dangerously close at hand!

The main perceived aim of rugby being to RUN LIKE HELL the full length of the playing field to the far distant touch line with the ball tucked firmly under your smelly armpits WITHOUT ACTUALLY INCURRING A FATAL ACCIDENT; a FOOTBALL game in which the BALL IS VERY RARELY, ACTUALLY KICKED WITH THE FOOT. So naturally, I can't help wondering why rugby is called "foot-ball!" "ARM-BALL" seems more to the point. But being a foreign South Australian completely out of my depth in rugby-mad South Africa, who was I to judge?

****

It was a lukewarm winter's day at Ellis Park, not a cloud in the azure blue sky, and I was surrounded by a tough looking bunch of heavies, most of whom I wouldn't like to meet after dark and who didn't speak much English. As we waited for the whistle to start the mayhem, I realised the language was mainly Afrikaans, a hybrid language of mainly old Dutch, a little contemporary Dutch, and various amounts of Portuguese, Malay, German, Bantu and Kitchen Kaffir, and the odd Yankee English "OK" thrown in from time-to-time in all tongues regardless.

Confusingly, the Springboks and the Wallabies were in their national colours, which happen to be the same; green and yellow. From where I was sitting, I couldn't tell one team from the other. I didn't know who was wearing green shorts or who was hiding in a yellow jumper, and the wording on the difficult-to-see-or-understand scoreboard was complete mumbo jumbo to me.

However, after a skilful passage of play, I thought I heard one of the green shorts shout something in English. Looking at him, it was easy to see he was a fine, suntanned, strong, outdoor specimen of a man, so now AT LEAST I KNEW WHO WAS WHO, and he made me rather PROUD TO BE AN AUSSIE.

Anyway, the game started with the kicker seemingly kicking the ball sideways and out of bounds – I would have thought dead – into the stands, while neither side seemed interested in actually playing. The umpire then blew his whistle for some other unknown reason and seemed happy with the situation. I then thought it may pay me to just PLAY DUMB – that is, dumber than usual – and in my confused mindless mesmerised state, just watch the blood and guts and the mayhem unfold.

However, it wasn't long before Australia scored. I think it was called a "field goal", which is about the first time I saw the under-arm carried ball actually kicked. I then thought they should rename this game "PARTLY-FOOTBALL", but for reasons of personal safety kept my thoughts closely to myself. Not long after, I was pleasantly surprised at the South African spectators who generously applauded an Australian "try", which was then "converted"; although I never did find out whatever it had actually been converted to!

I knew damn well that had that try been by a South African back home in Australia, we would not have been so generous with our applause. We would be saying something like "KILL THE BASTARDS!"

****

About this time, having established that I was not an English Rooineck but an Aussie, I struck up a conversation with an Afrikaans body builder called "Els" sitting beside me.

"An Aussie eh", he remarked, "WHEN ARE YOU GOING TO SCORE?" I WAS FLABBERGASTED. I said, "I thought we were leading". "Och mon", he said, "WE'RE THRASHING YOU!" It was then I said to him, "Look, I'm sorry, I thought the guys in green shorts were Australian. It's difficult when both sides wear the same colours". "It's not difficult at all", he said,

South African Stories 1969-1972

"IT'S PLAIN AS DAY. YOUR COLOURS ARE GREEN AND 'YELLOW'. OUR COLOURS ARE GREEN AND 'GOLD'!"

8.
AS CLOSE AS CLOSE COULD BE

I was selling Toyotas for Lawson Motors in the elevated, one-mile-high city of Johannesburg in South Africa's Transvaal. I was following up a sales lead to industrial premises in the old mining area called "Booysens" on the city's southern outskirts.

On the opposite side of the road was a very large mine tailings dump, and along the roadside were a few old twisted and gnarled Australian blue gum trees. The air was hot and humid, and seemingly expectant. I later learned Jo'burg was claimed to be the lightning strike capital of the world due to its elevation, latitude and other misunderstood (by me) reasons. On a previous occasion as I drove along the elevated highway on the West side of the city, I had seen lightning strike the high communications tower a couple of miles further West six times in about a minute. Forget that bunkum about lightning not striking the same place twice!

Back at Booysens, I was fascinated by the huge, quickly-forming cumulonimbus-type cloud steadily growing in size to the North of me. I then saw a few lightning strikes showing up within the eye-catching, incandescent cloud while the very top of the space-high cloud started to flatten out in typical anvil fashion. I was at the time wearing a fashionable SHORT SLEEVED SAFARI SUIT, the South African fashion of the seventies, and noticed with surprise the hairs on my arms seemed to be standing up. I was just about to get out of the Toyota when a large, eight-foot blue gum tree 30 yards across the road exploded in a simultaneous deafening clap of thunder and a brilliant flash of light as it was struck and split apart from top to bottom while its branches were instantly ignited by a fiery, forked bolt of super high voltage lightning.

This was about the time the standing hairs on my arms decided to relax and go back to their normal unthinking repose. In hindsight, when thinking back in 2013, I realised that that was really about as close to lightning as I actually ever needed to be!

9.
BOOMERANG BY STARLIGHT

Adele Maritz and I were invited to a night-time, underground inspection tour of the deepest mine of any type in the whole world; the Western Areas DEEP LEVELS GOLD MINE, at the time 13,500 feet vertically below ground, about 40 miles West of Johannesburg, South Africa, in 1970.

Everything about the mine was HUGE. The square lift, or "cage", had three decks, each about 20 X 20 ft, and holding about 250 miners per deck, which travelled UP or DOWN the main shaft, fully loaded, at more than 1,000 feet a minute.

The surface level of the mine, on the high-veldt, was situated at an altitude about 6,000 feet above sea level, and the bottom of the first shaft was in fact about sea level where it entered a horizontal underground cross-drive tunnel which extended a few miles both left and right of this junction. The cross-drive contained a number of other smaller cross-drive tunnels, ore chutes, underground railway lines, locomotives, ore carriages, jumbo drills and loaders etc.

A second vertical shaft started about a mile to one side of the first shaft, being about sea level, and dropped a further 7,500 feet below sea level, being a total vertical depth of 13,500 feet from top to bottom. We didn't go anywhere near the bottom of the second and deepest shaft. It was dangerous. Explosive pressure bursts sometimes occurred without warning at these lower levels when the wall of the mine, under the immense pressure of depth, seemingly and spontaneously exploded into the confined space of the mine, often causing much injury, or sometimes killing miners and causing great material damage.

South African Stories 1969-1972

The air was hot and humid, even with extensive, expensive air conditioning, without which the ambient air temperature was around a pressure cooker 150 degrees Fahrenheit. After returning to the surface, we returned our hard hats, overalls, boots, lights, helmets, etc. at the mine changing rooms, then showered and changed before re-entering the mine's canteen and bar. The majority of the various managers seemed Afrikaans, and me, being an Aussie, had a lot of interested questions to answer, as best I could, about rugby and cricket.

One of the managers asked whether I could throw a boomerang. "Yes I can", was my immediate answer. I was facetiously asked, "Have you by any chance got one with you?" To his great surprise, I answered "Yes", as believe it or not, making returning boomerangs and throwing them was a some-time, long-time hobby of mine. This came as a great surprise to the Afrikaner I was talking to. "Well, can we see one?" "Of course", I said, and went to my car in the visitors' car park, returned inside the canteen, and placed a South African, hand-made-by-me-in-Johannesburg boomerang on the bar.

A poorly-lit rugby field shedding feeble light was directly outside the bar "Could you give us a demo?" "Yes", I said, "but first I'll show you WHAT NOT TO DO". I then showed how to hold a boomerang at the moment of release, which is in a NEARLY VERTICAL ATTITUDE and NOT THROWN FLAT like skipping a flat stone over water, in which case a skimmed boomerang just rises straight up, high into the air, then crashes down vertically, like a stone to earth, and if the ground is hard, invariably breaks.

I then threw the boomerang. A good throw. A near horizontal trajectory into the calm night sky. I watched carefully for its return in poor light and luckily caught it with two hands as it momentarily hovered at shoulder height just a couple of feet from my launching position. Then I passed the boomerang to the most enthusiastic "barfly", and again, without throwing it, I showed carefully how it should be held and thrown. Half a dozen of his interested mates were standing around, too close for comfort, and I had to get them to stand much further back as the novice barfly prepared for his very first throw. We were all greatly surprised. He threw it powerfully, his launch was copybook, but it was a little too high and we lost sight of the boomerang in the dark folds of the starry night sky. We waited expectantly, maybe as long as 15 seconds, when out of the blue,

"WHACK!"

HE WAS CLOBBERED by the boomerang he had just thrown, which hit him in the forehead an inch above his right eye and blood spurted from a nasty, deep gash. Holding his bleeding head in one hand and the blood-spattered, offending boomerang in the other, we presented at the bar and asked,

"IS THERE A DOCTOR IN THE HOUSE?"

Not surprisingly, the mine doctor was right there.

The injured barfly, now sitting on a stool with a double Cane and Coke in one hand and my forever guilty boomerang in the other as the doctor stitched up the gaping flap of the TWO-INCH GASH in his forehead, said to me with half a laugh:

"THAT'S A BLOODY DANGEROUS WEAPON. IT SHOULD BE CONFISCATED".

"No need", I said, "it's yours".

****

P.S. The last I heard (in about 1990), the offending boomerang was still nailed to the wall behind the bar.

10.
AN UNCANNY COINCIDENCE

When I was a 16-year-old student at Prince Alfred College (P.A.C.) Adelaide, in 1950, and on the way home from rowing training on the River Torrens before the pubs shut at six o'clock, we sometimes popped into Eugene McMahon's Tavistock Hotel, with

P.A.C. school caps plainly evident, sticking out of our hip pockets. The Tavistock Hotel is where we had maybe a very small, very weak, very discrete whisky, lime and soda if no one was looking, or if they were looking, it was pure lemon, lime and bitters. Eugene's son Jack was an older fellow pupil at Princes.

****

Some years later, in 1955, I was working at Elder, Smith & Co. in their farm machinery department selling Blue Streak chain saws, copper phone lines, Dunlite electrical power generators, Vesta batteries, and electric fence units and the like. Dunlite and their gregarious sales manager Evan Jones were almost next to the Tavistock Hotel, which was just around the corner from Gerard and Goodman, prominent electrical retailers, fronting on to Rundle Street. When having the odd ale, we sometimes noticed a good-looking, middle-aged gentleman with a fine clipped moustache, reminiscent of the Hollywood actor Clark Gable of "Gone with the Wind" fame, having the odd drink. We knew him to be Jack Gerard from Gerard and Goodman's.

About 1960, I became aware of a popular young dimple-cheeked lady who was actively involved in fine living and Adelaide's restaurant fraternity. For some reason, "Chesser Cellars" comes to mind. She was FRAN, Jack Gerard's daughter, and sister of Tony (P.A.C.). Fran was a frivolous extrovert. She knew the restaurant business and nearly everybody in it, and was highly regarded in the industry. We had dinner a few times and were quite good friends, although I was living interstate or overseas much of the time. Fran was quite taken in by a young dingo I had brought back from the remote South Australian outback.

****

Coming forward in time to about 1970, I was living in South Africa at an obscure, out- of-the-way suburban address: No. 4 Pine Ave, Sandton, Johannesburg. Since I left Sandton it has become a very large white enclave in the sprawling, "more black than white" square miles of the biggest city in South Africa; JOHANNESBURG. I was successfully selling new cars in Eloff St, Jo'burg, in 1969-71, but for some obscure reason I just happened to be unexpectedly home at Sandton one day when Terry Alderton, a friend of mine I had met on the R.M.S. Oronsay on our way to Africa, pulled into my residence and, LO AND BEHOLD, OUT STEPPED FRAN GERARD from far off Adelaide onto my needle in a haystack, far off Southern African driveway. Until that moment I presume Fran had not the slightest idea I was in Africa, let alone in which country, which city, what suburb, which street and what number, plus the fact that surprisingly I just happened to be home on that particular working day.

It was AN ABSOLUTELY UNCANNY COINCIDENCE! I never did find out how or where in Johannesburg she happened to meet Terry. She may have been hitch- hiking, I don't know. It's a mystery and Terry was very surprised to realise that Fran and I actually knew each other in Adelaide and were old friends.

****

Well, a year or two later when I was living in Rhodesia with MY CURRENT LADY FRIEND JOY, Fran advised she was coming over.

Joy didn't mind, and in due course Fran arrived in Bulawayo and the three of us set off on a motor tour of Eastern Rhodesia for a few days to Umtali, visiting the tea and coffee plantations on the border with Portuguese Mozambique and going trout fishing in the high Inyangani Mountains, then driving back to Bulawayo. We also met up with Fran's Rhodesian friends, Ivan Light and family. Ivan was related to Adelaide's founding architect, Colonel William Light.

We had an interesting, important night gathering of white Rhodesians at Ivan's farm near Essexvale, who were concerned about the terrorist Mr. Mugabe and their possible uncertain future rights under a government run by him. An Australian political identity (whose name I have forgotten, but who was very much involved in the League of Rights) addressed the large gathering.

Not long after Fran left Rhodesia, JOY AND I WERE MARRIED AT ESSEXVALE by Mr Wilson, the District Commissioner, and not much longer after that, we decided it was indeed time to leave a beautiful, great and fast-sinking ship.

"G'bye Rhodesia, G'day Australia".

So, now middle aged and back in Adelaide, I had trouble finding a job, having been absent in Africa for almost 10 years. I sold new cars for a time until something better turned up, while Joy landed a well-paid position with the South Australian Government as a draftsperson, which was at the time very fortunate; times were tight. However, after a short time in Adelaide at her well-paid job, Joy took off against my wishes and returned to Rhodesia, her mother and her family in Bulawayo. A few months later she returned to Adelaide but things had changed between us. I had meanwhile landed a good position as manager of Mindrill Ltd. in distant Kalgoorlie, Western Australia. Joy, in her own good time, commenced hitch-hiking around Australia.

Joy's solicitor father in Rhodesia then took steps to have our marriage annulled. Joy divorced me and married my old friend John O. Brook and went on to live at Mt. Osmond as Mrs Brook. A few months later I went up to John's house at Mount Osmond for dinner, with my dear old mate Fran Gerard now as my Adelaide dinner partner, with my former Rhodesian wife Joy pouring the wine as our hostess. IT'S A FUNNY WORLD!

That was the last time I saw Fran. Within days of our dinner, I landed a managerial position with Ingersol-Rand in Tasmania. One thing leads to another, YOU DRIFT APART INTERSTATE or OVERSEAS, you lose track and time goes by without a backward glance, and the next thing you know it's Christmas.

I SHOULD POINT OUT THAT JOY WAS THE SECOND WIFE I HAD INTRODUCED

TO JOHN BROOK. His first wife, introduced by me about 1950, was Pat Steele, daughter of "Tinny" Steele, a P.A.C. teacher and father of Des. Though Joy and John Brook are also now divorced (since about 1990), WE ARE ALL THREE OF US STILL GOOD FRIENDS. We get together on a regular basis, about every ten years reliably, without fail, but from my remote outback New South Wales vantage point, I have sadly lost track of Fran under the hazy smoke of time and distance. The last I heard, Fran was running either an olive plantation somewhere North of Adelaide or a cosy restaurant somewhere in the Clare Valley.

"IF YOU EVER READ THIS, HI FRAN!"

RHODESIAN STORIES
1972-1977

11.
MATEBELELAND

Cecil John Rhodes was an English-born businessman of extraordinary talent operating in Southern Africa in the later part of the reign of Queen Victoria. As a major shareholder in De Beers Diamond mining companies, he made a very large personal fortune by amalgamating hundreds of small, difficult-to-work individually, diamond mining claims in Southern Africa as a large, controllable, workable, single entity.

At one time, Rhodes became the Prime Minister of South Africa but suffered a bad case of hiccups after the failed Jameson Raiders event in the Transvaal backfired and he came "a bit of a cropper" in 1895. He had been involved in the formation of Bechuanaland (now Botswana) and the possible northward expansion of South Africa's Transvaal across Africa in the general direction of Cairo. British controlled territories or colonies North of the Limpopo and Zambezi Rivers in the late 1800s were briefly called "Zambesia", but in 1895, during his lifetime, were renamed "NORTHERN RHODESIA" and "SOUTHERN RHODESIA" in his honour. Rhodes never married, was rich beyond the wildest dreams, and when he died early aged 49 in 1902, the same year as Queen Victoria, his estate provided funding for the still- ongoing Rhodes Oxford University Scholarships over a hundred years later. When he died he was interred in a cavity hewn out of a large granite boulder and covered with a large, full-body-length brass plaque in a bush area called the "Matopos", about 30 miles South of Bulawayo in Rhodesia (now Zimbabwe).

Rhodesia originally consisted of copper rich Northern Rhodesia on the northern side of the Zambezi River, which in 1964 became an independent Zambia under Dr. Kaunda. The territory South of the Zambezi River down to the Limpopo River was called Southern

Rhodesia and was later simply called "RHODESIA". The northern area of Rhodesia was mainly populated by the Mashona people and was called Mashonaland, which contained the capital city of Salisbury (now Harare). The southern portion of Rhodesia had, during the days of Queen Victoria, been at continuous loggerheads with the paramount warlike Matebele chief Lobengula, and years later his former region of activity was named "MATEBELELAND". The main southern city was Gubulawayo, later shortened to Bulawayo. In 1979, two years after I left Bulawayo and a crumbling Rhodesia, it fell into the hands of Mr MUGABE and his young African terrorists, and then became ZIMBABWE.[6]

****

The Rhodesia I knew was a small country with large mineral deposits, a big gold mining industry, and world class Nickel, Platinum, Diamond, Copper and Lithium deposits. At that time, Bikita Minerals was the main source of the rare-earth mineral Lithium for the whole world. To a large degree, Rhodesia was suffering badly as a result of outside world opinion, which I had not realised when I first arrived. This was because the minority white Rhodesian Government was very reluctant to hand the country over to Mr Mugabe and his henchmen, who made a hobby of beating-up, raping and murdering whites or others simply for expressing a different racial or political point of view.

****

As a result of Rhodesia's unpopularity, it had become a pariah state, a "persona non grata" on the international stage, and was boycotted mostly by the West. China, of course, went on trading with the struggling Rhodesia, behind the scenes, oblivious to any off-putting

---

[6] A cartoon about Mr Mugabe which was in the first edition has been removed due to copyright restrictions. For anyone interested, cartoons featuring Mr Mugabe can be found by searching Google for "cartoons about robert mugabe and zimbabwe 2007"

world opinion. The supply of petroleum-based fuel to land-locked Rhodesia was an ongoing problem and the only two ports were in Portuguese Mozambique. The major Indian Ocean Port at Laurenco Marques in Southern Mozambique, connected by rail to Bulawayo, was perpetually blocked by the British Royal Navy, in keeping with world opinion.

For some completely strange, unknown reason, perhaps geographical, the northern Port of Beira, connecting Rhodesia's capital city Salisbury to Beira by rail, was not blockaded by world opinion and adequate petroleum for industry managed to trickle in through the back door, although it was rationed to the public. Anyway, Rhodesians had to tighten their belts in order to make do, but like others in a tight situation, they were a resilient lot; IF YOU DIDN'T HAVE A NUT OR A BOLT YOU SIMPLY MADE

ONE. They used many ingenious means to keep their old British-made Rhodesian Airforce jet aircraft flying. During World War 2, Bulawayo was where a lot of allied personnel did their Airforce flying training, including Australians and New Zealanders.

I used to call on a fellow in Fort Victoria who overcame a simple problem caused by the import restrictions of the time. He played golf, and plastic golf tees were virtually unobtainable, so he bought an old woodworking spindle machine, and using Rhodesian-grown, Aussie gum trees, employed a couple of Africans to make thousands of golf tees, then started a small export business while buying his Norton abrasives from me.

About this time, I had to call on a very remote place in the African bush in the former tribal areas – a sort of no-man's land called BUCHWA and an isolated 1,000-foot-high mountain of solid iron ore– in relation to sharpening their worn Tungsten Carbide Percussion Drill bits. It was a spectacular spectacle, a more-or-less CONICAL SPIRE OF

SOLID IRON ORE, surrounded by a decreasing-diameter conical road which, near the top, ran slap bang into the vertical side of a natural solid iron cliff. Here the road entered an inclined tunnel and re-entered the open air near the top of the mountain, where continuous mining of the high-grade iron ore was taking place as it was being mined by quarrying progressively downwards.

****

As a point of interest, one day in Sydney Australia about 30 years later, my car broke down and I called the N.R.M.A. roadside service and received a visit from an African mechanic. I said, "Where are you from mate?", and he replied, "Zimbabwe". I then said I had lived in Rhodesia before it became Zimbabwe and asked whereabouts in Zimbabwe he came from. He said, "I don't think you will know it, but I came from a very small, isolated place called BUCHWA". Well as it turned out, I'm probably one of very few Australians who has ever heard of this isolated place and has actually been there.

12.
ROOFING GUTTERS

I was in Mrs Salmon's kitchen in Bulawayo, Rhodesia, about 1976, and for some obscure reason, long-since forgotten, I was idly holding a bottle sideways under the tap as water poured over and around the bottle and down into the sink. Although I had seen it many times before, as everyone has, something about the event at that particular time woke me up with a start. It was a Eureka, "I have it" moment. "ROOFING GUTTERS!"

****

Back home in Australia, WATER, or the lack of it, is the biggest problem. I grew up in Adelaide, the capital city of South Australia, the driest state in the driest and most waterless continent on Earth.

****

What I had just noticed was the way the stream of water flowed from the running tap as it poured vertically down, then over the horizontal held curves of the bottle and passed around the sides before flowing down into the sink. As the tap water flowed on to the actual top of the horizontal bottle, the down-flowing stream was divided in two and the two opposite streams CLUNG TO THE OPPOSITE SIDES before flowing around to the bottom, where both sides then met again, head-on, cancelled each other out, and fell away vertically from the underside of the bottle. This was when the penny dropped.

As I moved the horizontal-held bottle either to the left or the right of the down-flowing water, the physics of the situation changed. When the water flowed in a steady stream on to the UPPER LEFT side of the bottle, the flowing water still clung to the underside of the bottle before breaking free of what I have since found out is generally called the "TEA POT EFFECT" and fell right away, well out and away, on the lower right or opposite side of the bottle. This is when I thought, "Here's a method of retaining roof run-off rainwater, clean, in a roofing gutter, while at the same time discarding the blocking leaves, twigs and berries as they fall harmlessly off the roof and past the gutter to Earth. CLEAN ROOFING GUTTERS and CLEAN WATER the final aim.

****

Well that was my moment of inspiration. The trouble was, I was in Africa and a long way from Adelaide's rainwater problems. But events do change. Nothing is the same forever and a couple of years later, as a result of Mr MUGABE and his henchmen taking over Rhodesia and renaming it Zimbabwe, I found myself back home in Adelaide. I was, at this time, in my mid-forties. Jobs for my age group were not so easy and I wound up selling new cars in my old home town until I could find more suitable employment, hopefully in the mining or associated industry. Meanwhile, I was having a drink in Tony Mathews' (S.P.S.C.) FEATHERS HOTEL near my old Burnside home and met an interesting A.B.C. reporter. During the evening, I foolishly drew him a picture of my gutter concept on a serviette and promptly forgot about it!

Shortly after, I gained employment as the new manager of MINDRILL W.A. LTD in their Western Australia state branch office in Kalgoorlie, and again, Adelaide's water situation was far from my mind. A couple of years later, as a result of Mindrill being taken over by their American rivals Longyear, I was transferred to Mindrill's Melbourne head office to carry out various obscure sales duties in Victoria during their last gasp. While based in Melbourne I joined the INVENTORS ASSOCIATION and thought I would do something about MY OLD RAINWATER GUTTER IDEA. I filed a Provisional Patent application with the Patent office, I.P., Australia. I also started my own research into rainwater gutter matters, and when in contact with the Buildings Research Centre at Highett in Melbourne I was informed a medical doctor in Queensland had much earlier, back in the 1930s, designed and made rainwater gutters employing mainly what I had until then regarded as MY NEW PRINCIPLES for a Heron Island science facility on the Great Barrier Reef.

Heron Island is a small coral cay a few hundred yards across and has no permanent water, so all water either has to be shipped in or captured as rainwater collected from the roof. This was OK most of the time except that at certain times of the year certain trees released thousands of seed pods onto roofs, which, when wetted and washed by rain into gutters and tanks, turned the water slightly acidic. Although this water was safe, it was unpleasant to drink.

I was told at the time that the actual engineer (NOT THE ACTUAL INVENTOR!) who had originally installed the gutters on Heron Island in the late 1930s, and had long retired, was at this very time, years later, by chance, back on the island in a temporary caretaker mode, and I was given his phone number for my interest's sake. I phoned the old engineer and he said they still had some new, unused, "special" guttering in the store shed, and if I liked he would place some carbon paper over the end of a gutter and send me the exact carbon copy profile for my interest, which he did. I received the carbon copy profile and basically it was very similar, and as it had already been patented at that much earlier time, was now well past patent protection. It was, at this much later time, very old hat and just a part of recent history.

In the meantime, I had been in contact with a major gutter manufacturer, Monier, when we both became aware at the same time that the GUTTER CONCEPT under our joint discussion was NO LONGER NEW, and was, as a result, NO-ONE'S CONCEPT TO SELL.

****

About this time, I was watching the original A.B.C. "THE INVENTORS" on Channel 2, when I was surprised to see "my gutter" and the A.B.C. reporter I had previously spoken to in Adelaide claiming my invention as his. HE WON THAT WEEK'S EPISODE WITH MY CONCEPT!

****

Monier by this time had started making their "NEW MONIER LEAFLESS GUTTER" (badly!) and since they did a bad design job, after about 20 years it seems to have disappeared from their gutter range. I then had the dubious pleasure of phoning the Adelaide reporter and congratulating him on his discovery, without saying who I was, while I also pointed out the invention was unfortunately very old, no longer patentable, and indeed rather "old hat!"

****

P.S. Old ideas never die. A new A.B.C. T.V. inventors program called "The New Inventors" reappeared about 2005, and on it, SOMEBODY ELSE WITH THE SAME LEAFLESS GUTTER IDEA ONCE AGAIN WON the program.

I might wait another couple of years and have another go if THE INVENTORS is still around!

13.
JOHN MASEKO

I owned a small, gold mining/exploration operation, the DOWN-UNDER MINING CO, in the UMZINGWANE TRIBAL TRUST AREA near BULAWAYO, in Rhodesia (now Zimbabwe) in the early seventies. My main asset was a leftover from the days of Queen Victoria; the remains of a very rich mine, the INGUBO, which once yielded 1,800 ounces of gold from a single ton of rock the size of a large T.V. set, and then went on to produce a further 8,000 ounces from about 8,000 tons of still-rich, auriferous ore! When I repegged the long-abandoned Victorian workings in about 1973, the gold price was a low, United States Government-fixed $34 per ounce, where it had been since about 1934. I was NOT TO KNOW the price would be FREED, UNRESTRAINED and above $800 per ounce in 1977, $1,900 in 2011 and rapidly rising, JUST AFTER I BAILED OUT of a sadly crumbling Rhodesia. It has decreased slightly today (2021) to $1,775 U.S. per ounce.

When I left the Ingubo, I had outlined a surface outcrop 120 yards long x 8 yards wide, dipping about 30 degrees into the earth, being a deposit weighing about a thousand tons per single metre of depth, and containing two cross-cut trenches at a sampled, proven assay grade of 6 pennyweights per ton of rock/ore. This represents 6,000 pennyweights or 1,200 ounces of gold per metre depth of the deposit, which at the 2011 price of $1,900 per ounce was worth $2,280,000 per single three-foot depth. Today it would be worth $2,130,000. If I still had the INGUBO today, I WOULD TRULY BE SITTING ON A GOLD MINE containing well in excess of around $200,000,000 worth of easily-mined or quarried gold.

BUT, CURSES, I'M NOT!

Prior to leaving Rhodesia, my principal operation had been involved in establishing recoverable gold grades and proving recoverable tonnages from a number of leases held by me, on a financial shoestring, while I worked during the week for the I.M.F. Machinery Co., Nap, Colin and Ken Kendall, 35 miles away in Bulawayo.

Meanwhile, I supported two or three Africans to prospect and look for auriferous, in situ, rock outcrops to be sampled on my behalf by crushing rock samples to a powder with a steel pestle in a cast iron mortar, known as a "dolly pot" in Australia. The manual operator of the dolly pot was called a "gigger boy" in Rhodesia. The work could be tiring but was only intermittent. A "condensed milk" tin of sieved, crushed, pulverised, powdered rock sample, as the general industry yardstick, was then washed, swirled around and skilfully concentrated in a prospector's gold pan, sometimes leaving a long tail of gold in the pan, while values were investigated and confirmed by visiting various sites of interest and by further checking the dimensions of the outcrop etc. If interesting, datum posts were erected, and the claim pegged out, mapped and legally claimed, importantly in daylight hours!

****

JOHN MASEKO, born in MALAWI, was one of the best gigger boys, although a 70- year-old scallywag. I was not the only one to whom he showed and sold THE VERY SAME POTENTIAL GOLD PROSPECTS, as I found out later. On his way home from the Umzingwane Beer Hall late one night, he passed out drunk on the wet-grassed track through the bush. It rained overnight and he was found still lying in the grass the next morning in a bad way; unconscious, wet, shivering and in a deep fever, and admitted to the Essexvale Hospital with acute pneumonia.

****

The first I knew of this was mid-morning when I arrived at his small kraal, a settlement of about a dozen thatched-roof, wattle and daub, mud-walled buildings. I was advised John had died in hospital earlier that morning and his relations asked if I could take them to the morgue at the hospital to claim his body. I spoke to the District Commissioner in Essexvale, Mr Wilson, about legalities, and was advised it would cost money to have him interred in the cemetery or nothing if buried in the Umzingwane Tribal Trust lands, where he lived.

Back at the hospital I was taken to the outdoor morgue; a square, flywire-covered, wood-framed construction, a bit like a shade house, containing a rudimentary concrete slab (on which old John's naked body lay, simply covered with a sheet) with raised shallow sides and a large, central drainage hole under his backside for collecting and discharging excreted body waste. There was a water tap with a hose for washing the dished slab down afterwards.

We borrowed a stretcher and carried his body out to my open-backed L.W.B. Land Rover, laid him flat on the floor in the back and covered him with a blanket.

As we left the hospital, I realised the Land Rover was low on gas and so I swung into the nearby garage to fill up before leaving Essexvale. The Indigenous attendant was filling the tank when he suddenly stopped, looking slightly "ga-ga" as he discerned the giveaway toe of a dead body under the covering blanket in the back. We explained as best we could the circumstances surrounding the body, paid for the petrol, and drove off leaving the whiter than usual dark-skinned attendant in the rear vision mirror, standing alone to haunt himself!

Arriving back at old John's kraal, we looked around for his final resting spot and realised we had the perfect place. There was a sand-heap about 12 feet wide and two feet high at the place where he had tirelessly "giggered" tons of rock to sand, under the shade of a large mopani tree. WE WOULD BURY HIM IN A GRAVE BENEATH THE SAND HE HIMSELF HAD CREATED.

His family men-folk then set to work and had soon dug a six-foot-deep grave while the women gathered soft, broad-scented leaves, which the digger in the grave then spread out and arranged as a comfortable, springy, leafy green mattress. There was a momentary hiccup when it was realised we had encountered blue and green copper carbonate in the sides of the grave, which frequently means gold may also be present. It was then my common sense decided against the obvious impulse to dig another grave elsewhere. So, back to John.

Without further ado, his friends and relations gently lowered old John's now-dressed body down into the grave, while as an afterthought I added an old pillow from my Land Rover, which was placed comfortably under his unknowing head. I also added a packet of the African's favourite brand TEXAN TOBACCO and a box of matches, which was tucked under his soft pillow. This action seemed to be appreciated by some of the older African ladies, causing them to sob and wail louder than before.

So it was "GOODBYE OLD JOHN" as he was then covered with the very sand he had painstakingly created with his own labour, pulverised by him, grain by grain, from solid gold-containing rock, while as an afterthought I added a handful of some of the highest grade GOLD-RICH SAND WITH A PINCH CONTAINING EASILY-VISIBLE GOLD, as a SPARKLING, EASY-TO-SEE, STAR-LIKE, FINAL ADORNMENT.

> "Goodbye old John. Amen".

14.
IRENE MARY NIGHTINGALE

Irene Mary Nightingale was a near neighbour of mine in Kensington, an outer suburb of Bulawayo, in Rhodesia (now Zimbabwe) about 1976. Irene has a sad story to tell and now, many years later, I think it's worth re-telling before it's forgotten.

Irene and her husband were English. They had come to Africa, where he took up employment as a member of the BRITISH SOUTH AFRICAN POLICE FORCE (B.S.A.P.) based in Bulawayo. Her husband took up flying, first as a hobby and later, after resigning from the B.S.A.P., he obtained a commercial pilot's position as a full- time charter aircraft pilot. He was engaged flying old Douglas D.C. 4 piston engine aircraft, taking African mineworker recruits under contract from the central African country Malawi, VIA FRANCISTOWN, BOTSWANA, and ON TO JOHANNESBURG and the rich gold mines of South Africa.

On his fateful last flight, he had left Blantyre, Malawi in the morning and arrived at Francistown, Botswana about lunchtime, where the D.C. 4 had been topped-up by the African attendants with AVGAS (aviation gasoline) at the Shell fuel depot. After lunch, the loaded aircraft with AVGAS tanks full, took-off on time for Jo'burg, when suddenly, just after the end of the airstrip had been cleared, all four engines abruptly choked, coughed, spluttered and died. The engines ran out of compatible AVGAS fuel simultaneously. They stopped and all hope was lost. Without power and unable to return safely to the airstrip, the fully-loaded D.C. 4 dropped like a brick, crashed and burned in an EXPLOSIVE FIREBALL. About 50 passengers and crew, including Irene's husband, were killed, incinerated on the spot. There were NO SURVIVORS.

The eventual enquiry revealed a tragic tale of theft and corruption. The low-paid African Shell petroleum fuel attendants had, over time, stolen AVGAS from the depot and re-sold it, cheaply, to their mates to run their cars and taxis! In an attempt to cover the theft, they had TOPPED UP THE NOW-EMPTY AVGAS TANKS WITH JETFUEL; the aviation kerosene-based fuel only used in jet-powered aircraft and TOTALLY INCOMPATIBLE IN OLD FASHIONED PISTON ENGINE AIRCRAFT. The D.C. 4 had managed to take off with the last of the residual AVGAS gasoline type fuel remaining in the fuel system, but had choked to death the moment it received its FIRST FATAL DOSE OF INCOMPATIBLE KEROSENE-BASED JETFUEL. That is, JETFUEL flooding undetected, right through the aircraft's entire fuel system in a matter of moments.

My dear friend IRENE WAS A WIDOW.

15.
AFRICAN DUNG BEETLES

After visiting the WANKIE GAME RESERVE on the Botswana border, we were heading North up the highway from Bulawayo to the giant VICTORIA FALLS in Northern Rhodesia (now Zimbabwe). These great waterfalls are more than twice as high and twice as wide as the Niagara Falls in North America.

Quite suddenly, the road ahead dropped away, revealing the Zambezi River and its impressive escarpment maybe 1,000 feet below the elevated African teak wood forest. We were still about 10 miles South of the Victoria Falls and could see where they were by GREAT WHITE CLOUDS OF WATER VAPOUR rising up overhead, perhaps 2,000 or 3,000 feet into the background of a brilliant blue sky. It was at that time I was attacked by a most inopportune, premature, internal impulse, which required me pulling over to the verge, grabbing a roll of "loo"[7] paper and dashing into the thorny African bush to go about my urgent business A.S.A.P.

****

With Adele Maritz safely in the car, I uneasily scratched my way past the "wait-a- while" thorn trees and a tree snake of some sort about 100 yards from the car and into the shade of a large mopani tree. The ground under the great shady tree was littered with shovel-sized elephant dung and large, strong-smelling, rotting mopani fruit, which was a favourite of the wild elephants who sought its alcoholic, fermenting flesh every day for a "high" at this fruitful time of the year. I realised I was in marginal lion territory and didn't want to be there a second longer

---

[7] Toilet

than was really necessary. I did see and hear monkeys in the great tree, and they seemed a little too interested in my personal activities as I lowered my trousers. I did find their curiosity a bit off- putting!

Relief at last. "Bombs away!" And in seconds I heard a great buzzing noise like grasshoppers on steroids or cicadas on drugs, as a large, matchbox-size flying beetle homed in like radar on the delicious, natural, wafting aroma that told it "SOMETHING WAS COOKING".

The heavy beetle was a very poor flier and made an audible crash landing with a screaming thud about two feet downwind of the newfound object of its desires. I could see the beetle's "radar" antenna ears visibly activated with eager anticipation as it homed in on its target. Its next move was to charge blindly forward without an ounce of finesse and plunge its nose unerringly deep into its fresh, soft, warm, amorphous target, then back off an inch or two, and repeat the same encircling procedure over and over until the ground coordinates of the prize had been accurately centred, tasted and finally established.

Having established the position of its "TARGET FOR TONIGHT", it backed off about three inches to one side and started digging furiously as though there was no tomorrow; straight down. In a minute, "she" was gone out of sight while filling the tunnel behind her as she frantically burrowed downwards toward the centre of the Earth.

****

In the meantime, I had, without thinking, delivered a brother or sister additionally to this tender outdoor scene, but she remained steadfastly faithful to my first newborn while she remained ensconced and out of sight underground. Then suddenly, I noticed the ground under "you know what" start caving in. Employing a clever modern mining technique known as "BLOCK CAVING", her efforts led to the earth steadily collapsing under the additional weight of the rapidly cooling, homely, amorphous object. In seconds, it all started disappearing completely from view.

She was busy down below establishing an underground nursery in a very suitable, humid, scented habitat and gently laying her eggs in "IT". I really felt very proud to have played such an important donor part in her life's ongoing story, and to her forthcoming family of SPECIALISED AFRICAN ELEPHANT DUNG REMOVALISTS.

Elephant dung waiting for dung beetles

16.
ENTEBBE

I departed London on a United Arab Airlines flight in about 1976, destination Nairobi, Kenya.

Once seated in the early model Boeing, I had the immediate feeling I was already in Islam. Several sections of the aircraft seemed to be curtained into individual veiled apartments and seemed to be areas of somewhat limited secretive access. Various interesting smells wafted uncontained through the air conditioning, and the plane stank to high heaven of ingrained, scented, oriental cigarette smoke. I wondered if some of the older Muslims were still smoking the multi-patron use hookah while seated uncomfortably one on top of the other in the aircraft toilet?

I didn't see any prayer mats used in-flight; I guess that would be a sensible "no no". Many of the women wore Islamic type headwear and seemed to stick very much to themselves. I would not have been at all surprised to have seen a trussed-up goat kid peering down on us from an overhead luggage rack. I was surprised to see a couple of loose screws on the aircraft's interior panelling under my elbow, which I pointed out to the cabin staff, while of course also wondering about the general mechanical standard of the rest of the old model Boeing 707.

I didn't know the exact path of our flight to Nairobi and was interested to observe whatever happened as the flight unfolded. I just sat back, waited and watched. My fellow passengers were in the main of Islamic appearance, mostly Arabs, but included a number of Pakistanis and/or Indians, while very few were European.

****

Surprisingly, the in-flight coffee was particularly good! Our first brief stop was in Switzerland. I don't remember where. Then off again to land at Naples in Italy about 3:00 a.m., where they were undergoing one of their frequent SEAFOOD POISONING scares. I think we all stayed on the plane. There was no point in chancing Berri Berri or similar quite so early in the flight. Mid-morning we arrived in Cairo, which included a four-hour stopover. I was informed that by the time I passed through customs it would be time to leave, so time was inadequate for a good look at the Pyramids of Giza.

Instead, I had a meal of roast mutton in the dining room and was surprised to see a real Pharonic style cat, still existing, large as life, padding around the dining room walls under Pharonic murals. I quickly discovered the cat was not averse to a piece of mutton from my plate, just like any other cat. I have been told since that the mutton was probably Australian.

Looking around the duty-free shops, I was quite taken in by the attractive cartons of CLEOPATRA AND NEFERTITI CIGARETTES. Although I don't smoke, I bought a carton of both brands to give to my smoker mates. I asked where in Egypt the tobacco was grown and was told it all came from Turkey. I was later surprised to be approached by a plain clothes gentleman who showed me his photo I.D. and who informed me he was an airport employee engaged to make sure that transiting passengers were not overcharged. He looked at my cigarettes and my receipt and told me I had obviously been overcharged, and stayed with me until the supplying argumentative shopkeeper gave me quite a substantial refund; and …

SURPRISE, SURPRISE, HE WOULD NOT TAKE A REWARD FOR HIS REALLY CONSIDERABLE TROUBLE!

****

After lunch we flew South, with the NILE RIVER frequently in view on our left and glimpses of Abu Simbel before sighting the large LAKE NASSER. We landed at KHARTOUM near the junction of the White and Blue Niles in the Sudan later that night. I couldn't help my mind being cast back to a well-known painting in the Sydney Art Gallery showing General Gordon being killed by the Dervish, or whoever, on the steps of his British offices in Khartoum in about 1885, and a photo of him meeting Queen Victoria at Buckingham Palace at an earlier time, which is still on display at the General Gordon Hotel near Mackay in Queensland. Makes you think, "WHAT'S IT ALL ABOUT, ALFIE?"

Shortly after midnight we descended more-or-less right on the equator into Ugandan air space and landed at the ENTEBBE AIRPORT on the North-Western shore of LAKE VICTORIA; a giant freshwater African lake about the same size as the whole of Ireland or Tasmania. Uganda at that time was under the control of a certain GENERAL IDI AMIN, who had recently found favour with Arab states by generally upsetting the State of Israel.

We taxied to a standstill and many of us left the aircraft for a stroll almost right on the equator with a night view of the giant lake, while most of the Indian passengers elected to stay aboard as they were TOO FRIGHTENED TO STRETCH THEIR LEGS IN IDI AMIN'S UGANDA. Unknown to all of us, about 10 days later this airport was the site of the Israeli Airforce strike which in minutes destroyed most of the Ugandan Airforce on the ground, and carried out the successful recovery of Jewish and Israeli hostages that has since become known as THE ENTEBBE AFFAIR. Had we arrived 10 days later, things would have been quite different.

****

We then flew East across the 150-mile-wide Lake Victoria and landed at NAIROBI in Kenya, having no idea about the events that were to follow in Idi Amin's Uganda.

17.
DEVIL'S DICE

In the 1970s I controlled a number of gold mining leases in the Essexvale/ Bulawayo area of Rhodesia (now Zimbabwe). These leases had been repegged BEFORE the price of gold unexpectedly leapt from U.S. $34 an ounce up to a heady U.S. $800+ or so. My pride and joy was the still-rich, Victorian-era, INGUBO GOLD MINE, and I still remember seeing surface patches of oxidised specimens of iron pyrites, or "DEVILS DICE", which I found an interesting but otherwise unimportant feature of the low, scrubby terrain. Some of the larger cubes were an inch-or-more wide and bore obvious striations along the sides of the cube at right angles to each other.

I amassed a few pounds weight of these fascinating geological oddities and had a number of broken, imperfect Devils Dice in a reject box, when one day I was surprised to spy a tiny glint of gold in a broken and exposed striation. Out of curiosity I placed the rejects in a cast iron pestle and mortar, known as a "dolly pot" in Australia, and quickly pulverised the cubes to brown powder and passed the crushed material through a 400-mesh laboratory screen. I discovered that a quantity of coarser material that was too big to pass, was in fact, when panned in water, GOLD. Likewise, the minus 400 mesh crushed cubic dice was equally blessed with the yellow metal.

The result was a long tail of yellow gold in the bottom of the gold pan, roughly equating to about ten ounces of gold to a ton of virgin oxidised concentrated pyritic material. The DEVIL'S DICE WERE RICH IN GOLD.

****

Failed Times and Twisted Follies

Unfortunately, I was in Rhodesia at the wrong time. The price of gold was still pegged at U.S. $34 an ounce, where it had been since 1934, and the Guerrilla "FREEDOM FIGHTERS" under ROBERT MUGABE were close to taking over the country. A NUMBER OF CIVILIAN PEOPLE I KNEW HAD ALREADY BEEN KILLED in the

voluntary Rhodesian Army, fighting a losing battle against overall impossible losing odds. The guy behind the counter selling you a pie and Coke at lunch time was possibly laying land mines around your house at night.

I abandoned my mining machinery, my crushers, ball-mill, Gallagher and James tables, amalgam barrels, jackhammers etc., as well as my gold leases, sold my Land Rover for a song, and RETURNED EMPTY-HANDED AND BROKE, BUT ALIVE, TO

AUSTRALIA in about 1977.

****

When I went back to Australia, I was employed as manager of Mindrill, in Kalgoorlie, a company which manufactured diamond drilling apparatus in Heidelberg, Victoria.

Six months after returning to Australia, the price of gold was freed from U.S. Government price control and in a couple of days was priced over U.S. $800 per ounce.

IF I WAS STILL IN RHODESIA I WOULD HAVE BEEN VERY RICH, BASED ON THE PRICE OF GOLD, BUT MORE PROBABLY DEAD, BASED ON MR MUGABE!

Back safely in Australia, with gold above U.S. $800 per ounce, I couldn't help thinking back to the strewn patches of Devils Dice I remembered seeing near the Warburton Ranges about 15 or so years before when I was engaged in mineral exploration duties by the Western Mining Corporation (W.M.C.). MEMORIES OF THOSE UNOXIDISED, BRASSY CUBIC FORM DEVIL'S DICE, not assayed as far as i know, perhaps still lying on the ground in outback Western Australia, similar in form to the oxidised Rhodesian cubes, STILL HAUNT ME; and prod me as outstanding, untried, unfinished business!

AN ENGLISH STORY

18.
EL-SHERANA PITCHBLENDE

I left Melbourne, Australia late in the afternoon on a British Airways flight. After eight hours, we landed at Hong Kong, were on the ground about an hour and took off again well before dawn. Later I saw the sun rise between Hong Kong and Bangkok as we flew more-or-less West, crossing right over a plainly-visible, postage-stamp-sized India, and landed at Bahrain hours later.

All that time the sun above was relatively lazy and very reluctant to move as our ground speed closely matched the Earth's rotation. After many continuous daylight hours, we finally arrived at London while the sun was still in its overhead midday position.

****

On landing, I phoned my English mate Richard Maxwell Chalmers whom I had known earlier in South Africa, and his opening words were, "Have you got your tennis racquet with you?" I said, "Yes". "Good", he said, "catch a train to Dorking in Surrey and meet me at the station, then we can finish that game of tennis interrupted by rain in Johannesburg about six months ago. I still have the score in my notebook. You were leading at the time!"

We arrived at his mother's house, "Holmbury", Saint Marys, in a very comfortable garden setting with a little-used grass tennis court nestling among the oak trees; a court patiently, desperately waiting for a little real tennis action. I tried to explain to Richard as politely as I could that I had been on the long 31-hour flight to London from Melbourne via Hong Kong, Bangkok, Bahrain, etc., and was tired and really not quite up to it. "Excuses, excuses", said Richard as he wiped me off the court.

****

A day or two later we relocated to Richard's London address in Abbey Road, St Johns Wood, in the same building as the Beatles' Abbey Road studios. The famous zebra crossing was directly outside the front door. I believe an illegal gambling casino was also hiding somewhere in the large rabbit warren of a building!

While Richard went to work, I wandered around London. The West Indies were playing a cricket test match just around the corner at Lords and the nearby Knights of St John hotel was a lively place to be. We had a few beers with the long-retired Australian cricketer Keith Miller and Wally Rayburn, a New Zealand writer and author of his tongue-in-cheek book, "The Inferior Sex" (my lips are sealed!).

Richard Chalmers and daughter Sophie

I later found myself quite unexpectedly in the Natural History Museum, where I came across a large, black, ominous rock, the size of a T.V. set, displayed in a large, refrigerator-sized glass case, lying on its side. A large sign proclaimed this to be the "LARGEST HIGH-GRADE SPECIMEN of URANINITE, URANIUM ORE" (called "PITCHBLENDE" by the discoverer Madam Curie) ON DISPLAY IN ANY MUSEUM IN THE WORLD, donated by Joe Fisher from the El-Sherana Uranium Mine on the South Alligator River, Northern Territory, Australia. I'm sure Madame Curie would have loved to have lived to see it. The glass case was equipped with an electronic device, a Geiger counter, with instructions for the observer to press the button to hear the very loud crackling sounds of NATURAL RADIOACTIVITY emanating from the large, since found to be extremely dangerous, uranium ore geological specimen.

I was very surprised. I had no idea a large chunk of the El-Sherana was here in London. It was then I noticed a well-dressed gentleman standing beside me in a pin- striped suit and London fashionable bowler hat looking studiously at the crackling "pitchblende" exhibit. I simply could not stop myself remarking, "I know you may not believe it, but I am actually a CO-DISCOVERER of this mine, and until this very moment I had no idea a piece of the El-Sherana was here!" "How frightfully interesting", he said, as he turned his back on me and walked away. I could have kicked myself. He probably went home and said something like, "You know, some of those colonial chappies will say just about anything for a bit of attention".

****

Ten years later I was walking down a very wide stone staircase in the Australian Museum in Sydney, Australia and came across an even bigger pitchblende specimen than the one I had seen earlier in London, once again with an attendant Geiger counter and a notice stating, surprise, surprise, "THIS SPECIMEN IS THE LARGEST PITCHBLENDE

An English Story

SPECIMEN ON DISPLAY IN THE WHOLE WORLD", from the very same El-Sherana! A further three years later I was back again in the Sydney Museum, and to my surprise noticed the pitchblende exhibit was MISSING! So I asked an attendant why and was ushered into the basement Geology Department where the museum geologist asked, "Who wants to know?" I then explained my long El-Sherana connection and details of the discovery by the six prospectors, including me, and the £25,000 REWARD paid to us by the Commonwealth of Australia Government in 1954. And so, being a co-discoverer of the El-Sherana Uranium Mine, I was not unnaturally interested in the whereabouts of the largest mined pitchblende specimen in the world, which had formerly been on prominent display in the Australian Museum until the early 1980s, together with its attendant Geiger counter.

It was then the geologist in charge told me the story, which, had it become public knowledge, would have been embarrassing for the museum at those rather unenlightened times. Some time between 1983 and 1986, someone in the basement Geology Department turned on an old museum Geiger counter after fortuitously finding fresh batteries. SURPRISE, SURPRISE! THE GEIGER COUNTER RESPONDED IN FULL VOICE, with a full-blooded screaming staccato noise, enough to wake the dead, in the buried subterranean basement of the museum, indicating A VERY HIGH LEVEL OF UNSAFE RADIOACTIVITY WAS VERY, VERY CLOSE AT HAND.

It was not hard to find a usual suspect. The largest uraninite or pitchblende example anywhere in the world, weighing seven-eighths of a ton, was close by in a glass case only two floors above and less than 30 yards to one side from the museum's underground basement captive-gravity trap, no-escape location. Heavier than air, glass penetrating, radioactive Radon gas had been escaping unseen from the pitchblende through the glass case and gravitating down the stairwell. For years it had been dangerously, invisibly pooling in the no-escape underground Geology Department. This department was clearly an unsafe work environment and IT WAS OBVIOUS THE PITCHBLENDE WOULD HAVE TO GO.

****

On a Sunday morning soon afterwards, able-bodied museum attendants, with the help of a strong trolley, lifting jacks, ropes, slings and levers etc., man-handled the heavy pitchblende, on its tough trolley, down the wide, gently-sloping steps of the staircase to the William Street side museum entrance where a taxi truck with a crane was waiting. When trying to raise the pitchblende from its trolley, however, a miscalculation saw the very heavy "rock" drop about a foot onto the concrete sidewalk and break apart, revealing an enclosed, head-sized open cavity inside containing RARE URANIUM CRYSTALS, SOME NOT PREVIOUSLY DESCRIBED, hidden within. The now broken pieces of the once unique specimen were then loosely placed on a pallet on the back of the taxi truck and taken to the Lucas Heights Atomic Research facility about 12 miles South of Sydney. There, they were simply placed without fanfare in storage building number 59 and covered with a non-protective, plastic dustsheet. As of March 2010, it still sat on its old pallet at this location, and its ultimate fate and future were undecided. I was led to believe it may be returned to a dump for radioactive materials, planned for the Northern Territory (still undecided), not far from its original South Alligator River source. It seems clear to me it ought to be fed back into the fuel chain for overseas atomic power stations, which seems to make more common sense.

****

Recently I couldn't help wondering about the "sister" pitchblende specimen I had originally seen in the Science Museum in London in 1973. I thought, "If it's still there, THEY MUST ALSO HAVE A NO-ESCAPE BASEMENT FULL OF HEAVY, RADIOACTIVE RADON

An English Story

GAS, POOLED and TRAPPED and HELD IN PLACE BY GRAVITY, WITH NOWHERE TO GO!"

I then wrote on 28-5-09 to Jane Davies, Curator of Minerals at the Science Museum and received an answer from Rory Cook (ref. scm/01/2583) stating they were unaware of the large pitchblende exhibit to which I referred. However, he stated that the Natural History Museum may know something and had forwarded my letter to them. I received a letter dated 8-6-09 from Peter Tandy, Curator of Minerals at the Natural History Museum, and all was revealed. Peter remembered seeing the London-based pitchblende specimen and its attendant Geiger counter years ago, and believes IT WAS QUIETLY AND DISCREETLY REMOVED FROM PUBLIC VIEW AND CONTAMINATING RADIOACTIVE PERSONAL CONTACT IN ABOUT 1985 ; about the same time as the Sydney Museum-based exhibit was clandestinely relocated to Lucas Heights. He stated in his letter that, I quote:

"Ever changing legislation on exposure to ionizing radiation would not now permit us to own such an item, still less display it! Where it went, I don't know, but I suspect it went to one of the atomic weapons establishments in this country (Harwell?), either for safe keeping or for destruction. It's anybody's guess whether it would still exist".

Well, as far as I can find out, that's the current U.K. pitchblende exhibit situation.

World's Largest Pitchblende Specimen at Museum

By R. O. CHALMERS

THE needs of the times stimulate the search for minerals. Uranium minerals had been found in South Australia as early as 1906, but nowhere had pitchblende, an oxide of uranium and the richest source of the metal uranium, been found in Australia until after the second World War. Even the great demand for uranium for the atom bomb project in the closing years of the war failed to reveal the great abundance of high-grade uranium ore in Australia.

Post-war demand for uranium led to an intensification of the search on the part of both the prospector and the geologist. A prospector found Rum Jungle, Northern Territory, in 1949, and four years later a geologist, B. P. Walpole, of the Commonwealth Bureau of Mineral Resources, found uranium minerals at Coronation Hill, in the upper South Alligator River, about 140 air miles south-east of Darwin. Prospecting in this rugged terrain, mostly on the sides of steep cliffs, revealed further lodes, the richest of which was named El Sherana, a compound of abbreviations of the names of the three daughters of the discoverer.

Specimen Weighs 1875 lb.

The El Sherana lode contained lens-shaped masses of high-grade pitchblende, and the company, United Uranium, was able to mine intact some very large masses, the largest of which, weighing 1875 lb., was brought to the surface in May, 1956. The sheer impressive bulk of this monster spared it from being crushed immediately and shipped off with thousands more tons of uranium ore. Yet it was by no means an economic proposition to retain it as a specimen because it is probably worth something in the order of £A5,000. The scientists of the Australian Atomic Energy Commission, realizing the great educational and scientific value of the specimen, advised that the Commission should purchase it from the company, which was done. After being

The largest piece of pitchblende ever mined, now on display at the Australian Museum, is here seen ready for loading on to a truck at the El Sherana Mine, South Alligator River, Northern Territory, where it was found. The specimen weighs just on seven-eighths of a ton. Pitchblende is the richest source of the radioactive metal uranium.

Photo.—"Walkabout."

World's Largest Pitchblende Specimen at Museum

By R. O. CHALMERS

A long "twisted" tale,

STILL WAITING FOR A BANG!

BOTSWANA STORIES
(Formerly the British Bechuanaland Protectorate or B.P.)

19.
A SHOWER OF SPARKS

Travelling to England on the R.M.S. Oronsay in 1979, I met Terry Alderton, who was going to South Africa to join his brother Danny, a new and used car dealer and distributor in Johannesburg. Terry thought I might make a useful new car salesman, so when the ship docked at Durban, all things being equal, I had a job assured in Johannesburg.

Joining Aldertons, I was engaged selling Alfa Romeo and Lotus sports cars, until one day, after winning the Formula Ford event at the Kylami Racetrack, MY EMPLOYER, DANNY ALDERTON, VANISHED FROM THE COMPANY AND SOUTH AFRICA

OVERNIGHT, never to return. The company was insolvent, so I joined Lawson Motors, which sold Toyota, Mazda, Renault and Volvo vehicles. While at Lawsons, I built up a good rapport with the South African branch of the General Electric Company and had assurances they would soon buy a fleet of 52 Toyota Hi-Ace vans from me, as well as two Dyna light trucks. In the meantime, Lawsons had decided to relinquish their Toyota franchise in order to take over the South African assembly and distribution of Mazda, which left me in a bit of a bind.

After certain assurances, I went on to join the NEW TOYOTA DEALERS for JOHANNESBURG, IMPERIAL MOTORS, controlled by Percy Abelkop. They offered very good commissions on the 54 vehicles that I subsequently went on to deliver from their new Toyota showrooms in Commissioner Street. I also sold a number of 4-wheel drive (4WD) Toyotas to the United States Steel Company, which was just about to set up mineral exploration activities in the Northern Chobe region of neighbouring Botswana.

As I had considerable previous mineral exploration experience in Australia and New Zealand, I offered my services, and so, after discussions, they offered me an interesting field position operating in a bush area of Botswana; an area just earmarked as the forthcoming, soon-to-be Chobe Game Reserve, to be located about *A Shower of Sparks* 100 miles West of the Victoria Falls in adjacent Rhodesia (now Zimbabwe).

****

So here I was, at the end of a long drive a few days later IN BOTSWANA, driving North past the small modern capital city Gaberones, then Francistown, then on the dirt Nata-Kasane Track into the about-to-be Chobe Game Reserve, bordering the Zambezi River, South of Zambia. Our base camp was about 90 miles south of Kasane, well within the about-to-be game reserve, which at this point in time was a game reserve in name only as the resident animals of Northern Botswana didn't really know they were in it!

****

Our own United States Steel surveyors had previously cut and roughly graded about 30 miles of a sandy, seismic road access to the Shinamba Hills; two little isolated tits in the bush, 50 feet high with a 300-yard cleavage between which we finally arrived about dusk. We had on site a Bedford 4 X 4 truck and Toyota Land Cruisers (which as a car salesman I had previously sold to my new employers), plus a few trailers, about 10 United States Steel geological staff members and about 25 African manual workers.

On arrival, we immediately set to work stringing long ropes and tarpaulins between trees, and tent pegging the sides and securing them firmly, and then assembling our camp stretchers for the night. By about 10:00 p.m. we were all in bed and nodding off when we realised the Africans were making a lot of noise in their separate camp; a lot of yelling, hitting tin cans, which seemed quite odd.

The African workers were camped about a hundred yards away, where they cooked their own traditional food and observed their customary toilet rules. It was then we became aware of certain dull, low, vibrating, guttural animal noises and realised we had an unwelcome visitor in our midst. We lay silently, unprotected in our beds, while the Africans continually made a lot of noise and had the theoretical safety of numbers, crowbars, picks and shovels on their side. We had a number of large trunks, wooden boxes etc. heaped at the ends of our long tarpaulin-covered TENT-LIKE HOUSING, which more or less covered the vulnerable ends. However, the guy roped sides were only about six inches high and were not much of a physical barrier; of that we were fully aware. At this point in time, an inquisitive lion sniffing around on the outside of our thin canvas tent sprang a taut guy rope with a "T'WANG", which made us all jump and realise our quite vulnerable position.

We lay uneasily for an hour or so, but by about midnight, after no further sounds of "Felis Leo", I simply had to go. I was closest to one end of our tent and by now I WAS REALLY, REALLY BUSTING. I cautiously crawled past our flimsy packing case fortifications and emerged outside in my birthday suit near the still-burning embers of what had earlier been a substantial log fire, and at last relieved my internal hydraulic pressure. It was only then, with the pressure finally relieved, that I tossed a large piece of fibrous firewood onto the fire, creating an INSTANT SHOWER OF FIREWORKS-LIKE SPARKS, which was SIMULTANEOUSLY ACCOMPANIED BY THE SUDDEN ABRUPT, VERY HEALTHY, STARTLED "GR'MPPH" OF A LION, which, unknown to me, had obviously been SIZING UP THE CALORIFIC VALUE OF MY NAKED BODY from behind the bushes just 20 feet away!

The timely sparks surprised the sneaky lion, the sneaky lion's close proximity surprised me, and maybe in the end,

> I WAS SAVED FROM A STICKY SITUATION BY A SHOWER
> OF SPARKS!

20.
THE SHINAMBA HILLS TRACK

We left the United States Steel Company's SHINAMBA HILLS base camp in CHOBE, Botswana after breakfast, heading East towards our nearest water source; the jet- pump-equipped bore and its temperamental engine 30 miles away, East of the Nata road. We had only gone about 8 miles and successfully negotiated the only really heavy sand-impaired left, right, zig-zag bend in the road, and were building up a slight, though frustratingly slow, increase in our vehicle speed when we ran straight past a lion kill which had recently taken place on our right about 50 yards away from the bush track. Lions had just killed a zebra, and as we drove past a possessive lioness detached herself from the group and charged towards the front of the Bedford 4 X 4 truck I was driving. I accelerated as fast as I could but only managed about 30 miles per hour in the very heavy loose sand conditions. The lioness actually had a couple of swipes with her lethal clawed paw at the driver's side front tyre of the truck before the open bush we were driving through closed in like a fence, causing her to veer away at the last moment.

Meanwhile, one of the Africans on the back of the truck had managed somehow to enter the truck's cabin through the passenger-side window and impose himself, completely uninvited and uncomfortably, on the lap of the verbally-reluctant, original, squashed-underneath, now-suffering occupant. This was while closing the window to other like-minded mates still unhappily ensconced on the back of the truck, and who presumably, if given the opportunity, might also have been inclined to follow suit. A couple of hundred yards later I started to slow down and check that all was OK but the boys on the back yelled out, "KEEP GOING", so I did for a further mile. It was only after stopping I learnt the full story! While I had only seen one lioness on my side of the truck, TWO OTHER LIONS I HAD NOT SEEN had run up behind the constantly receding truck and on at least one occasion had tried to leap up, unsuccessfully, onto the back of it, leaving their hard claw marks deep in the new truck's paint. Meanwhile the boys had thrown all the tyre levers, jacks, ladders, jerry cans – anything and everything loose – over the back of the truck at the persistent, pursuing and annoyed lions.

****

Coming back a couple of hours later was the problem. It was I who had to stop the truck in the formerly lion-infested area and tentatively recover the flotsam and jetsam each time we came across another discarded piece of United States Steel Company's equipment.

A couple of vultures sitting on a mopane tree and a scavenging black-backed jackal were all that was left at the scene of the zebra kill on our return.

21.
LIONS: IT HAPPENS

While picking my way along the wheel tracks through the bush to the Shinamba Hills near Chobe in Northern Botswana, I observed a sad situation. An old and feeble lioness was trying to catch her dinner by charging into small groups of ducks loosely scattered about the shallow, ankle-deep waters of a swamp. The nimble ducks just fluttered 20 yards and settled down again completely unperturbed, for the lioness was old, though her claws were still as sharp as ever. HER OLD TEETH WERE SIMPLY WORN STUMPS. SHE COULD NOT CHEW MEAT EFFECTIVELY, SHE WAS FRAIL, EXHAUSTED, ALONE AND OBVIOUSLY ON HER LAST LEGS, while a small group of hyenas was gathering for her undoubted final, merciful (I hoped) execution!

When I returned the next morning, there was little left; tufts of lion hair, the chewed remains of her skull, the barely evident stumps of her worn canine teeth and a few of her still, surprisingly, just as-sharp-as-ever, scattered claws. I collected a few loose claws, cleaned them up and soaked them in a formalin solution for a while before drying them and mailing them to David Engel's daughter Treena back home in Adelaide, Australia, where she has since had them mounted in a silver setting and wears them sometimes as an unusual, mounted brooch with an African theme.

At least she knows the true story.

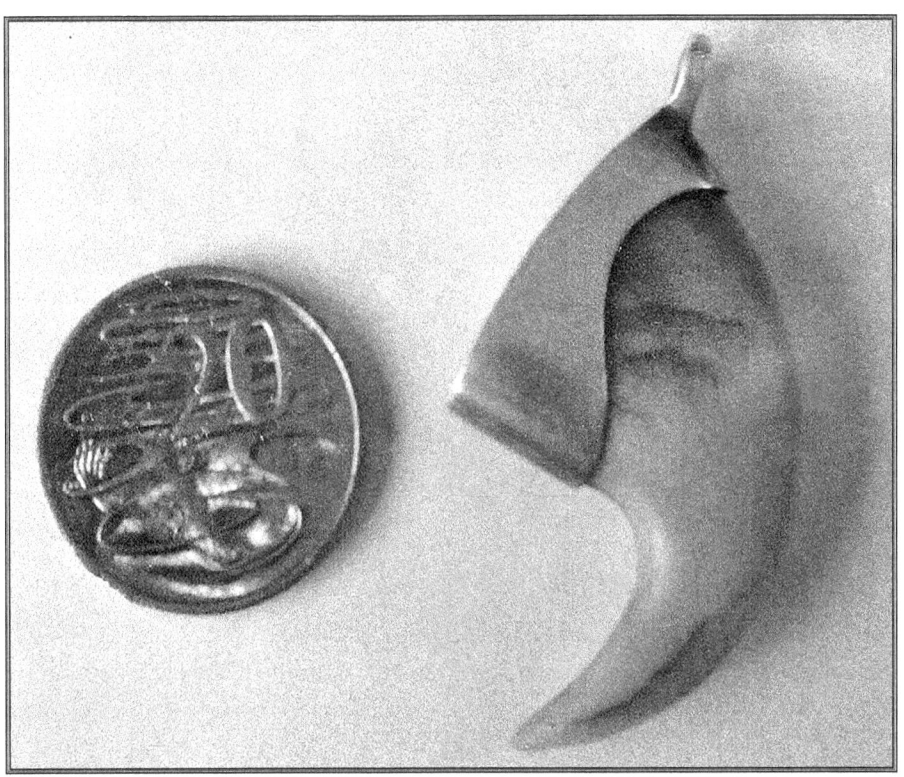

Treena Engel's mounted lion claw brooch

22.
SIESTA INTERRUPTUS

Threading my way down an isolated sandy bush track in the Eastern Kalahari, I came across a clump of small trees and a bit of shade and pulled into the cool shadows for an out-of-the-vehicle PIT STOP; A PEE,[8] A SANDWICH AND A NAP. I left the windows of the Land Cruiser half down for ventilation and half up for a little bit of security. I had then quietly read a week-old South African "Rand Daily Mail" newspaper, finished a cold Coke from the ice box and dozed off for a bit of a nap.

****

A little later I was alerted by a certain low guttural sound I recognised from another time and place. I turned my eyes to the left to see standing, right there in all his full majesty just ten feet from the passenger's door, a magnificent FULL-MANED MALE AFRICAN LION, many miles away from the protective Chobe game park. I quietly removed the lens cover from my Canon "Pellix" camera, quickly focussed the lens and pressed the shutter. This small CLICK unfortunately alerted the lion to my presence as I quickly wound the window right up for security. Although I was alone, I felt very safe and secure as I had in my lap a loaded .458 F.N. Elephant Gun, which gave me a great overall undoubted feeling of total security. I was not in any danger!

The lion then gave a sort of a SNUFFLING SNORT, so I stupidly verbally answered with my best rendition of a lion's ROAR! Well, it worked. The lion didn't roar but became agitated and ill at ease as he moved a step towards the passenger's door while looking directly at me through the glass side window. WE WERE THREE FEET APART EYE TO EYE, which is when I thought maybe I'd better go. This was

---

[8] Urination

mainly because I didn't want to get into a sticky situation where I might have to shoot an innocent lion, which I had been foolish enough to provoke and antagonise without a lawful, justifiable reason. It would be hard to explain the circumstances.

The LION WAS LEGITIMATELY PISSED OFF![9] And I couldn't blame him. At least I got a very good close-up photo of the lion in the African bush, outside a game park, and as a result the photo and its copyright are forever mine.

---

[9] Extremely angry

23.
CATTLE COUNTRY LIONS OF NATA

I was employed by the United States Steel Company (U.S. Steel) and engaged in DIAMOND AND COPPER MINERAL EXPLORATION ACTIVITIES IN THE CHOBE REGION OF NORTHERN BOTSWANA, formerly known as the "B. P." (British Bechuanaland Protectorate), bordering the North-West boundary of South Africa. In 1972, we were returning South from the Shinamba Hills to Johannesburg, South Africa, in our reliable old friend the Bedford 4 X 4 truck. The Shinamba Hills are a twinned pair of "tit-shaped",[10] stony 50-foot rises, remotely situated in the newly- designated game park area now called Chobe.

It was summer and the tinder-dry elephant grass was still 10 feet high, even while drooping wisplike half over the undefined sandy edge of our narrow, two-wheel, single file, sandy track. Thunderheads, thunderstorms and incessant lightning strikes lit up the twilight sky in the distance ahead as we set off in the still-warm but starting to cool air of a dry, African early evening; two of our tribal African workers, plus my good Aussie mate Ian Temme (ex S.P.S.C.) and me (ex P.A.C.), with most of our gear lying loosely sprawled in the back of the open truck, and a hessian sugar bag enclosing a loaf of fresh bread, margarine, and important and hard-to-get AUSSIE VEGEMITE AND OUR APRICOT JAM, plus my last, highly-treasured, breakable, heavily-padded, strongly-wrapped, African-sourced and RARE BOTTLE OF SOUTH AUSSIE COOPERS ALE. Not to mention a large bunch of slowly ripening bananas plus a few inedible blankets, kitbags, fuel, spare wheels, jacks, and the usual crowbars, tyre levers, jack handles, tins of preserved food and water (Manzi) etc. All these items were held loosely in place by the constant force of gravity and the solid steel, no- escaping-sideways, 18-inch-high sides of the truck.

---

[10] Breast-shaped

We had only been travelling about an hour when we were startled by an influx of small GAME ANIMALS EXPLODING WITHOUT WARNING FROM THE HIDDEN BLACK OF THE AFRICAN BUSH in front of us, mainly from the left, or East side, of the narrow, loose, sandy, indistinct wheel-tracks we were carefully following.

Impala pouring out of the thick bush; some out-of-place waterbuck; a small mob of zebra; small, timid-minded, big-eared, bat-eared foxes; a disoriented Jabiru-sized secretary bird; a large eagle owl followed by a couple of magnificent long, spiral- horned kudu antelopes; and a split-second glimpse of a leopard as it sprang across our path without leaving a single paw-print in the soft, night-cooled African sand.

A strengthening breeze was also coming from our left. We could smell, and sometimes see, wisps of smoke, and had ever-increasing glimpses of the steadily- brightening, rapidly-approaching, illuminated fiery red sky on the South-Eastern horizon, effectively backlighting the strange, gnarled, stark, twisted ghost-like silhouettes of the midnight black mopani, boab, fig and teak tree forest.

Next, a small herd of great heavy-horned African buffalo came thundering out of a small clearing, dangerously scraping obliquely past us; large, race-horse-sized, light- framed eland antelope leaping right across our path, just missing our high, dirty, insect-smeared windscreen – leaping maybe 10 feet high, clearly intent on achieving, somehow, an unofficial African OUTER SPACE, FREE FLIGHT ORBIT OR OUTER SPACE HEIGHT RECORD. They leapt right across our track, their "winged feet" seemingly never touching the ground. If we were not crawling along at a very shuffling pedestrian 10 miles per hour, we would surely have hit them fair and square with our high windscreen while they were still mid-air.

At this time, we saw a few RED AND EVEN MORE BRILLIANT WHITE-HOT BURNING, SHOOTING-STAR-LIKE EMBERS STREAKING PAST

ABOVE THE TREES, high overhead, and realised we were getting dangerously close to the fire front or fronts. It was just thick, African bush all around. IT WAS NIGHT. We were not at that time carrying two-way radios and if something untoward happened we were completely on our own in the dubious hands of our as-yet-unknown, untried and untested devices. We were hours from our base camp and the comfort of our cosy camp stretchers in our galvanised, barbed-wire-protected, wooden-pole, lion-proof huts that were now way back behind us in the remote Shinamba Hills in Chobe, 50 miles south of Kasane on the Zambezi river in Northern Botswana. (Kasane is where Elizabeth Taylor the actress re-married Richard Burton in 1975).

****

THEN IN MINUTES WE WERE RIGHT IN IT!

Luckily for us it was shortly after the fire front had crossed over and safely burnt both sides of the track, which still fleetingly lay just ahead of us.

****

We were now passing, picking up and removing fallen burning branches and twisted saplings, and sometimes going completely off-road, fender bashing our way over the cinders through the bush, past the remnant, blackened, still-smouldering logs, larger tree trunks, stumps and burning embers. At the same time we couldn't miss seeing the remnant charred, still-smouldering, still tentatively-hanging remains of the INTRICATELY WOVEN, HIGHLY-FLAMMABLE, THREAD-SUSPENDED WEAVER BIRDS' NESTS AND THEIR INCINERATED NESTLINGS in the all-vanquishing ashes of the jet black, scorched earth of the night … the flammable bush now rendered common black and neutrally harmless by the sterile ashes on both sides of the track.

There was NO MOON. The sides of the track ahead were an invisible carbon black, with a few odd, still-burning, glowing, twinkling, sprinkling-red and fiery-yellow flickering embers. We felt the worst was over. We were breathing easy and now doing a heady 20 miles per hour-plus in the gradually-firming, more positive wheel- contacting, retentive sands of the underlying track, and gradually, gradually accelerating. At last the road ahead was really good and it was "full steam ahead!"

Which is precisely when IT nearly happened.

THE GREAT, BLACK, REAR END of the last member of a string of night-black elephants – "ELEPHANTS WITHOUT TAIL-LIGHTS" – just ambling along the single- file track, in a single "one way" file, the largest five-ton bull elephant bringing up the rear. Surrounded as we were on both sides by sparkling, ember-lit, contrasting charcoal-black country, why we did not hit him squarely in the "bum" I do not know; but we didn't. All we could express moments after was a very relieved "P'HEW!" The great elephants wisely and magically sidestepped and disappeared mysteriously into the black of the night, and we sensibly slowed down for a while longer.

****

After an hour or so we had left the burning bush, the lightning bolts, a few very large , promising drops of rain and the cacophony of thunder well behind, while the masking bushfire smoke had finally blown right away revealing THE MOST BEAUTIFUL CONTRASTING, CRYSTAL-CLEAR, DEEPEST MIDNIGHT-BLUE SKY. The jewelled stars of Africa hung down like brilliant, dazzling glow-worms in immediately-recognisable constellations. A BRILLIANT SOUTHERN CROSS, other crystal-clear, space-hanging celestial chandeliers, and the ALWAYS MYSTERIOUS SWORD OF ORION hypnotically held our out-of-this-world attention, while inducing a dreamy, serene, wispy type of mental pleasure as our souls somehow soared spiritually above our earth-bound, disconnected, subconscious bodies.

With our wandering thoughts back on earth again and mentally in one piece, our mortal bodies and bruised bums kept on driving south, over the washaways, the corrugations, the rutted bumps and the snaking, twisted, intertwining, bodily- and mentally-tiring wheel tracks of the KALAHARI. This was until we reached the more open, semi-civilised cattle-grazing ranch lands of Eastern Botswana, past the odd fence, a fox terrier-sized Duiker antelope, an impala or two, and a long-dead, thoroughly on-the-nose giraffe, its squashed, flattened neck lying right across the dirt track, its tail presumably removed by someone for making long, coarse-haired "Sjamboks" (African whips), and finally a few civilising, reassuring road signs. The cattle were locally sparse because, generally unknown to outsiders, they were still on the sometime menu of the small but still present local pride of lions (completely unknown to us weary, night-time travellers). These were lions who didn't seem to know they were not supposed to be there; they hadn't read the book!

****

We were only at this time about 20 miles North of the small African village of NATA. It was probably about 3.00 a.m, Tired and sleepy, I finally pulled the Bedford over to the side of the now-formed, graded and recognisable but still unfenced dirt road for a bit of a snooze. The four of us settled down on old moth-eaten thin blankets on the hard, unyielding, "soft" concrete-like, side-sloping steel floor of the truck, with me personally wishing, despairingly, for an accommodating, matching, comforting "hip-hole", kangaroo style, to somehow magically impress itself into the steel deck of the truck for my own personal hip comfort. This was together with the aid of a very solid, uncomfortable, wedge-shaped, hard teak, wooden wheel-chocking block, which was at least seemingly "WARMER, IF NOT SOFTER" than the hard, cold steel deck of the truck, put to use as a completely unsatisfying "incompressible pillow", yet in seconds I was, in spite of all and sundry, fast asleep.

I slept briefly but after a while, in my sub-conscious, I gradually became aware of certain low, deep, throaty, meaty, vibrating sounds gnawing in my ears, coming from large vibrating feline tonsils close by; or was I dreaming? Then I thought, "NO, THIS IS CATTLE COUNTRY, IT COULDN'T BE?", and tried to get back to sleep. But then I heard Ian whisper, "You awake John?" This woke me right up. "Yes Ian! DID YOU HEAR IT TOO?" Then one of the until-now-silent Africans lying on the back of the truck beside us, said, "We better go boss, dem lions is gett'n close". We then realised by their soft, yet penetrating snuffling, guttural, grunting noises that prowling lions were nearby, perhaps 50 yards away. And so, without a second's delay, as quick as a flash, Ian got down to the ground on his, and the lions', unprotected and more vulnerable side of the truck in order to obtain access to the door, all the while peering apprehensively over his shoulder into the unseen black of the night as he tried to enter the cabin and wind the window up in full view of the very NOCTURNALLY- EFFICIENT, WIDE-OPEN-EYED LIONS HE COULD NOT SEE. Meanwhile, I got down to the ground on the safer right-hand side of the truck, then up again in an instant onto the high side-steps, through the door and settled into my seat in the high cabin, with the bulk of the truck between me and the hungry lions.

In the cabin I found a torch but the old batteries were nearly flat. I was just dimly able to see the eyes of at least three prowling lions about 80 yards away before the feeble torch flickered briefly, gave up the ghost and expired. Behind me on the open back of the truck, THE TWO AFRICANS, BY THEIR OWN CHOICE, WERE ACTUALLY LOOKING EXPECTANTLY FOR A FIGHT; A FIGHT WITH THE MARAUDING LIONS while standing up, totally vulnerable and blinded by darkness, on the high deck of the truck while looking eagerly into the hidden gloom for a probably fruitless life and death battle against their still-unseen, sharp-clawed feline adversaries. All this while pitifully armed with heavy but slow-wielding, agricultural type picks, crowbars, shovels and a "panga" or two (big heavy-bladed cane knives), and as a final impossible resort, big, eight-foot-long, heavy teak-wood fencing posts, which, unfortunately, would have been completely unmanageable in a fray with lions except in the hands of giants. All this potentially HEAVY, SLOW-TO-HANDLE, SELF-DEFENSIVE TYPE, PUNY FIREPOWER IN THE HANDS OF THOSE WHO COULD NOT SEE IN THE DARK, AGAINST THE LIGHTNING-FAST REFLEXES OF THE LIONS, WHO COULD SEE PERFECTLY WELL, DAY OR NIGHT. (I think in hindsight this was a stupid, non- thinking act of bravado).

Reassuringly, with Ian and I now ensconced back in the safety of the cabin and freely breathing again, our two African warriors were doing a challenging, vocal, mumbo-jumbo, foot-stomping, sabre-rattling war dance or Maori-style "HAKA" on the wide- open, unprotected, absolutely freely-lion-accessible back of the truck.

Thankfully, the motor started at the very first touch and tickle of the starter. Off with the handbrake, foot on the clutch, an impatient, roughly-handled, gearbox-shattering CLUNK and "Oops", into gear, foot off the clutch, truck moving cautiously ahead, and moments later, greatly relieved, we roared off down the road, just like the lions themselves, and in for the kill.

****

Lion memories … buried where no one really cares in the stacked and endless pages of living/ dying history while standing under the almost perpetual starry African night, and mentally commiserating, lion-like, on the whisper-quiet, endless, timeless, drifting sands of the Kalahari.

****

As our brightly-contrasting headlight beams sliced their way like a razor through the instantly-parting black folds of the remnant African night, THE REAL, PISSED-OFF, NOCTURNAL LIONS OF NATA WERE LEFT IN THE DARK TO LICK THEIR LIPS, while possibly, in the end, stalking off with empty stomachs in a thoroughly frustrated mood in search of a rancher's cow.

EVENTS IN OZ

24.
GERMS AND OTHER ADULT "CRAP"

It was 1939. My Grandmother and I were at her new beach house on Whitton Bluff at Port Noarlunga, 21 miles South of Adelaide, Australia.

My Mother then arrived in her Mother's brand-new Hudson Terraplane with two MOUNTAINOUS DOUBLE ICE CREAM CONES recessed in a perforated cardboard tray from the "deli"[11] around the corner. I was a five-year-old boy and had never before had a six-penny double ice cream, just the usual small one-penny serve and occasionally the larger three-penny model. A double ice cream at that time to a five-year-old was like winning the lottery and I reached out expectantly to my Grandmother to receive my prize.

But in a fraction of an instant I was beaten to the punch by my Grandmother who usually didn't eat sweets! On this august occasion, with all the reserved hesitation of "Lightning Pedro", she took immediate, unquestioned possession of MY PRIZE before I could even blink. This was followed by her HUGE, DROOLING, SLURPY, SALIVA- GUSHING, VACUUM CLEANER-LIKE, ALL CONSUMING MOUTHFUL, which is the time she finally handed the now rendered poisonous ice cream remnants back to me for a lick! Then, without a word, she silently left the scene of her unwitting "crime" and went inside the house as though nothing untoward had ever happened. This left a very DISILLUSIONED ME, a five-year-old boy, between a rock and a hard place.

Adults, mainly orchestrated by my Grandmother, had been drumming into me right from the start the inherent danger of fleeting contact with

---

[11] "Deli" slang for delicatessen; a small shop, usually situated on a street corner, selling mainly things like milk, bread, ice cream, fizzy drinks and lollies/ sweets

invisible unseen nasties called "GERMS!" Opportunistic germs which lurked anywhere and everywhere; on used knives, forks, spoons, cups, drinking vessels and other persons' bodies. Especially their fingers, tongues, saliva, teeth, hair and lips, and other UNMENTIONABLE PRIVATE PARTS.

I just stood in the driveway balling my eyes out as my ice cream slowly melted in and over my hands, and formed long vanilla-flavoured stalactites hanging, dripping, all the way to the ground. Which is when my Grandmother, noticing my absence from the house, came out and found me standing in A FOOT-WIDE ICE CREAM PUDDLE and said,

"WHAT ARE YOU DOING YOU STUPID CHILD? WHY DON'T YOU EAT YOUR ICE CREAM?"

I said,

"Because you licked it!"

To which, without obvious considered thought on her part, she replied,

"BUT I'M YOUR GRANNIE!"

****

I was totally confused. I didn't know what to think.

These thoroughly "failed times" bring me to the end of this unfortunate confusing episode, which will forever remain locked in my memory as the

"NEFARIOUS DOUBLE ICE CREAM AFFAIR".

****

This brings me to another load of ADULT CRAP.

There was a very successful child actor in Hollywood in the '30s, the darling of the cinema with long, sissy, golden curls: SHIRLEY TEMPLE. My dear old Grandmother and other uncles and aunts were persistently drumming into me the absolute need to "EAT YOUR BREAD CRUSTS. IF YOU DON'T, YOUR HAIR WON'T GO CURLY". I don't remember any adult asking me if I wanted long, sissy, curly hair. I didn't. I was a five-year-old, red-blooded boy. LOOK LIKE SHIRLEY TEMPLE? NO WAY!

****

Reminds me of another adult-orchestrated furphy pounded into my impressionable young mind by my dear old, unthinking Grannie.

"YOU MUST CHEW EVERY MOUTHFUL OF FOOD ONE HUNDRED TIMES".

I tried to but was left still chewing my cud at the table when the others had all finished and left. Which is about the time my Grannie said to my mother,

"THERE MUST BE SOMETHING WRONG WITH HIM, HE'S SUCH A SLOW EATER!"

****

I was now a little older and along came my 8th birthday, and with it, out of the blue, a HALF-SIZED VIOLIN and a prepaid term of violin lessons conducted by Lilli Palmer in Rose Park. This seems to have happened because of an earlier exploratory question by my Grandmother who, posing it as a clever trick question, had asked me, "WHAT'S YOUR FAVOURITE MUSICAL INSTRUMENT?" Off the top of my head I had said "the VIOLIN".

I'm sorry Nana, but I was not the least bit interested in actually playing the fiddle, either in my time, for you or for anyone else, and especially after school!

****

I've included these stories on behalf of young kids who are maybe not as dumb as you think and would rather receive STRAIGHT TALK from adults and NOT SO MUCH COMPLETE GIBBERISH.

P.S. Eat your vegetables, especially cauliflower, swedes, turnips, cabbage and broccoli.

25.
DAISY BATES 1941

I was a seven-year-old Cub Boy Scout in 1941, and Lord Baden Powell, the esteemed founder and leader of the Boy Scouts and Girl Guides movements had recently died in England. A Memorial Service was being held in Adelaide at the St. Peters Anglican Cathedral, where I accompanied my Grandmother on a warm summer's day.

After the service, a sea of ancient people mingled on the spacious, adjacent lawns, and my Nana was engaged in conversations with various people she presumably knew. I must have wandered away, when suddenly I realised I had somehow lost my Grandmother in an impenetrable forest of tall, overshadowing, overpowering adults. Before I had time to worry, I was rescued by an 81-year-old lady, a living remnant of the past, straight from the late 1800s, who held me firmly by the hand. I realised her dress and appearance was 100% Victorian in fashion, and that she, in fact, was really somewhat out of step with the contemporary times in which we were presently immersed. She asked my name, if I was a Cub Scout, and said, "Your Gran can't be far away". A minute or two of chit-chat, when after about five minutes my Nana reappeared and reassumed control of me, after first having quite a long conversation with my kindly, ancient, Victorian-era benefactor.

My Grandmother asked if I knew who my rescuer was. I had no idea. She told me the Victorian lady was Daisy Bates, a famous lady who usually lived in a tent on the desolate Nullarbor Plain in a small, still-surviving, Australian tribal Aboriginal group, and was recording their history while she still had time. It was eventually published as "The Passing of the Aborigines: A Lifetime Spent Among the Natives of Australia".

Whenever in Adelaide, Daisy Bates had the honour of staying at Government House as a highly respected member of society and a guest of the Governor. Long after she had died in 1951, and with the later popularity of the Anglo/ Boer War film "Breaker Morant", it turned out that SHE AND BREAKER MORANT HAD IN FACT BEEN MARRIED to each other for a time in the late 1880s. As a point of interest, it was pointed out to me, much later, that I may be one of the last living people to have actually held the living hand of Daisy Bates, who, as his wife, had earlier held the living hand of her husband "The Breaker". Therefore …

I GUESS I AM CONNECTED EVER SO TENUOUSLY TO THE BREAKER, DAISY BATES AND THE ANGLO/ BOER WAR BY TWO HANDSHAKES!

26.
DIAMOND JIM 1943

When I was about four, in 1938, my Grandmother took me along on a visit to the 10,000 ton liner R.M.S. Manoora berthed at Port Adelaide.

My Aunt Mary, nee Welch, was married to Bill Brady, who was the ship's Purser in the '30s and succeeding war years. During the war, the Manoora was pressed into service in the Australian Navy as an armed merchant cruiser and served throughout the war in the South Pacific.

The Manoora was painted battleship grey for its naval service; that is, all except Uncle Bill's brightly painted cabin, which looked and smelt of cigars and expressed an ambience well above its lowly status. Maybe he did a private job with commandeered Japanese paint? He was also known to be able to produce the odd bottle of Scotch in an emergency.

I remember him telling us of an encounter in the South Pacific with an American cruiser whose Captain enquired whether the Manoora had any spare mutton on board. They were willing to exchange their turkey for our mutton on a pound-for- pound basis. An exchange took place; they were happy, we were happy, and both sides considered they had the better of the deal.

By about this time, Uncle Bill had become known to the American Navy as "DIAMOND JIM", and to this day I still can't help wondering why. Maybe I shouldn't ask? Post war, Uncle Bill shipped shore-side as the Providore for the Adelaide Steamship Company, owner operators of the Manoora and a fleet of other ships, at their Currie Street Adelaide headquarters, and remained there until he retired. His widow, my Aunt Mary, lived on and died at Semaphore, South Australia, at age 97 in about 2005.

27.
JOHNNIE SNOWBALL 1946

It was about 1946, I was about 13, wandering about the interesting trading ships visiting Port Adelaide, occasionally being invited aboard to look over a vessel, including the bridge, the hold, or the engine room, etc. The S.S. Fort Deaslake was a typical, small, post-war trading vessel, or "TRAMP-SHIP", flagged I think, in Panama. A twentyish, well-spoken, BLACK AFRICAN-AMERICAN sailor, JOHNNIE SNOWBALL, was pleased to show me over the vessel from stem to stern, which I really appreciated.

As it was early afternoon, I asked whether he had ever seen a kangaroo. The answer being, "NO", I said I could show him around the Adelaide Zoo if he liked. He seemed pleased to accept my suggestion. We caught a trolley bus to the city and enjoyed a pleasant visit to the Australian section of the zoo, and since it was still only mid- afternoon, I asked would he like to come back to my mother's house at Burnside for tea. My mother was used to me sometimes arriving home with interesting characters I had just met and I knew she would not mind.

We got off the bus at Tusmore and walked the half mile past Hazelwood Park to our large house on Greenhill Road, passing some of my schoolmates' fathers in their front gardens. "Good afternoon Mr. YOUNG". Instant frozen silence. That's odd! "Good afternoon Mr INWOOD". A funny look and not a word spoken? I started to feel uneasy. We crossed Burnside Road and arrived at 282 where my uncle, a discharged army captain, Rolfe Sabine, was staying with us, and on this day was also working in the garden.

Taking one look at the new-found situation I had presented, my uncle said in a very stern voice, "Your mother's been looking all over for you, she wants you INSIDE, IMMEDIATLEY!"

Wondering what was so urgent, I raced inside. "What did you want to see me about Mum?" To which she said, "I didn't want to see you!" Smelling one very big rat, I ran to the drawing room window and looked out in time to see my uncle gesticulating and telling Johnnie Snowball, in no uncertain obvious terms, to "GET OUT AND GET LOST!" I saw an UNHAPPY, CRESTFALLEN, JOHNNIE SNOWBALL shrugging his shoulders as he despondently walked out the gate, without looking back, trudging forlornly back to the Tusmore terminus, the bus to the city and another bus back to Port Adelaide.

About six weeks later, I received a very nice letter from Johnnie, mailed from Port Lytellton, the port for Christchurch in New Zealand, in which he said he was SORRY he couldn't accept my kind offer to dinner, as UNFORTUNATELY SOMETHING CAME UP AND HE HAD TO GO!

It was then I was pleasantly surprised to realise that in spite of his bad experience at our house, he had very THOUGHTFULLY NOTED, REMEMBERED and then LATER WRITTEN DOWN the NUMBER OF OUR HOUSE and the NAME OF THE STREET, and had somehow found the NAME OF OUR SUBURB!

It's because of this 1946 event, the memory of which has always bugged me, that I have recounted this letter. Johnnie could still be alive, in his 80s, probably in the U.S.A.? President Obama might know!

28.
HOME AGAIN 1947

Ian Brook and I were riding "Dolly" and "Robin" home, about 25 miles from Woodside, after they'd had an eight-months spell in the green and grassy ADELAIDE HILLS. We were mostly walking, the horses occasionally stopping to grab a bite of tempting, succulent grass, sometimes trotting (Dolly was an ex-pacer) even a mile or two at the canter when on good ground. We ambled down the high, narrow, ridge of the O ld Norton Summit Road while watching a pair of wedge tailed eagles gliding past closely overhead, and then turned South over the Eastern Adelaide foothills towards Burnside, past the still-operating Penfolds Winery and its associated, still-functioning acres of vineyards, and the GREAT SCAR of Quarries Ltd's 1950s STONYFELL QUARRY, imposing itself for all to see.

At this time, we were about three miles from home, when without any input or directional or instructional guidance from either of us, our PACE VISIBLY QUICKENED as the horses in their eagerness attempted to take control. We allowed them to trot a bit since they clearly wanted to go faster and turn a trot into a canter or even faster. As they got closer to home they became very hard to hold. Penfolds Road, Kensington Road, Halletts Road, a sudden right turn into the top of Godfrey Street at the canter and scraping my shoulder on the LARGE GUM TREE that still stands, GUILTY TO THIS DAY, on the verge near the top North-East corner of Godfrey Street.

They knew where they were. They had a lust for home. They were hard to hold at more than a fast trot and they were really pulling at the bit. Pulling South down Lockwood Road and a fast, sharp, right-hand turn into busy Greenhill Road, 100 yards down the hill, opposite Mrs Cooper's FERNILEE LODGE, hardly seeing with a lump in my throat in the sudden emotion of the moment and wind-induced teary eyes as the horses quickened their race to home.

Left turn into our open home driveway, 100 yards up the driveway, straight past the house at a canter, past the kitchen and straight through the doors of the wooden stables out the back! Dolly bypassed Robin's temptingly-full feed box and went directly to her old feed box a few steps further on, just as though she had never really left – she had forgotten nothing. Her feed box was full of the choicest chaff, warm bran and pollard, with a tasty apple on top, as was Robin's, placed there by my thoughtful Mother a short time before. At this point, we dismounted, unsaddled, and the horses were HOME, JUST AS THOUGH TO ALL INTENTS THEY HAD NEVER BEEN AWAY!

Me on Robin

29.
KLEINEBOOFYHAUSEN 1948

If you, the reader, know the meaning of the above, you are either Donald or Walter "Wally" Brown Junior.

In 1948, Walter Brown Senior employed a Germanic speaking housemaid. The Brown family owned a black Kelpie dog by the name of "Boofy" and the maid always referred to Boofy's dog kennel as the "KLEINEBOOFYHAUSEN".

Walter Brown Senior was Eve's, Don's and Wally Brown Junior's father. Don was a friend of mine at P.A.C. In 1948, '49 and '50, we knocked around quite a bit at school and after school, and did the odd foolish thing, such as nearly being caught by the caretaker from his pedestrian speed rowing boat when unlawfully fishing for Redfin perch in one of Adelaide's fresh water supply dams, the Thorndon Park Reservoir.

Gary Wight and I left P.A.C. midway through 1950 to join News Ltd., Adelaide, as cadet reporters (e.g. COPY BOYS), shortly before a certain Rupert Murdoch arrived on the scene. Don also left P.A.C. the same year but I'm not sure when Malcolm Cooper or Ian Burridge did. I do know that in 1955 I was employed by Elder, Smith & Co. in their machinery division, selling, among other things, AUSTRALIAN-MADE, BLUE STREAK CHAIN SAWS, when I was approached about chain saws by Malcolm Cooper.

Don Brown, meanwhile, was working his way up through the family business, W. Brown & Sons, having started at the bottom shovelling coal in the foundry to learn every part of the business before proceeding further up the long ladder of success, one hard-earned rung at a time.

Meanwhile, Malcolm Cooper had fallen on hard times, as had Ian Burridge, P.A.C., and Don Brown was at loggerheads with Walter Brown Senior over some obscure reason, so Don had, as a result of an argument over something, suddenly decided to leave the company, turn his back on the family business of W. Brown & Sons once and for all, and seek his fortune elsewhere in the big wide world.

Malcolm Cooper, meanwhile, had hit on the idea of making a small fortune by hard work, cutting down pine trees with axes and well-known Spaniard "Manuel Labour" in the Kuitpo Forest, deep in the Adelaide Hills. He had recruited Ian Burridge and Don Brown to join in this great, modern-times, free-enterprise venture. Malcolm was trying to work up a plan of some sort to buy a chain saw from me, but from memory nothing ever came of it. I believe it was decided axes were the simple and practical way to go.

In due course, they were teamed-up, set to start in the morning and raring to go at 5:00 a.m. The first arranged pick-up point was at Walter Brown's house in Sprod Avenue, Toorak Gardens, and right on time a large truck pulled up outside, laden with mean, lean and hungry woodcutters, and the driver got out to look at the street number. He was a little perplexed. It didn't really look like a typical woodcutter's house. There was a Rolls Royce in the driveway and the ex-Tommy Trinder's[12] Jaguar XK120, a rare and snarling "CAT", was menacingly growling behind the Rolls.

The ever-so-tentative driver knocked on Walter Brown's door at precisely 5:00 a.m. and seconds later Walter Brown Senior opened the beautifully-polished, handcrafted walnut door and said loudly, "WHADDA'YA'WANT?"

---

[12] Tommy Trinder was a famous English comedian and entertainer, particularly during World War 2

The driver sheepishly explained he was looking for a team of "ACE" woodcutters and had been given this address. Walter Brown exploded, "DOES THIS LOOK LIKE A WOODCUTTER'S HOUSE?", walked inside and closed the door behind him.

The woodcutters drove off.
DON REMAINED WITH W. BROWN & SONS.

****

Casting my mind back to about 1949, Don Brown was driving his father Walter, young Wally and Me in his father's Buick 8 down to Cape Jervis to look at kangaroos in the pine forests. We had minutes before left Sprod Avenue and were on Greenhill Road, and we were already about halfway across the Goodwood Road intersection without actually, legally stopping.

This was when we heard a loud YELL from under a tree from a middle-aged policeman, the spitting image of Jimmy Edwards, mounted on an old-fashioned bicycle with big coil springs under the seat. Being law abiding, Don naturally stopped for a moment halfway across Goodwood Road, when the irritated policeman said, "YOU WEREN'T GOING TO STOP!"

Don's father Walter Brown piped up, "HE STOPPED DIDN'T HE? DRIVE ON SON". And so we did, leaving a puzzled ancient policeman scratching his noggin[13] on the side of the road.

****

---

[13] Noggin is slang for "head"

WALTER BROWN SENIOR, WALTER BROWN JUNIOR, DONALD CAMERON BROWN AND I were on school holidays down the South-East of South Australia about 1948.

A Millicent fish shop owner and commercial fisherman, Mick Peters, with fishing rights over Lake George and its lake-bound Jack Salmon, had us out in the middle of the lake, baited up and ready to go. The lake was about six miles long and three miles wide, a couple of miles inland from the sea, but closed off from the saltwater most of the time by low water and sandbars.

I was a bit "GREEN" when it came to the ways of the world when I asked Mr. Peters how could he be sure the fish would be exactly where we were. "It's BERLEY son", he said. I said, "What's Berley Mr Peters?" So Walter Brown Senior said to Mr Peters, "Show him, Mick", and pulled up a very lifeless, long-deceased, waterlogged Black Swan from the depths of the lake. I said, without a moment's thought, "IT'S A SWAN". Walter Brown Senior said, "IT'S A RABBIT". At 14, I could not understand how an adult person could ever mistake a "Rabbit" for a "Swan", but then I was young, still learning the ways of the world and didn't quite know everything.

****

This reminds me of a story I heard at that time about Walter Brown Senior and his younger brother Alf, who sailed on the Queen Elizabeth shortly after it re-commenced sailing the Atlantic, not long after the end of World War 2. After a day at sea, it was obvious the Brown brothers represented substance and were invited to join the ship's Captain at the Captain's table for the remainder of the Atlantic crossing, which they seemed to enjoy. On their return to Adelaide, when asked what it was like on the Queen Elizabeth, Walter Senior was heard to remark, "IT WASN'T BAD, EXCEPT WE HAD TO EAT WITH THE CREW".

****

Don and I were active members of the Game Fishing Club of South Australia and used Don's "Bell-Boy" boat, Evinrude-powered, for our shark fishing attempts, mainly in association with Ray and Margaret Hambly-Clark. We spent a fair bit of time anchored around the back of Port Adelaide's Torrens Island without much luck. Knowing what I do now, I realise we were only about five miles shoreward of the Great Whites' regular stamping ground.

About 1965, Don and I were in Sydney for the Australian Game Fishing Competition on different allocated boats each day. On one day, we had Bob Dyer's crewed boat "Tennessee" allocated to us for our use, which wasn't all that hard to take! Don hooked but later lost a large fish, presumably a shark, at a submerged pinnacle known to Sydney Game Fishermen as "THE PEAK".

Years later, near Ceduna, I successfully hooked and played one Great White for eight hours but retired hurt with a bad hernia after losing two Great White Sharks in one day, one of them a likely new world record, from the same boat, the "Victory", in the same Franklin Island waters from which the five other largest Great Whites had previously been caught, including the long-standing record of 2,664 pounds. The title of this book, "FAILED TIMES and TWISTED FOLLIES", is largely based on my all- failed Great White Shark fishing attempts and numerous other unmentionable stuff- ups.

30.
THE ROCKET'S RED GLARE 1948

About 1946, some of our pre-teenage mates had been looking around the UNGUARDED, WIDE-OPEN, DOORLESS EXPLOSIVES SHED ABOVE THE GREAT SCAR-LIKE QUARRY FACE OF STONYFELL QUARRIES on Adelaide's Eastern hills' outskirts.

By their account, the magazine was a large, open, 20 X 30-foot galvanised steel shed, situated about 700 feet high up in the scrub above Slapes Gully. The GELIGNITE explosive was generally held in bulk in secure, well-made, dovetailed wooden boxes, where the individual plugs just sat loosely awaiting inspection by the local inquisitive lads. I seem to have forgotten individual names but subsequently

P.A.C. and S.P.S.C. names, many years later, still come surprisingly to mind. Waterproof WAX VESTA MATCHES and waterproof safety fuse shared the same box as the No. 6 detonators, which the fuse was ultimately intended to ignite. The safety fuse was uncanny, as when lit, it burnt safely (?) underwater.

Cubic black No. 6 tins of detonators were loosely arrayed around the frame of the shed, right next to the UNGUARDED, HIGHLY VULNERABLE, GELIGNITE they were intended ultimately to ignite and explode. Most of the local lads had "filched" a stick or two of gelignite, which is similar to dynamite. Most of the purloined explosive matter ultimately met an inglorious end, EITHER IN THE GARBAGE BIN OR BURIED IN THE BACK REACHES OF A FATHER'S GARDEN. This, however, caused a bit of a furore in a father's garden when a single plug of GELIGNITE INSTEAD OF A POTATO turned up on the sharp end of the father's fork!

About this time, some errant youths managed to blow up the brick letterbox of a house near the Anderson's, facing Hazelwood Park, more-or-less exactly behind the Burnside Police Station, and that of Ken Stacy, the easy-going policeman. This episode made local news in the paper and on the radio, which was well before the introduction of T.V. The suspected, unidentified miscreants were many.

At this time, my mate Donnel Shepley (P.A.C.) somehow seems to have come across A SINGLE PLUG OF GELIGNITE; a softish, dampish, pliable, amorphous NITRO- GLYCERINE-BASED MATERIAL. We were inquisitive and being scientifically-minded, conducted safe tests on the "gelly". We cautiously peeled away the paper greaseproof wrapping and removed a chewing-gum-sized piece for further investigation. As part of our investigation, we placed the small piece of gelly on a long piece of twisted newspaper, about a foot long, lit the paper and stood back about 10 feet away to see if, when the flame reached the gelly, it either exploded or burnt.

Well, IT WAS A "FIZZER"!

Nothing happened. It simply burnt softly with a slightly effervescent yellowish flame and a slightly FIZZING sort of sound. This passive, effervescent fizzing reaction caused me to wonder what would happen if the gelignite was enclosed in a confined space, with the lower open orifice pointing down and tied to a stick, like a real skyrocket. There was only one way to find out.

MAKE ONE.

I couldn't find a suitable, ready-made hollow container in which to place a small amount of fizzing gelignite propellant. But then I was overjoyed to see an empty .303 bullet case on my mantelpiece. We taped the .303 case to a small stick with its open orifice pointing down and stuffed it full of gelignite, cleverly leaving a small "daggy- snot-like" piece hanging down to act as a SLOW BURNING IGNITION FUSE.

There was a good open rocket launch place behind the house in my Grandmother's rose garden, where we stood the "ROCKET" up in a tin of dry, loose sand. Losing the toss, it was up to Donnel to light the daggy looking fuse. He lit it and it fizzed for the largest part of a second as we envisaged a fiery red rocket "STREAKING" over Mrs Cooper's Fernilee Lodge on the opposite side of Greenhill Road

BLAM!

It exploded with the noise of a .303 rifle in my eardrum. DON WAS HOLDING HIS BLOODIED NOSE, which was a mess and required plastic surgery, while his legs were peppered with fine shrapnel. Blood dripping on my shoulder told me my left ear was bleeding.

It was about then we stopped stuffing around with gelignite. The "ROCKET'S RED GLARE" was for us an explosive non-event.

EXIT ANOTHER THOROUGHLY TWISTED FOLLY!

31.
KYM BONYTHON AND THE YELLOW SUBMARINE

John Brook and I were pioneer members of the Underwater Spear Fishing Club of South Australia in 1950. The word SCUBA was unknown at that time. We were living in the days of "AQUALUNGS", the name coined by their inventor Jacques Cousteau.

Wet suits were not under consideration at that time because common sense of the day told us they WERE WET AND COLD! Swim flippers haven't changed much, except they are bigger, and face masks still employ the same principles.

A few of us had WARM and DRY, thin rubber PIRELLI suits, inside which you could actually wear a warm woollen garment. Unfortunately, they were more easily punctured than the wet suits which ultimately followed, and LEAKING DRY SUITS immediately became amorphous, useless bags of non-radioactive "heavy water".

At the time, there was a profusion of harpoon-shooting spearguns available, including the French "Le Fusil Américaine" compressed, spring-powered gun and a few compressed air or CO_2 guns, but most were rubber-powered.

Independently, my friend Jack Conquest had converted an 1878 Martini-action .303 for use as an underwater speargun by boring out most of the barrel and removing the rifling. He then removed surplus metal from around the firing pin so that it would not be held back by the hydraulic cushioning effect of water and had all the parts cadmium plated. With a black powder charge of about a quarter-full cartridge case, suitably sealed and water-proofed, the gun fired a three-foot-long metal rod straight up in the air, and at times out of sight, something like 1,000 feet.

****

Sometime about 1958, the well-known Adelaide entrepreneur Kym Bonython was toying with the idea of buying a ONE-MAN YELLOW SUBMARINE but realised he would first have to learn the rudimentary ropes of the new sport of "skin diving", so he got in touch with my friend John Brook. John arranged to meet Kym on the overseas wharf at Outer Harbour one Sunday morning and I brought Joan Sainsbury along for the ride. John, Kym and I spent about an hour in and out of the harbour, which was about 60 feet deep, and Kym departed the scene having learned all he had to know. A little while later, he bought his yellow submarine. As I was writing this in 2013, Kym was recently deceased at about 91 years old. I was not too sure about the yellow submarine?

32.
THE SUPERGUN 1950

John Brook (J.B.) would have been 18. I would have been 16. I had an idea about making a gunpowder-powered, underwater speargun from my perfectly good single shot Lithgow .22 rifle. My idea was to remove the .22 bullet and propellant powder from its cartridge case and put the empty case back in the breech. Then, holding the rifle in a vertical position, trickle a small amount of the original propellant back down through a glass funnel into the open barrel and down into the lightly-loaded cartridge case as a LIGHT PRIMING CHARGE, and top it up with a greater amount of the presumably less powerful black gunpowder.

This I did, then using the cleaning rod as a "rammer", I forced toilet paper right down the barrel to seal the various powders in their newly-housed position. I then inserted a long length of close-fitting wooden dowelling down the barrel as a shaft for my experimental underwater spear, or harpoon gun. This was taking place in my small discrete workshop in Burnside, South Australia, and out of earshot of my mother's nearby house. As an afterthought, I wrapped an old bath towel right around and around the breech of the rifle, just in case my intentions were in any way misguided.

THIS IS ABOUT THE TIME I REALISED J.B. WAS MISSING. "Must have gone to the toilet", I thought. Anyway, finding the "trigger" buried deep in the bulky folds of the towel, I gently pulled it and THE LITTLE .22 LITERALLY EXPLODED with the noise of a very much larger .303 military rifle.

The cocking handle of the bolt of the small rifle sheared off. The body of the bolt escaped its towelling shroud and shot rearwards, smashing a glass jar of nuts and bolts to pieces on a shelf behind me, while my instant tingling hands felt as though I was back at Princes and had been on the receiving end of A THOUSAND CUTS OF THE CANE from Tex Dillon.

About this time, having missed the fun, J.B. came back into my shed as the smoke cleared. It was really very interesting as I unwrapped the rifle from its towelling shroud; the beautifully-grained rifle stock was no more. Just a longish, loose bundle of fibrous wood splinters, none of which individually could ever claim to have earlier been part of a rifle stock.

The interesting feature of my somewhat misguided "TWISTED FOLLY" experiment was the fact that the wooden dowelling shaft did not appear to have moved a fraction of an inch in its intended forward direction; it was jammed lock-solid in the barrel.

> I DIDN'T USE THE OLD "LITHGOW" AFTER THIS.
> I DIDN'T TRUST IT!

33.
DELMORE DOWNS 1950

After returning from England about 1948, my sister Pamela was employed as a governess by Geoff and Jessie Holt to help with the care of their son Donald on their station (ranch) called "DELMORE DOWNS", 160 miles North-East of the Alice[14] in Australia's Northern Territory. At 150 square miles or about 100,000 acres, Delmore was not large by Australian standards but big by most overseas' comparisons.

I was at that time a student at Prince Alfred College (P.A.C.), and the May school holidays were coming up, when I was invited up to Delmore by Geoff and Jessie for the two-week holidays, probably to humour my sister. I flew up from Adelaide with Trans Australian Airways (T.A.A.) in the latest hot shot Convair 240, a 300-miles per hour, piston-engine aircraft with a rearward-facing, internally-enclosed rear passenger access ramp. We landed at Leigh Creek, then Oodnadatta before circling and landing at Alice Springs four hours later. On arrival at the Alice, I was met by Jessie's brother Donald Chalmers and Millicent, his wife, who put me up for the night in their modern East-side home. The next day, Geoff and Jessie Holt arrived at Mrs Chalmers', his- sister-in law's home, in Bath Street, then after shopping in the morning we set off to Delmore Downs, calling in at Scotsman Alec Kerr's Delny Station on the way.

****

As a 16-year-old, I had a very interesting time at Delmore. It was different to life in suburban Adelaide and I guess it started my wander lust. Geoff's pride and joy at the time was his 998 c.c., 130 miles per

---
[14] Colloquial term for Alice Springs

hour VINCENT BLACK SHADOW MOTORCYCLE, which seemed a little lost in its unlikely off-road, rough dirt track surroundings. I had no idea at that time that I would soon have my own Vincent Black Shadow collection, starting within two years and ending early, in one piece, when I safely gave up motor bikes at age 21.

****

Delmore was running sheep at that time. The cold-climate Korean War was in full swing and warm wool was selling at record prices. But Geoff had one big problem caused by sheep losses at the hands of wild dogs and dingoes, or losing lambs wholesale to the numerous, large wedge tailed eagles, not to mention hordes of grass-eating kangaroos. Once or twice he employed a professional kangaroo shooter to reduce their numbers to a more acceptable level, while using some of their kangaroo carcasses laced with cyanide to attract and poison the eagles. For dingo control, it was an endless battle setting leg traps or poisoning kangaroo carcasses with tasteless, odourless strychnine rubbed into open cuts on the kangaroo bodies. Dingoes would not touch a carcass laced with smelly cyanide.

The other stations surrounding Delmore were all cattle stations, where dingoes and eagles were not a problem. So Geoff really had an unresolved problem unique to the few sheep ranchers like him in the area.

****

I had never been on the back of a motor bike when Geoff said, "Hop on the pillion seat of the Black Shadow", handed me a cocked and loaded, long-barrelled German 9 m.m. Luger pistol, and set off in search of kangaroos.

Well, AT 40- OR 50-MILES PER HOUR WITHOUT GOGGLES, MY COMPLETELY UNACCUSTOMED EYES STREAMED A NON-STOP RIVER OF BLINDING TEARS, so that when we came up alongside a fast-moving blur of kangaroo, I couldn't see a thing. I blindly shot the earth, rocks, trees and stumps. I EMPTIED THE MAGAZINE OF THE LUGER ON EVERYTHING EXCEPT A KANGAROO! I guess, as a result of my marksmanship, I was not exactly flavour of the month in Geoff's humble opinion.

****

Later we were in a World War 2, 1.5 ton International truck about 15 miles from the homestead when the engine went dead. Geoff said, "Wait here, I'll be back in two or three hours with a new condenser". Sure enough, he walked or jogged 15 miles home through the bush, gathered various electrical vehicle items and arrived back in a utility, all in less than three hours, fitted a new condenser and fixed our problem.

****

About 1950, the Ford Motor Company in Australia produced a number of 1938 model V8 Ford cars using existing old, but new, Ford parts, and the newly-assembled vehicles were SOLD AS NEW FORD V8 "PILOTS", one of which Geoff bought. About this time, Geoff was also captivated by another pre-war American car, sold as the "CORD", and had one delivered by rail 500 miles from Melbourne on the OVERLAND TRAIN to Adelaide and 1,000 miles on the GHAN TRAIN from Adelaide to the Alice. Geoff took one look at the CORD when it arrived, didn't like what he saw, and RETURNED IT TO SENDER, 1,500 miles back in Melbourne, Victoria without actually removing the vehicle from the Ghan. The dealer in far off Melbourne was not a happy chappie.

****

A side trip on to McDonald Downs Station, owned by another of Jessie's brothers, Mack Chalmers, saw me fascinated by various strange insects, such as the Masked Wood Moth and the Masked Wood Swallow, as well as the new-to-me, seven-foot- long PERENTIE[15] – the largest GOANNA – a less bulky, smaller cousin of the GIANT KOMODO DRAGON in nearby Indonesia.

****

Geoff gave me a pair of Aboriginal "KADAITCHA" boots; shoes actually made from soft bird under-feathers, cemented together with dried kangaroo blood in a feathered slipper shape. They were traditionally worn by an Aboriginal assassin when doing his dirty work and usually left no guilty tracks or footprints behind after a clandestine murderous mission in the darkness of the night.

****

My week at Delmore was over, and now it was time to go the 160 miles back to the Alice, overnight at Mrs Chalmers' in Bath Street, and watch a movie at one of the open-air, deck-chair-seated picture theatres with flying ants, mosquitoes and huge stinking Christmas Beetles farting and shitting in flight and endlessly crashing on to one and all of the sundry, seated, tolerant movie goers. Then back to Adelaide on the Convair 240 in the morning, with my appetite for all things new and outback interests thoroughly whetted.

****

I went out to Delmore about 30 years later after winning the inventors' prize on Channel Nine with my CARR-B-Q bush barbecue.[16] After

---

[15] A large lizard

[16] Often shortened to B.B.Q. in Australia, hence my naming it the "CARR-B-Q"

seeing a Carr-B-Q for the first time, Donald Holt, Geoff and Jessie's son, was quite taken with THE BARBECUE CONCEPT and purchased a few from me to give his friends and relations as presents. Geoff and Jessie at that time were living in retirement in the Alice. They both passed away sometime about the year 2000 and are buried out at Delmore, while Donald, his wife Janet and family are still in occupation at Delmore, raising hardy, dingo-resisting, big-framed cattle, and/ or wholesaling Aboriginal paintings from nearby UTOPIA,[17] while at 80, at the time of writing, I am now in outback New South Wales and actually making some more "Carr-B-Qs" before I finally slip off the perch.

---

[17] Utopia is a remote Aboriginal community

34.
THE GHAN 1950

From the mid-1800s until 1929, in the case of Alice Springs, AFGHAN CAMEL TRAINS were employed in outback Australia to convey all types of food and material goods to the distant INLAND; to new settlements, towns, mines, cattle or sheep stations (ranches) and other isolated missions, etc. The camel drivers were mostly experienced natives of Afghanistan or the present Pakistan, from where the single - humped, dromedary camels and their Afghan cameleers were originally sourced.

One of the last Marree-based Afghan cameleers was Bejah Dervish, about 105 years old, who died in 1957. He had actually served under Lord Roberts at the Khyber Pass. When the railway line was extended from Oodnadatta in northern South Australia to Alice Springs in the southern part of the Northern Territory in 1929, it broadly followed the route of the earlier camel trains over the generally soft, sandy, arid, spiky, spinifex-bordered track. The new train retracing the old Afghan camel drivers' route quickly became known unofficially as the "GHAN"; the NOW OFFICIAL NAME IT PROUDLY CARRIES TODAY.

****

In December 1950, I met a fellow pupil on the Ghan, Ben Smith, from P.A.C., the school I had attended in Adelaide. He was returning to his parents' home in Alice Springs for Christmas and his annual school holidays. Ben's father was D. D. SMITH, the long-time head of the Northern Territory Works and Housing Department, who, during World War 2, undertook the construction of – BUILT – THE SEALED STUART HIGHWAY, 954 miles from Alice Springs to Darwin in the Territory's top end (a road still ignorantly believed by some to have been built by the Americans).

The Ghan journey at that time would be UNIMAGINABLE TODAY. It was THREE WHOLE DAYS, starting with a five-foot-three-inch broad gauge rail from Adelaide, about 140 miles to the silver-lead smelting town of Port Pirie, where we changed trains, then stepped down for a short 60 miles stint on the "International" standard four-foot-eight-and-a-half-inch gauge line to Quorn at the base of the Flinders Ranges, not far from Port Augusta. As a point of interest, I have since learned the "International" gauge was derived from the WIDTH OF THE ALMOST FOSSIL WHEEL RUTS DISCOVERED IN ENGLAND, dating from the Roman occupation, and the actual confirming remains of original chariots, discovered still intact, in Pompeii, ITALY, in the 1800s.

After changing trains again, the final 760 miles from Quorn to Alice Springs was a cheap, plus or minus 20 miles per hour, antiquated, "clickety-clack" line even before it was built; a cheap, narrow, three-foot-six-inch gauge line, using LIGHTER RAILS DATED 1872, and SHORTER, MORE ECONOMIC-LENGTH WOODEN RAIL SLEEPERS IN THE ABSENCE OF LOCAL, SUITABLE, LONG, WHITE-ANT/TERMITE-RESISTANT TIMBER.

In places where washaways were common, the line was only lightly ballasted or not ballasted at all for the sake of money. The route was initially mountain scenic, as the Flinders Ranges were to the East of the train line and were visible for about 100 miles, well North of the Parachilna Gorge but disappeared from view well before the old camel settlement of Marree. Before the train reached Oodnadatta, we crossed an impressive steel girder railway bridge over the usually-dry Neales River, a permanent gum tree-lined, fish-filled (then!) waterhole called Algebuckina. This long bridge, originally planned for crossing the Murray River at Murray Bridge I was told, was completely out of character with the arid surrounding countryside, which had an annual rainfall of about four inches.

OODNADATTA was a small settlement of maybe 250 people, a pub and an important airfield, a couple of shops, stock and station agents, a garage, Police station, T.A.A. aviation personnel, a "Native Affairs" officer, a small first-aid station, railways staff, a vital meteorological station and not much else, but it was the vital hub of a very remote area of outback Central Australia. Standing in the open space near the road/railway station interface was an upright four-inch bore pipe, with an on-off tap, which, when turned on, gushed steaming hot artesian water through a shower rose for the public to use; NOT MUCH USE ON A HOT 120 DEGREES-PLUS FARENHEIT

SUMMER'S DAY when your only desire was to cool off!

Over the imaginary border and into the Northern Territory, the Ghan rattled along at its usual 20 miles per hour, then slowed down again to a mundane walking speed crawl as it approached the wide, shallow, sandy, many-channelled Finke River crossing, where the rails and sleepers just simply lay on the bare river sandy bed without the usual benefit of reassuring, underlying stone ballast.

In these periodic circumstances, it was therefore necessary for the Ghan to crawl about a mile, slowly, as there had been recent rain and the line over the Finke was mostly free and UNBALLASTED, and PASSENGERS NECESSARILY JUST WALKED

AHEAD OF THE TRAIN TO ENSURE ALL WAS WELL. Walking ahead of the train was quite off-putting, however. It was then that passengers, staff and tourists came face to face with the sordid, very solid reality of truly old-fashioned rail travel. The Ghan, like country trains of the time, was NOT EQUIPPED WITH ENCLOSED FLUSH TOILETS and HUMAN EXCRETA JUST PASSED THROUGH AN OPEN, SEE- THROUGH PIPE TO SPLATTER DIRECTLY ON THE ENDLESS STEEL RAILS, while the area both sides of the line was festooned and decorated with sometimes airborne, multi-coloured, very second-hand toilet paper blowing about all over the place; AN UNPLEASANT SITUATION that drew unfavourable comment from the few foreign and other quite enlightened tourists of the day.

Meanwhile, some of the other teenagers had been collecting GREEN, ROCK HARD, INEDIBLE, "PADDY" MELONS and began throwing them around. One of the boys lost a tooth owing to a direct hit from a fellow idiot.

As the Ghan again accelerated up to its earth shattering 20 miles per hour heading North, not very far South of Alice Springs we saw, a few hundred yards away on the Eastern side, a pair of suggestive, shapely, well-formed desert hills, which Ben Smith referred to as "tits".[18]

As we got closer to the Alice, the guard told me a story about a woman who, AFTER THREE DAYS TRAVEL on the old, tortoise-speed Ghan, asked the guard if he could tell her, "Just when do we get to Alice Springs?" The guard said, "Why, madam, what's your problem?" She said, "Well, I'm pregnant!", to which he replied, "Well madam, you shouldn't have got on the train in that condition", to which she replied, "When I got on the train, I wasn't in that condition!" They were still telling this story word-for-word in 2017.

An hour later we passed through the picturesque HEAVITREE GAP at the Northern, dead-end of the railway line and crawled past the stark white ghost gums lining the Todd River, then into Alice Springs, population about 2,000 at the time, where I quickly unloaded my 1968 350 c.c. B.S.A. motor bike, engine number XB 31 1407, and my clobber, and unknowingly started my first ADULT (?) chapter in my forthcoming, slowly-gathering, unknown future, knockabout life. I was just about to turn 17.

---

[18] Breasts

35.
ALICE SPRINGS AND DARWIN 1950

My B.S.A. motor bike and I arrived in the Alice, population about 2,000, on the Ghan. It was December 1950, and I had just met another Princes (P.A.C.) pupil, Ben Smith, on that old CLICKETY-CLICK train. Ben invited me to his parents' place in Alice Springs, pre-Christmas, for a home-cooked dinner. Ben's father, D. D. Smith, affectionately known to one and all as "D.D.", offered me a job as an electrician's off- sider to Bob Tunk in the Northern Territory Works and Housing Department, of which he was the head – the Chief, the Lord and the Master. During the recently-ended World War 2, D.D. had been in charge of the construction of the all-sealed Stuart Highway; 954 miles from Alice Springs to Darwin.

I was accommodated at a single men's quarters and mess, which backed onto the usually bone-dry Todd River, where the gardener one day dug up a .45 Colt Frontier model revolver and gave it to me. I then started work with the Works and Housing Department and had no sooner done so than along came Christmas and a couple of weeks' leave on full pay, and I was invited to tag along with a couple of old Saints (S.P.S.C.) Alice Springs' boys, Ian Lovegrove and Geoff McCrae, on a trip to Darwin on our B.S.A. motorbikes. Ian had a brand new 1949 "Gold Flash" 650 c.c. twin- cylinder bike, and had made a very impressive, all-enclosed, two-wheel trailer to go with it. All loaded up, we set off late in the afternoon, riding past the sign about 15 miles North of the Alice proclaiming the "Tropic of Capricorn", and slept in sleeping bags on sand hills near Ti Tree, about 60 miles north of the Alice, and had an early 6:00 a.m. start on the road next morning.

The day was bright and sunny, but some distance away in the East we caught sight of a thunderstorm and lightning but thought little of it. The terrain was generally flat and open, with a few short, 20-foot-high bloodwood and mulga trees, and spiky spinifex grass as we approached a slight depression in the road just ahead. I read the name "Maclaren Creek" on a road sign. Just at this moment a guy came out from the shadows of a tree waving at us to stop. It was lucky he did. Had we gone over the dip in the road we would have been in strife. The Maclaren Creek was in flood, flowing full tilt from low hills just visible in the East and running a banker, that is, it was almost the height of the surrounding country and must have been 20-feet deep.

Unfortunately, across the creek and out of reach or help from us was an International- make truck lying on its side with its driver lying presumably dead alongside. He must have been travelling fast; too fast to stop when he saw the floodwaters in the previously out-of-sight creek ahead, swerved, rolled over, was thrown out and killed.

We had to wait three or four hours for the flash flood to dissipate and the water level to go down, during which time an ambulance arrived from Tennant Creek, about 50 miles North, and removed the body from that side of the river.

After this unfortunate episode we pressed on past the great granite, many-feet-wide boulders called the "Devils Dice". Then a brief stop for fuel, sandwiches and a Coke at "Handlebars" (Ken Macintyre's Tennant Creek Hotel). Past Tennant Creek's numerous gold mines, including the rich, one-ounce-to-the-ton "Noble Knob" and "Peko" mines. We pressed on North. Ian had a brother, Craig, living and working at Elliot, a fairly remote agricultural research station, so we kept riding until late, arrived there about 10.00 p.m. and stopped the night. Elliot, I remember, is about halfway between Darwin and the Alice; about 500 miles either way.

Pressing on the next day past Daly Waters, Dunmara, Katherine and Pine Creek, we arrived at Adelaide River where Ian's aunt, Mrs

Forsaith, owned the Adelaide River Hotel, adorned over the door by a set of seven-foot-wide, tip-to-tip, locally-shot buffalo horns. We had Christmas dinner and the next day rode into Darwin, population about 6,000 (during hostilities, Darwin had received 79 Japanese air raids). Now being a government employee, I was able to stay at one of the single men's quarters, of which there were several, two of which were nicknamed "Belsen" and "Buchenwald" as a mark of THOROUGH DISRESPECT.

Though small, Darwin was very cosmopolitan. Greeks such as Haritos, Antonas, Raptis and Paspaley, Italians such as Favaro, and Chinese such as Alec, Richard and Arthur FONG-LIM and others were representative of the wider population. Riding past the rice gardens one day, about 10 miles south of Darwin, I was surprised to see a black-as-the-ace-of-spades, full-blooded Aboriginal carrying a long, wooden-shafted, steel-headed, shovel-nose spear. The steel blade had been fashioned from the steel leaf-spring of a light truck and ground to its sharp, shovel-nose shape painstakingly, presumably on abrasive rocks; or by a mate in a garage on an abrasive wheel. The steel head itself was about a foot long and three inches broad, fastened with kangaroo-leg sinews to a long wooden spear shaft, made using woodfire-heated and water-straightened tree roots.

I clearly saw the spear was a working model and had recently been used, as it was heavily blood-stained. Enquiring as best I could, he more or less explained he used it to spear and kill the local buffalo, of which I had seen dozens, some just standing near the road. When using the spear as a hunting weapon, the object of the stalking Aborigine was to creep up to a preferably younger buffalo, say within 20 yards, and spear it in the forward part of its body, inducing heavy internal bleeding, then to back off and wait. Cruel it was, but that is the way it was. In a short time the buffalo quietly bled, succumbed, collapsed and expired through loss of blood, and the hunter and his many mates cut up and apportioned the meat, and/ or cooked much of it and ate it on the spot. … After haggling, he sold the spear to me for five shillings. I was stuck with carrying its full 12-foot length about, disconcertingly, on my motor bike when changing addresses, until I eventually arrived back in Adelaide about six months later.

I was probably lucky the road laws were more easy-going then!

****

Back in Adelaide, I found that when thrown by hand, even without the aid of an extended arm WOOMERA, the full length of the steel spear head EASILY PENETRATED A CORRUGATED, GALVANISED-STEEL FENCE about 30 feet away.

****

Returning to Darwin, I enjoyed the foreign-to-me, cosmopolitan goings on, and spent a lot of time drinking thick, black and sugary coffee at the Greek club; so thick the spoon had difficulty just trying to fall over in the little coffee cup. Walking around the wartime wrecks in Darwin's harbour, I was interested in the ship the "Neptunia", still lying next to the wharf where it had been torpedoed by the Japanese. It was also interesting watching the four-foot-long, pike-like "Long-Tom" fish as they drifted past, usually in pairs, just under the oily green surface. Sharks, crocodiles, sea snakes and groper were still plentiful in the deep natural harbour, as were the manatee-like Australian counterparts, the DUGONG.

"Doctors' Gully", "the Don", "the Fanny Bay", "the Parap" and "the Victoria" hotels are still with me as part of my 16-years-old, juvenile fond memories. Also, the various wartime army camps and fighter aircraft airstrips every few miles alongside the Stuart Highway, many still festooned with their slowly-rotting wartime camouflage nets hanging in disarray. Post-war auctions of redundant military equipment were in full swing. You could buy a military tank, a naval ship or an R.A.A.F.[19] aircraft for a song.

****

After our 10-day holiday in Darwin, we retraced our tracks uneventfully back to the Alice, where I returned for a while to the Works and Housing Department. I then heard about a position being advertised for a clerk at CONNELLAN AIRWAYS at their town- site aerodrome, just West of the Alice township. This seemed interesting, and I joined them.

---

[19] Royal Australian Air Force

36.
A MEANS TO AN END: DARWIN 1950

"Pancho Price" was an illegal Darwin S.P. bookmaker in the early 1950s. He had problems with some of his illegal punter clients who were threatening to break his legs over certain unpaid gambling matters, which had occurred through the undoubted slowness of certain of the thoroughbreds and/ or a lack of business acumen on the part of Pancho.

Pancho was an intelligent man and saw no future in trying to walk on useless broken legs. He recognised an urgent need for a source of extra cash and invited me to give him a hand, rowing a dinghy, while he leant over the bow, holding a torch in one hand and grabbing juvenile fish crocodiles around the neck with the other. We went out on the Finnis River one night and caught about thirty small "crocs", mostly under two feet, as well as a 14-foot olive python swimming in the crocodile-infested river shortly after a 10-foot shark had swum past; a river clearly quite unsafe for midnight skinny- dipping. The fish crocs were placed in a large sack on the floor of the dinghy until we thought we had enough. We returned safely back to our 4WD on the riverbank after midnight. We had seen a couple of very big saltwater crocodiles, well over 20-feet long, and knew it would have been curtains for us if we had fallen in.

Back in Darwin at Pancho's place, he lowered his bag of juvenile crocodiles into his chest-type deep freeze overnight, where they painlessly and quietly (we hoped!) went to sleep. The next day Pancho set to work with his scalpel, delicately skinning the little crocs and soaking the skins in a formalin solution for a time before fitting glass eyes and mounting the crocs in lifelike poses, adding a clear lacquer coating and sometimes painting their open mouths pink or red. A couple of days selling the crocs as souvenirs to tourist shops and Pancho paid his gambling debts in full!

In hindsight, I AM SORRY I took part in this MIS-ADVENTURE over 50 years ago but it happened, and I've told the story as it was.

37.
GROUND LEVEL 1951

In 1951, I was 17, living in Alice Springs, Central Australia, and employed by CONNELLAN AIRWAYS in a clerical position. Connellan was A SMALL OPERATION IN A LARGE TERRITORY, and operated general, regular and charter light aviation services throughout the Northern Territory of Australia, including scheduled services to large, isolated cattle stations (ranches), sometimes hundreds of miles apart, in the vast grazing areas of the AUSTRALIAN OUTBACK.

Connellan operated a small, irregular fleet of mainly older, pre-World War 2 bi-plane aircraft, such as the De Havilland Dragonfly, the De Havilland Rapide, a Fox Moth, a Tiger Moth and one or two fairly modern, pre-war, all metal, twin-engine Lockheed aircraft. Ian Leslie was chief hands-on manager of operations, while Eddie Connellan was the owner. Eddie was active with the airline as well as with his Narwietooma Station, other station properties and various commercial interests.

Peter Leunig also played an important part, as did Sam Calder, who used to fly, and, I think, also managed Narwietooma Station for Eddie. THEN THERE WAS THE INVISIBLE DOROTHY. Sam Calder was later a Federal Government politician and husband of Daphne Campbell, the actress and star of the classic post-war movie "THE OVERLANDERS", alongside Chips Rafferty, which was released about 1946. I had been to the film's premiere at Adelaide's Wests Theatre.

Being young, green and curious, when the chance arose and in the absence of paying passengers, I was offered a free, three-day flight – probably to keep the pilot awake – on the scheduled Borroloola service in a twin engine, D.H. Rapide bi-plane from the Alice via a number of cattle station airstrips, and staying overnight in Queensland at Boyds Hotel, Mount Isa. I do remember being told the D.H. Rapide was THE FIRST PASSENGER AIRCRAFT WEIGHING A TON ABLE TO CARRY ITS OWN WEIGHT IN COMMERCIAL PAYLOAD. It first flew the year that I, the venerable Douglas DC3 and Russian cosmonaut Yuri Gagarin were born; 1934.

The second day, we flew generally North-West and back into the Northern Territory to the scattered cattle stations on the Barkly Tableland, delivering mail, medicines, perishables, car batteries, springs, axles, etc., and overnighted at Borroloola, with its crocodile-infested McArthur River and the still-visible, wartime aircraft wreckage on the other side of the river. The stations were large by world standards. The largest at that time (Victoria River Downs) would have been over 13,000 square miles in area, and bigger than many small countries. A few of the INDIVIDUAL PADDOCKS WERE OVER A HUNDRED MILES WIDE, and adjoining homesteads were similar distances apart.

The pilot and fellow employee was Jim Manley, an American ex-World War 2 U.S.A.A.F.[20] Mustang fighter pilot, who must have been bored to death flying these ancient, pre-war, wood, string and canvas 1930s aircraft in isolated 1950s outback Australia. I do remember an episode at Brunette Downs Station when Jim was having a technical conversation with the station manager about the possibility of somehow putting a ROLLS-ROYCE MERLIN AIRCRAFT ENGINE to useful work! A R.A.A.F. Mosquito aircraft, used post war for photo reconnaissance, had made an INJURY- FREE CRASH LANDING on the station a year or two before, and the wreck, including the still-serviceable engines, had been abandoned by the Air Force and resigned to the station. The station manager was wondering if he could somehow mount an eight-foot diameter circular saw blade directly on the Merlin, in place of the propeller, to cut the extremely hard, local Ironwood timber! However,

---

[20] Unites States of America Air Force

I did not hear any more on this subject. I guess sleep, or common sense, may have prevailed.

****

Anyway, it was near the end of the DRY SEASON, the remnant grass was sparse or non-existent, and the ground was as flat as a pancake. We were flying from Creswell Downs Station to Brunette Downs, the next-door neighbour's (about 40 miles apart), at a cruising air speed of about 85 very pedestrian miles an hour. SINCE I WAS STAFF AND COULD BE TRUSTED NOT TO TELL TALES – besides which, life was otherwise boring – JIM TOOK THE OLD WOOD AND CANVAS-COVERED D.H. RAPIDE DOWN LOWER AND LOWER, INCH-BY-INCH, UNTIL THE WHEELS ON THE FIXED UNDERCARRIAGE SOMETIMES "BRUSHED" OR EVEN RAN ALONG

THE HARD, FLAT, BARE, SUN-BAKED, OUTBACK EARTH, sending up explosive powder puffs of dust, revealing our somewhat irregular on-road or in-flight path, and our highly-suspect, very low, ground-level altitude!

We mainly flew, or really, drove at this adrenalin-positive, touch-and-go level for maybe five minutes before giving way to A THREATENING, APPROACHING STATION FENCE, which looked like a mountain range when seen from our low, zero- level, cruising height vantage point.

IT WAS THEN WE RETURNED TO NORMALITY, common sense and a lower blood pressure environment as WE LIFTED UP, ALL OF TEN FEET, OVER THE LOOMING FENCE, before returning to our correct, more positive altitude and finally, at the end of a long day, about five o'clock, arrived back home in Alice Springs at Connellan's town site aerodrome.

It had been another BORING "BOROLOOLA RUN" or "day at the office"!

****

After rain, the days in the Alice were still fairly hot. It was swimming after work at the "Junction" or the "Wigley Waterholes" just North of the Alice that kept us cool, as there was no public swimming pool in town

Connellan Airways baggage label

Outback adventure flying Connellan Airways

at that time. As a money-making variation, early on Sunday mornings myself and a few others unpacked and repacked perishable fruit and vegetables from the just-arrived Ghan. Working for F.B.C. Heenan and Company, we earned ourselves £10 EACH in three or four hours, which was more than my weekly pay at Connellan Airways.

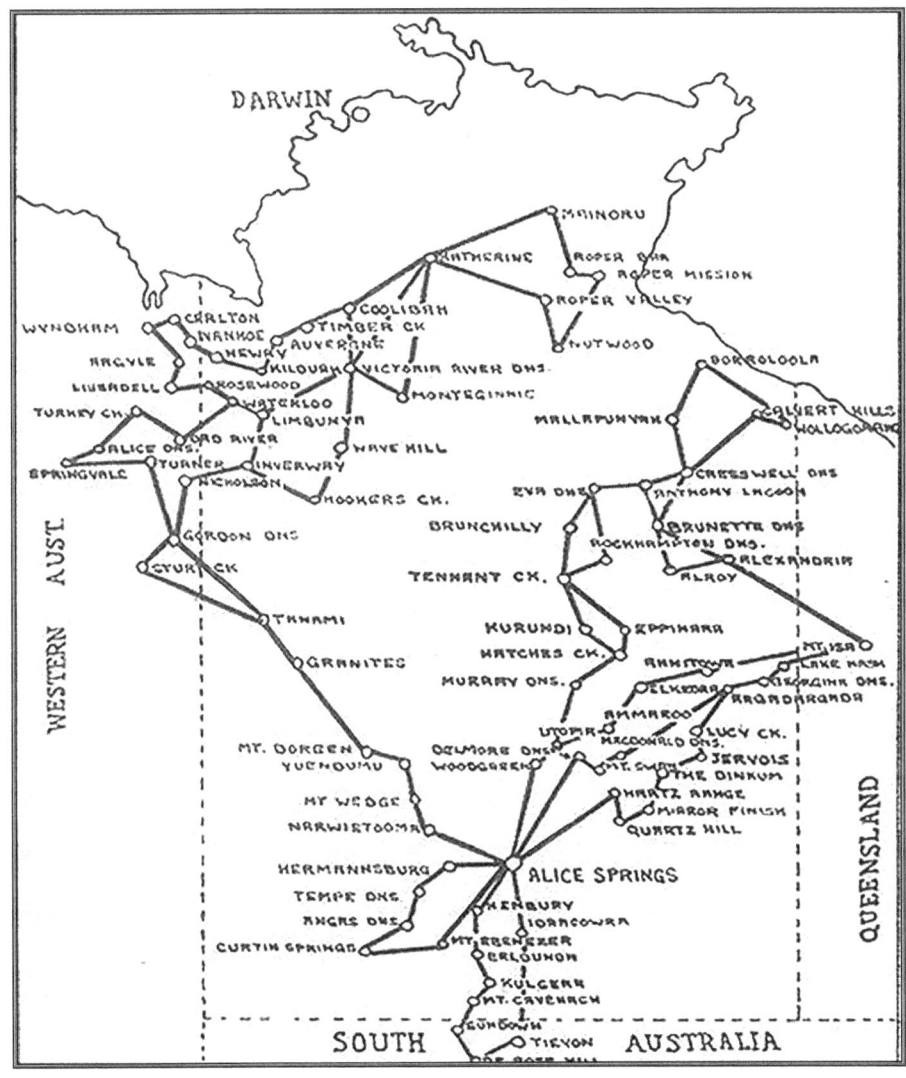

Connellan Airways Northern Territory Route Map, 1955

While I was in the Alice, I met up with Bob Hamilton (P.A.C.), a few years older than me, who lived over the road from Mrs Chalmers. Bob was a nephew of Mr. Chapman, the owner of the Granites Gold Mine, about 400 miles to the North-West. Bob had a Vincent Comet motor bike and we rode out to Delmore Downs Station to see Geoff Holt, where my sister Pam had been the governess. A few years later, Bob was in a dinghy when the "DRY" TODD RIVER WAS IN FLOOD. Unfortunately, HE FELL INTO THE TODD AND WAS PRESUMABLY DROWNED, lost in the muddy waters. No trace of him was ever found. His body was presumably swept along by the river as it slowly petered out and dissipated maybe 300 miles away in the lonely silent wastes of the Simpson Desert.

****

After about six months in the Alice, I caught the Ghan back nearly 1,000 miles South to Adelaide to rejoin the Adelaide "News" as a cadet reporter at a salary of £3 10s a week. This was one year before Rupert Murdoch came on the scene. And so, at 17, I ended my first independent trip into the still-mysterious adult fray.

38.
COLT 45 1951

I was staying at the administration hostel in Alice Springs in 1951 while employed at Connellan Airways in a clerical position. The back of the hostel fronted the banks of the generally dry Todd River and had been put to use as an extended vegetable plot by the gardener. I was 17 and was pleasantly surprised one day when the gardener presented me with a revolver he had just encountered and dug up in the garden. The wooden part of the handle had slowly rotted away and the metal was lightly pitted, but it was a genuine Frontier Model Colt .45. I remember the date, 1872, stamped clearly on the action.

I was then told the area near the riverbank was where the Afghan camel drivers used to camp with their camels after walking the heavily laden animals 400 miles from Oodnadatta. This was before 1929 when the railway was further extended to the Alice. The pre-1929 history of the Colt is in your imagination; it's anybody's guess.

I stupidly soaked the Colt in kerosene and "Penetrene",[21] and buffed it to a reasonable finish on a wire buff, whereas I shouldn't have touched it; but at 17 you don't quite know everything! After my rough cleaning, the action went through all the mechanical firing sequences. When the trigger was pulled, the hammer fell and the cylinder rotated. It worked, although I NEVER HAD ANY AMMUNITION TO ACTUALLY TRY IT! I returned to Adelaide later that same year and was persistently hounded by a friend to part with the Colt, and so I eventually sold it to Don Thompson for 10 shillings. A few years later, DON WAS TRAGICALLY IMPALED at 29 by the normally passive bridge rail on his way home,

---

[21] Fishing attracting bait released steadily into the water

presumably overtired from his job as an engineer at Ansett Airlines, as he passed West Beach Airport at speed.

My drinking mate FRANCIS D. HANNAN acquired the Colt somehow from Don Thompson's estate, then quickly DRANK HIMSELF TO DEATH on "Teachers Whisky," which is when our old MATE BOB SANDERS (S.P.S.C.) OF VIRGINIA, PHONE NUMBER VIRGINIA ONE, acquired it from Frank's deceased estate.

Then BOB DIED OF SOMETHING AGE-RELATED. He would have been in his early 70s. Presumably the Colt would have wound up in the possession of his son Robert (S.P.S.C) in the early 1970s, and that's now over 40 years ago. I can't help wondering where Robert Sanders and "IT" are now.

"G'DAY ROBERT!"

39.
T. S. PEARCE 1951

I was 17. Trevor Pearce was 29 and studying for a postgraduate Degree in Agricultural Science at the Adelaide University while he stayed with us at Burnside.

Apart from building an F.M. radio when they were unheard of, other than their new, secretive, clandestine use by the right up-to-date Police, Trevor had somehow acquired a large .575 calibre, muzzle-loading, black powder rifle and had a healthy desire to see if it worked. I was naturally like-minded.

Being an inquisitive, scientific-minded person, TREVOR THOUGHT HE WOULD MANUFACTURE HIS OWN HOMEMADE GUNPOWDER propellant since it was hard to obtain otherwise at the time. Using a chemist's pestle and mortar, he individually finely ground the sulphur, saltpetre and charcoal, then placing all the parts in their correct proportions in the porcelain mortar, added a safe amount of water and reground the lot to a smooth grey slurry. The slurry was then spread out, about an eighth of an inch thick, on a smooth pane of glass, about a yard square, and placed in the sun to dry. After a few hours, the mix was bone dry and curling up at the edges, lifting cleanly away from the glass. Using the safe, non-static edge of a wooden ruler, Trevor easily scraped the dry gunpowder onto a pre-folded crease in a sheet of paper and slid the newly-made gunpowder into an open glass container.

THE BONE DRY, BLACK GUNPOWDER was then passed gently backwards and forwards through a "non-sparking" brass laboratory sieve and poured in a smooth stream from cup to cup to see just how beautifully smooth it really was. Locating a flush-fitting test projectile for our experiment was difficult, so we dismantled a World War 2,

.5-inch calibre Browning machine gun bullet and with some difficulty extracted the large, half-inch-diameter projectile from the clinging, retentive brass case. Trevor carefully measured out and loaded an estimated minimal charge of OUR BEAUTIFUL BLACK ALCHEMIST'S POWDER, pouring it gently through a laboratory funnel down through the muzzle, plus a little bit extra for luck. We then stuffed a fair bit of paper wadding behind and around the loose-fitting projectile in the somewhat oversized barrel. Since the gun and its charge were an unknown quantity, WE WISELY THOUGHT IT BEST TO LASH THE LARGE MUZZLE-LOADING GUN WITH ROPE

TO THE OLD PEPPERCORN TREE near the stables and remotely fire it by a long string tied about 10 feet away, and out of direct sight of the old fashioned but still highly sensitive hair trigger.

With a new percussion cap fitted, IT WAS ALL SYSTEMS UP AND READY TO GO when Trevor remotely pulled the trigger with its long, intricately attached Heath Robinson-type string line. Surprisingly, there was NOT A DISTINCT BANG, just a large healthy-sounding F'WOOSH! Something like a Blue Whale breathing out, accompanied simultaneously by successive **CLUNK**, **BONG**, *BLING* and BLAM noises in rapidly descending order of volume.

At first appearance, the whole exercise seemed to be a bit of a FIZZER, but a step- by-step investigation quickly showed otherwise. Step-by-step, the one-inch-thick timber door to the stable had been penetrated at about a 45-degree angle, then the same one-inch-thickness timber wall of the stable was penetrated about two feet above the ground, followed by the corrugated, galvanised steel other wall, shared by the hen house next door.

ENTERING THE HEN HOUSE, THE .5-INCH PROJECTILE HAD PASSED STRAIGHT THROUGH BOTH SIDES OF A HALF 44-GALLON DRUM STANDING ON END, A FOOT ABOVE A FOWL SITTING ON

EGGS, WHICH REMAINED COMPLETELY UNPERTURBED BY THE CRASHING, POTENTIALLY DISASTROUS EVENT TAKING PLACE JUST INCHES ABOVE HER HEAD!

It then travelled 15 feet past the clucky hen, hammered a jagged hole through the outside galvanised wall of the hen house and went fittingly footloose and fancy free somewhere into the freedom of the outside world; but not before it first left a three-foot long gouge mark in the grassy, external earth outside in High Street.

That was, I thought, the end of the story until I received a PHONE CALL FROM SERGEANT STACY OF THE BURNSIDE POLICE, who asked me point blank if I had been firing my .22 again, to which I honestly answered, "NO, MR STACY".

It turned out that A BURNSIDE COUNCIL EMPLOYEE working in the street about 200 yards down the road, wearing his ex-Australian army felt slouch hat, HAD HEARD A "F'FIZZING NOISE" AS SOMETHING WENT PAST and took a healthy nick of material out of the crown of his hat. I hate to think of the various disastrous possibilities which are best left latent, safely untouched, in the imagination.

Luckily for me I was only an interested spectator in this non-fatal event. Over 60 years later, my lips are still trembling.

IT CERTAINLY WASN'T ME.

40.
HAND SIGNALS 1952

At the time of this true event, electronic motor vehicle signalling devices were in their infancy. A DRIVER'S ARM, extended through the open window and the possibly pouring rain TO SIGNAL WHETHER STOPPING or TURNING RIGHT, was the written law of the day. THERE WAS NO HAND SIGNAL REQUIRED IF TURNING LEFT.

I was driving up the Port Road towards Adelaide late on a Saturday afternoon with Robert Temme and John Harvey as passengers in my Land Rover. It would have been about 1952. I was 18 and hand signals through the driver's open window were the law and mandatory at the time. The Port Road itself was very quiet but a few hundred yards ahead I could see a lot of traffic coming from Woodville Road on the right from the nearby football oval shortly after the game had finished.

I was probably driving at my usual 45/ 50 miles per hour on the 40-miles per hour open highway before I started to slow down, when to my great surprise I discovered my brakes had failed and an unbroken line of football traffic was crossing the rapidly- looming Woodville Road intersection still a hundred yards straight ahead. This was a very sudden and serious matter as I instantly started to change down to the lowest available gear of my rather tired Land Rover. It became blindingly obvious I would still be left right in the middle of the Woodville Road traffic before the Land Rover had actually stopped, and that thoroughly unappealing prospect was a very definite "no no" to me!

Fortunately, I saw a lone car on the highway ahead which had already stopped at the intersection, which provided us with a fortuitous, one and only solid barrier between us and probable tangled, mangled destruction on the highway. Luckily, I had in fact been able to slow the

Land Rover down to about a very pedestrian 5 miles per hour crawl when, without a single moment's warning to the other driver since my horn was also "up shit creek",[22] I banged solidly into the rear of his long-stationary "jalopy".

He leapt out of his car like a frog out of hot water, exclaiming something like , "WHAT THE HELL!", when without thinking, I responded, "YOU DIDN'T GIVE A HAND SIGNAL!"

At this idiotic remark on my part, he was stunned. HIS FACE WAS FLUSHED AN INCANDESCENT PURPLE, he obviously found it hard to fully comprehend the sense of my flippant remarks and couldn't understand a single word of what I had just clearly said. Then he indignantly exploded, "BUT I WAS STOPPED", which was about the time Harvey chipped in, saying again, "YOU DIDN'T GIVE A HAND SIGNAL!"

Quite clearly we had the other driver on the hop. He was not a very happy chappie. He was thoroughly dismayed by our united front and our statement that "he" had NOT SIGNALLED HIS INTENTION TO STOP, since we would have been at least 100 yards behind him and almost out of sight when he had already been long stopped.

Looking back over the sixty years since this minor event, it is conceivable, with the blurring of time, that HE WAS JUST A LITTLE MORE THAN IRATE!

Anyway, we exchanged our drivers' licence details and did not fail to notice his car did not have a rear bumper bar or fender, as required by law. After our thoroughly negative conversation, the RIGHTEOUSLY INDIGNANT DRIVER drove off, no doubt mumbling under his breath, over and over, "BUT I WAS STOPPED. I WAS STOPPED".

---

[22] Broken/ useless

Some weeks later I was approached by a long suffering, at the hands of idiots like me, South Australian policeman about a sworn statement by the other driver, which stated I had collided with the rear of his car and DAMAGED HIS IMAGINARY BUMPER BAR. This fortuitous statement by him was to me like manna from Heaven. I said to the policeman,

"This not only proves what a liar he is, he is not only fibbing about his failure to signal, he is stretching it to the limit by claiming damage to his bumper bar because we noticed he didn't have one!"

In the meantime, Harvey was back at his Marine Engineering studies at B.H.P. Whyalla, where in due course he was contacted by the Police. He independently confirmed the other driver's statement was false:

"HE QUITE DEFINITELY DID NOT HAVE A REAR BUMPER BAR".

And so, in the end, that was the very final dead end of this ever so minor, unmentionable, sordid matter.

41.
A MATTER OF MANNERS

In the early and mid-fifties, I was a teenager and in my early twenties driving from Adelaide to Alice Springs on the various parallel, and/or criss-crossing, dirt wheel tracks which collectively, when mentally assembled as one on a road map at the time was GRANDIOSELY CALLED THE STUART HIGHWAY. COOBER PEDY was then a very small, sparse, outback settlement – a mostly underground, PRECIOUS OPAL- MINING TOWN, situated halfway between Adelaide and the Alice – a small town with a population of about 200 in and about the town, and maybe 1,000 others scattered, mostly out of sight, underground in the outlying areas of the MARS-LIKE TERRAIN. All that could be seen from the road at that time was a square tin shed, about 30 X 30 feet, with a petrol pump outside and a small door. I bought petrol plus the usual young man's diet (a HOT PIE, an ICE CREAM and a COKE) and headed off up the main Alice Springs road, about half a mile, when I was surprised by the unexpected, very unmoving appearance of a second building, which was also masquerading as a shop, complete with another petrol pump and with no obvious road leading beyond!

So I naturally stopped and went inside the second shop to enquire about the location of the missing road to the Alice, which seemed somehow to have vanished. Then I was asked by the LADY (???) behind the counter, "HAVE YOU GOT FOOD AND PETROL?" To which I answered, "YES!" She said, "WHERE DID YOU GET IT?" I said, "AT THE OTHER SHOP". "WELL", she said, "GO BACK AND ASK THEM!"

It turned out that the short, half-mile length of highway through Coober Pedy was well used, locally, and looked very much like a real road, whereas the so-called highway itself was relatively unused, being the lesser of the two tracks branching away to the left at the first shop.

I had unwittingly become an innocent party in the 20-year, ongoing, never-ending feud between the "Wilsons" and the "Brewsters".

42.
GHAN AGAIN, MINING AND EL-SHERANA DISCOVERY 1954

I was on the "Ghan" again en route from Adelaide, South Australia, to Alice Springs and the large "UNDOOLYA" AND "OWEN SPRINGS" CATTLE STATIONS (ranches) in Australia's Northern Territory. I was now 20 years old and going North to gain work experience on Undoolya Station, owned by "Old" Ted Hayes, with Eugene Knicker as his sidekick.

At this time, Ted was about to move approximately 2,000 head of cattle 50 miles from Undoolya Station near Alice Springs, West to neighbouring Owen Springs Station (Ted owned both). I thought I was engaged to ride horses for this cattle droving excursion but instead was handed the keys to the Land Rover and told to drive ahead to the next stage and set up camp for the night. The cattle were coaxed along in very easy stages, feeding, ruminating and farting as they leisurely accomplished seven or eight miles a day.

After a week on the trail, the cattle were turned out into their 100 square mile-or-so paddock and I remained for a couple of weeks longer to pump water up from the Owen Springs waterhole to the 50-foot long, galvanised drinking trough. Owen Springs is a natural, near permanent waterhole in the bed of a river, set in a very picturesque rocky-bordered gorge on the Hugh River (I think). The waterhole was about 200 yards long, maybe 40 yards wide, bordered by stark white, Central Australian ghost gums near the water and drying off towards the dry climate gidgee and mulga trees over 500 yards away from the water. The whole length of the water source was fenced off to keep the cattle out of it and the necessary cattle drinking water was pumped up and out of the river by a large "Lister" diesel engine and a long belt. My sole duty was to stand by and frequently dress the belt with a sticky, tar-like paste to stop it from "slipping"; a paste which reminded me very much of Golden Syrup.

****

I thought Owen Springs waterhole would be a popular tourist attraction if it was open to the public but it was on a privately-owned cattle station in my time and was taboo to tourists. Today, as part of Owen Springs Reserve, it has become a popular destination for 4WD and camping tours.

****

Well, I wasn't getting any horse riding on the station and the wages were a pittance, so I moved on. I came across a truck in the Alice Springs railyards loading 14 tons of South Australian West End beer, destined ultimately for Jim Boyd's Hotel in Mount Isa in Queensland, about 800 miles away. Mount Isa was a major silver, lead and copper mining town 601 miles inland from Townsville on the Pacific coast. It was a booming, prosperous town; three pubs and full employment. But it had been cut off from its usual Queensland beer supplies by the flooded North Queensland Burdekin River.

The owner/ driver of the large Fiat truck was FRANK FAVARO, FROM DARWIN, who, after I helped load the beer, gave me a lift the 800 miles to Mount Isa, probably just to unload the beer with help from Jim Boyd's son Marshall.

****

Thinking back, I remembered talking to a fellow student, PETER FISHER, when at Prince Alfred College (P.A.C.) a few years before. Peter was a quiet student and led me to believe his father had a managerial position of some sort at the town's main employer, Mount

Isa Mines, and so after my unannounced arrival, I fronted up at the mines office and asked if I could see "a Mr George Fisher".

"Who wants to see 'Sir George'?" the receptionist asked. So I told her that I had been at school with George Fisher's son Peter in Adelaide. I was then shown into the sumptuous office of SIR GEORGE FISHER, the Managing Director of Mount Isa Mines. (Sir George died in about 2010 at the age of just over 100). I explained I was just working my way around Australia and Sir George told me Peter was not in Mount Isa but "If you like you can start work tomorrow, underground, as a MULLOCKER, clearing the fallen rocks and mullock from between the underground railway lines".

The lowest status job in the mine, but good money. So I took it.

****

Frank Favaro had a lot of Italian friends where he stayed in Mount Isa and they said I could stay with them while I worked at the big mine. So I stayed with the Mazzonis and the Morbellis.

Mount Isa Mines Me, Stan Trcka and Lotha Tischman in 1954

Fresh homemade pasta, sliced on the table into strips of flat spaghetti, garlic and top knot pigeons washed down by rather nice, and rather potent, homemade "grappa" were often on the menu. This was because one of the other ex-Italian Army soldiers (our former enemy!) was a keen hunter and SHOT AND ATE EVERYTHING, INCLUDING "HA HA PIGEON" – our national protected bird, the KOOKABURRA!

After a couple of months, I upped anchor and caught a Queensland Railways train 601 miles to Townsville. As the train arrived in Townsville, it passed the airfield a few days after a cyclone had devastated the area, and I saw a number of Australian Air Force planes in various states of destruction, including an upside-down four-Rolls- Royce-engined "Merlin" Lincoln Bomber lying on its broken back.

In Townsville, I caught up with my Aunt Rene's brother-in-law Eric Kito, the manager of the Queensland Insurance Company, in his grand office, which was walled entirely with nothing but foot-wide Queensland timber cabinet panels. I looked around Townsville for a couple of days, caught another train 300 miles up to tropical CAIRNS, and had a few enjoyable days visiting the Barron Falls, Kuranda and Green Island on the Great Barrier Reef just a few weeks after Vince Vlassoff had opened his new underwater Green Island Coral Reef Observatory.

****

Walking along the Cairns foreshore with a young Canadian about my age, he looked up at the coconuts on their host trees and asked me if they were pineapple trees!

****

About this time, I looked at my finances, which caused me to look at "situations vacant" and quickly seek a job. "Wanted, dozens of positions as cane cutters", the old-fashioned way, with large cane knives like machetes or pangas. This was a few years before mechanical cane harvesting became the order of the day. Then I SAW AN UNUSUAL JOB ADVERTISED FOR A "URANIUM PROSPECTOR" for exploration work in North-West Queensland and the Northern Territory.

****

I caught the train about 40 miles South to GORDONVALE and met the exploration manager, Joe Fisher, at his house. I told Joe I had been working on cattle stations in Alice Springs and more recently underground at Mount Isa Mines. I was immediately given a job to start with the Northern Uranium Development Company (N.U.D.), a substantial cash advance and an airline ticket to fly down to Brisbane 1,000 miles South the very next day. In BRISBANE, I picked up a new Land Rover from Annand and Thompson's, then tarpaulins, "Austronic" Geiger counters, "Brades" wooden- handled geological hammers/picks, camp stretchers, a vehicle trailer, etc., then headed on up the KNEE-DEEP, BULL-DUST-COVERED BRUCE HIGHWAY another 1,000 miles back towards Townsville then West and inland 601 miles back to MOUNT ISA, which was now a hive of activity.

A couple of taxi drivers had made a rich uranium strike about 70 miles East of the town and called it THE "MARY KATHLEEN" after one of their wives. They were in line for the Commonwealth Government's £25,000 reward, which they eventually received. Meanwhile, they formed a company which earned tens of millions in profit over many years before commercially exhausting the uranium deposit. Anybody and EVERYBODY in the area WAS "URANIUM HUNGRY". Before work, after work and at weekends everybody was prospecting for uranium. Geiger counters were in very short supply and heavily price-inflated.

****

Joe Fisher arrived in Mount Isa at this time and spent most of his time writing five- figure cheques to all and sundry for the slightest "SNIFF" OF RADIOACTIVITY, paid out to keep our perceived rivals at bay. At this time, Jim Boyd told me that IF I WISHED TO REMAIN IN MY ROOM AT BOYDS HOTEL, MY 10-FOOT OLIVE PYTHON WOULD HAVE TO GO. I was sad as I released him, with a bulging belly full of rats, back into the bush.

****

We then got further instructions to proceed 940 miles to the Northern Territory to an area just a little South of the existing Rum Jungle Uranium Mine, and about 90 or so miles South of Darwin. We set up camp on a sprawling agricultural property which, because of the presence of a very large and very wide Banyan tree with many large, tree-top-connected, interjoined branches and many interconnected tree trunks, was naturally called "BANYAN FARM". We were close to the purpose-built town called "BATCHELOR", where everything was controlled and run by Territory Enterprises (T.E.P.). Batchelor was a modern town with all mod cons and provided a popular, after-hours' watering hole; the tropical Rum Jungle Hotel bar.

The farm was being set up to grow pineapples and early season mangoes, and was managed by popular, well-known Northern Territorian Boyne Litchfield. Talking to Boyne, I told him I had a friend in Adelaide called Warren Litchfield and he said he thought they were related. We then left the Rum Jungle area and set up our exploration duties near STAPLETON SIDING, maybe 20 miles or so South, and nearer the small town of ADELAIDE RIVER, where Mrs Fawcett still ran her "pub".

****

We were camped alongside a clear-water river full of tropical Archer fish. If a person "drew" on a cigarette when sitting by the river, invariably within seconds his cigarette was extinguished by a healthy squirt of water, ejected accurately from as far as 10 feet away, from the rifle-shaped mouth of the Archer fish. The stream was also home to a plentiful population of harmless-to-man, narrow-nosed, fish-eating freshwater crocodiles, which only grow to about 10 feet.

One evening, I was watching an eel or a snake, maybe six feet long, gliding across the river when its head emerged on the bank, right where I was sitting. I was able to grasp it around its just-emerged neck below its head before it really woke up to what was happening. THERE WAS A BIT OF A PROBLEM, however, as I found that THE OLIVE PYTHON I HAD GRABBED WAS NOT SIX FEET LONG. HE WAS 12 FEET LONG AND NOT ALL THAT HAPPY! But after a friendly wrestle, while not letting go of his head, I got him into a hessian sugar bag. He was more docile in the morning. I kept him for a couple of days and let him go again where I had found him.

As a point of interest, around the campfire one night, one of the other prospectors, "Bluey" Kaye, stated that if we ever struck it lucky he had dreamed up a name for such a discovery. He had daughters back in Darwin – Sharon and Elizabeth come immediately to mind – and HIS PROPOSED NAME FOR A MINE WAS "EL- SHERANA". We said we had no objection, IF EVER WE "STRUCK IT", and later of course, WE DID!

****

There was a certain air of concern at Stapleton Siding about a local man, Terry Stapleton, who had recently killed someone and had just been JAILED FOR LIFE, and we were in his family's territory. Although he was in prison, you couldn't help wondering …

We were then re-assigned to the KATHERINE REGION, about 20 miles East of the town and alongside the large Katherine River. This is where we were joined by MONTY O'SULLIVAN, about 65 years old, who had formerly owned stations in the general area and pock-mark mined a number of copper and gold deposits. He had formerly owned Goodparla Station out of Pine Creek, but lost it over time to women, wine and cheats.

During World War 2, while trapping dingoes for a reasonable living and camped nightly under a two-wheel donkey cart, Monty lost his mate to an accidental strychnine dingo poisoning event. Monty received much more of an overdose than his mate but vomited and luckily survived. Monty was either talkative, interesting and good to know or "pissed out of his mind" on methylated spirits, vinegar, sugar and powdered milk, and totally immobile, lying on the ground under his cart. The last I heard was when he was found unconscious with his pants down around his knees lying on a diagonal track cutting across a vacant corner block of land near the Katherine Hotel (more about Monty is in the next chapter).

****

Another uranium prospecting company, the North Australian Uranium Company (N.A.U.C.), was a fair way upstream from us on an interesting prospect they named "SLEISBECK" after George Sleise and Toby Becker. They were the "FLAVOUR OF THE MONTH" as at that time their five-shilling shares were selling at 55 shillings, and they could do no wrong according to the Australian stock exchange!

****

It was cold down South, yet we slept in our underpants on bare sheets out in the open on our camp stretchers just a few feet from the Katherine River. No "alligators" this far upstream from the large saltwater crocodile habitat. It was mid-winter, or the "dry season", with rarely a cloud in the sky. And we did not see a single mosquito. At the time, it was uncanny!

It was then that matters started to get interesting and we received fresh instructions to battle our way Eastwards through the bush to ARNHEM LAND'S SOUTH ALLIGATOR RIVER. (A point of interest being there are no Indigenous alligators in Australia, and so, in order to distinguish between the giant saltwater, man-eating crocodiles, "Crocodilus Porosus", the locals called them the more fashionable name at the time, "alligators". The smaller, mainly fish-eating "Crocodilus Johnstonni" was left as a "croc". But in these more contemporary times, "salties" are "crocs" and "man eaters", while freshwater "fish eaters" are just "fishies").

Importantly, N.U.D. had just received brand new maps showing areas of HIGH RADIOACTIVITY about 60 odd miles North of Sleisbeck, and we had been granted a "Sole Prospecting Authority" or "P.A." over a large area along the South Alligator River. THIS MAP WAS "RED HOT!" It showed areas of very high radioactive interest and we moved in via Pine Creek, where we stocked up at Jimmy Ah Toy's General Store, and I bought a .30 calibre, ex U.S. Army Rockola-make auto-loading carbine for £10.

Leaving Pine Creek, we proceeded past Monty's old "stud" cattle station, Goodparla, past a mineral-rich hill named "Coronation Hill", and within days were setting up camp on the West bank of the South Alligator River. After setting up camp, we fanned out and got to work prospecting, an Austronic brand Geiger counter in one hand and a Brades geological pick in the other.

Day one resulted in the location of a number of interesting, high-value anomalies being sampled and mapped. A few days later, we crossed to the Eastern side of the river under the shadow of the high, rugged escarpment. Things started to hot up. We encountered higher readings and saw uranium mineralisation in the form of yellow carnotite and green torbernite under numerous sheltered rock faces. This was about the time A PARTY OF N.A.U.C. PROSPECTORS ARRIVED SLAP BANG

IN THE MIDDLE OF OUR SO-CALLED SOLE AND EXCLUSIVE P.A. AND SET UP CAMP HALF A MILE UPSTREAM FROM US, WHICH LATER LED TO THE "URANIUM WAR OF '54", involving the Police, the press, company management and us!

A couple of weeks later, Jack Smith stumbled into an area of radioactivity which was right at the top-end scale of the hard-working Austronic Geiger counter. Yellow carnotite, green torbernite and heavy dark rocks later identified as uraninite, or "Madam Curie's pitchblende", were literally liberally scattered all over the ground below the high cliff face. N.U.D. had, in the meantime, applied for the maximum reward of £25,000 for a uranium discovery on "WE, THE PROSPECTORS'" behalf.

In days the word was out: "ANOTHER MAJOR URANIUM DISCOVERY MADE IN NEW AREA"; the same area where, a lot later, far greater discoveries were made, such as the still operational Ranger, Jabiluka and Kakadu mines.

Within days, heavy machinery started to arrive on site; a large cable-operated Allis- Chalmers bulldozer, compressors, generators, large surface-situated drill rigs, jackhammers, front-end loaders, massive diesel fuel tanks and the like … and the place got busy. THE MINING CREW HAD NO SOONER STARTED "MINING" THAN THEY HAD TO STOP. WE RECEIVED OUR FIRST "WET SEASON" RAINS and were close to being marooned for the duration of the wet season on the wrong side of the South Alligator River if we were not careful. In a few days, the river would start running and we might be cut off for about six months. We were then offered leave or redundancy. I took the latter and returned home to Adelaide, family and friends for Christmas 1954.

(Early in 1955, we were each paid our share of the £25,000 reward).

Earthen termite mound and Me, Arnhem Land, 1954

43.
MONTY O'SULLIVAN: THE FULL STORY 1954

Our 1954 El-Sherana uranium discovery, not far past the outlying Goodparla cattle station, which had belonged to Monty O'Sullivan and the buffalo shooter and author Tom Cole before him, gave me the chance to get to know Monty well. Monty, of course, knew the country like the back of his hand and the location of many of the old mineral occurrences. In the past, he had sporadically mined some of them on a small scale.

At the time, MONTY WAS DOWN ON HIS LUCK. He had long since lost control of Goodparla, he was pushing 65/70 and was thankful for any extra, hard-to-get-at-his- age income, helped out by the sometime generosity of N.U.D, Joe Fisher and others. Monty was, however, sometimes hard to find, but a search of his tent usually found him LYING UNCONSCIOUS ON HIS BED with the remains of his staple drink, concocted from methylated spirits, vinegar, powdered milk and sugar. When he was completely sober he was a good guy.

In his sober moments, Monty told me in detail an unusual story which occurred during the early days of World War 2. Monty and his mate were just getting by trapping dingoes for their scalps at about £1 each, which wasn't bad money at the time if you were unemployed. They lived in the bush and had no overheads. Their sole, simple transport was a donkey-drawn, two-wheel cart with a loose, old canvas cover as protection from the dew; during the dry season it rarely rained.

Dingoes were mostly obtained by poisoning, using baits – usually strychnine- poisoned meat, such as kangaroo, pig, buffalo or crocodile

Events In Oz

– and although the strychnine was slow acting and agonising for the poor dingo, it was necessarily tasteless and odourless, and readily accepted by wild dogs, dingoes, cats and all other animals, Indigenous or introduced.

One evening during the late dry season, Monte and his mate received an unseasonal shower of rain, which caused the two of them to dive under the two-wheeled wagon for shelter after quickly covering the load above with the old canvas cover. In the morning, after stretching their legs and gathering sparse dry wood from somewhere under the wet wood, they got the fire burning and made HOT "JOHNNIE CAKES" WITH GOLDEN SYRUP, WASHED DOWN BY COPIOUS AMOUNTS OF SUGAR- RICH, BLACK COFFEE.

In a short time, MONTY FELT TERRIBLE, WALKED OUT IN THE BUSH AND WAS SICK AS A DOG within seconds, involuntarily emptying the contents of his stomach in what he said was a "technicolour yawn".[23] HIS MATE WAS IN WORSE KNOTTED AGONY, clutching his stomach, and lying and squirming around on the ground in THE IDENTICAL AGONY TO THAT OF A POISONED DINGO. Unfortunately for him, he did not vomit and/ or expel the deadly strychnine poison, which was irreversibly gnawing at his insides. He quickly lapsed mercifully into unconsciousness and was dead in 20 minutes.

At the subsequent post-mortem enquiry, it was revealed that some of the rainwater falling on the canvas cover had run directly into the open, old treacle tin containing the lethal strychnine, and overflowed, some of it, into the uncovered, open sugar tin sitting immediately below, which then wound up in the coffee.

Monty had received a total overdose from two cups of coffee, causing him to quickly throw up. His mate, unfortunately, had received just

---

[23] Projectile vomit containing many colourful bits of undigested food

157

the right amount of poison from just one cup of coffee; not enough to involuntarily expel but just the right amount to kill.

THE VERDICT: "DEATH BY MISADVENTURE".

44.
URANIUM WAR OF '54

Towards the end of 1954, we were sitting on our laurels. We had just discovered the very rich, high grade El-Sherana uranium deposit in Australia's Northern Territory (N.T.) and were looking for more. There was a race for uranium between our company, Northern Uranium Development, N.L. (N.U.D.) and the North Australian Uranium Corporation (N.A.U.C.) in the South Alligator River/ Katherine region of "the Territory".

The N.T. Government had drawn up a series of maps of possible areas of uranium mineralisation. These were known as "Prospecting Authority Areas" (P.A.A.).

Companies who had expressed interest in such areas and had been granted their P.A.A., having received their new maps, were itching to start looking on the ground "in" their respective AREAS OF AUTHORITY. The main reason for the current rush of activity in the area was a result of the Australian Government's Bureau of Mineral Resources release of aerial scintillometer maps showing quite specific areas of promising RADIOACTIVITY in the South Alligator River region, which included our P.A.A. These scintillometer maps showed a number of promising areas of much higher-than-usual radioactivity about two miles from our present location, which at that early time was on the West bank of the South Alligator River.

****

There were six of us in our prospecting party: "Snowy" Anderson our party leader; Jack Smith, in his fifties; "Bluey" Kaye (who provided the name of the new mine, based on the names of his daughters); and

Ross Snowden, Jim Bowes and me. At 20, I was the youngest. We fanned out in specific areas of interest each day, armed with maps, Austronic brand Geiger counters, geological hammers/ picks, sample bags, sharp pocket knives, and the since proven useless Condy's crystals for snake- bite.

We had no sooner discovered the El-Sherana and applied for the Australian Government's maximum reward of £25,000 (the basic wage was then a princely £6 per week), which in time we received, when, to our great surprise, A TEAM OF N.A.U.C. PROSPECTORS ARRIVED, ILLEGALLY, ON OUR P.A.A. and set up their camp half a mile upstream, on our side of "our river", the South Alligator. Now at that time the rule was a company could hold no more P.A.A. territory at one time other than what had been granted in the first place. So, in order to acquire more land, they would first have to surrender an equal area of land they already held legally. but the N.A.U.C. prospectors had surrendered exactly nothing!

As a result of our hard earned "El-Sherana" discovery, N.A.U.C. thought they would just move into OUR PATCH, like the pirates of old, and somehow look around for our SCRAPS and LEFT-OVERS. A few days later we discovered that the N.A.U.C. party had discovered a uranium occurrence about two miles away on our P.A.A. and had started the work of ILLEGALLY PEGGING THEIR CLAIM ON OUR LAND!

It was at my suggestion that WE THEN SET TO WORK AND OVERPEGGED THEIR ILLEGAL CLAIM, even before they had actually finished their nefarious deed but not before we had a few unpleasant words with them. When we subsequently met the

N.A.U.C. guys in the bush, they were not very friendly but agreed with us that the matter would have to be settled peacefully in the Mining Wardens' Court 160 miles away in Darwin. In due course, it was the Mining Wardens' decision that if the claims were ever commercial, any income would be divided between us. That possibility never eventuated.

In the meantime, WE WERE STILL RED HOT ABOUT THE ILLEGAL ACTIONS OF N.A.U.C. and there is no doubt there was a bit of bad blood between us. On the evening of our confrontation, after our run-in with the "PIRATES" and our actions in over-pegging their claim, we had a few beers in our camp as we spoke of their unpopular, illegal actions, and talked ourselves up a bit. Apparently, the general feeling in their camp was similar to ours and later that night we heard an outbreak of gunfire coming from their camp, which woke us up. That was THE START OF SOMETHING BIG!

TIT FOR TAT, WE OPENED UP WITH A .303 FIRING A FEW EX-MILITARY TRACER BULLETS, leaving their brilliant shining path displayed for all to see high in the sky above their camp. Next, we were aware they were firing other firearms up and over our camp, so we retaliated with our considerable arsenal of mini-artillery, made up, as I remember, of a .45 Browning automatic pistol, a 9 m.m. Luger pistol, a .22 Lithgow single shot rifle (mine!), a Browning automatic 12-gauge shotgun, a U.S. "Rockola" make .30 carbine, bought by me for £5 from Jimmy Ah Toy in Pine Creek, and a couple of army issue .303s. WORLD WAR 2 WAS RE-ENACTED FOR ALL OF ABOUT FIVE MINUTES, when we seem to have decided we had had our fun and were running out of our expensive, hard-to-get ammunition, so we both ceased firing at about the same time.

****

To our surprise, about two days later, a newspaper reporter from "WYKIKAMOOKOW" or somewhere in New Zealand, who was a freelance reporter based in Darwin and looking for a good story, arrived at our camp on his autocycle to find out the truth of the rumours he had freshly heard in Darwin, which was about 200 difficult, mainly dirt- track miles and two days travel on an autocycle away.

We told "our enemies", the N.A.U.C. guys, about our visitor and WE BOTH AGREED TO PUT ON A GOOD SHOW FOR HIM THAT NIGHT, after elaborating and concocting stories of "layabouts, claim jumpers, crocodiles, buffaloes, Kadaitcha Men and hoop snakes" for his ardent Australasian and overseas readers. So that night, for a brief moment in time, all of about five minutes again, the sky lit up, the noise was horrendous (we thought!), and we used up most of our expensive, hard-to-obtain ammunition, including Brenneke slugs and a couple of plugs of gelignite set off in the bush between our camps, so we could both honestly blame each other. And that was that!

The next day, "Sir Galahad" on his autocycle set off early in the morning with tape recordings of our gunfire, bombs, bells and whistles, the sounds themselves desperately trying to somehow break out from his tight, sound-enclosed Grundig tape recorder, plus vivid Kodachromes of our last few remaining tracer bullets arcing past the stars and into the dark blue folds of the brilliant Northern Territory night sky.

****

A day later sensational stories appeared in the "Northern Territory News", syndicated throughout the world (I was later told) … stories about a URANIUM WAR breaking out between N.U.D. (us) and N.A.U.C. (them) on the South Alligator River. We then had radio calls from our general manager, Joe Fisher, company director Frank Jones, other newspaper scribes and a visit from the Pine Creek policeman a hundred or so miles away!

We told them it was just a bit of light-hearted fun that got more attention than it was ever meant to deserve, and …

GRADUALLY … WE THOUGHT …. WITH TIME … THE CURER OF MOST ILLS, WE'D LAUGH OUR WAY OUT OF IT!

45.
FRUIT SALAD 1955

We (me and my friend Geoffrey Lionel Banbury Hewetson (G.L.B.H.) who I met while working in the Peko Copper Mine) left Darwin and headed South down the road to the 54-mile peg and turned left into Ginger Palmer's camp about three miles or so to the Adelaide River. Ginger wasn't home. Just a white sulphur crested cockatoo in its crap- fouled cage incessantly uttering lewd obscenities, and an old, nearly blind, stupidly friendly, black "woofy" dog covered in numerous bloody-bloated, septic blue, yuckie ticks. This was next to a scrawny, eight-foot captive broken-toothed saltwater crocodile, twisted awkwardly in an ancient half-empty, once-white, six-foot iron bath full of stinking, slimy, pea-soup green, foul, dampish liquid masquerading hopelessly as water. The captive croc was thoroughly demoralised and going nowhere in a grossly undersized, all-surrounding, rusty steel weld-mesh cage, while a large attendant malevolent-looking, brainless green tree frog was sitting oblivious to any perceived danger to itself on the top of the annoyed, pissed-off crocodile's head.

Large letters in metallic silver paint on a battered, rusty-brown, perforated sheet of corrugated galvanised iron, wired loosely to the old shed with rusty barbed wire, were the supposedly awe-inspiring, facetious words proclaiming the run-down, ramshackle property to be the "GULP, GULP, GONE! CROCODILE FARM".

****

Herbie Griffin and Snowy Fabian had earlier said if Ginger was not about, which was invariably the case because he quite often had important drinking business at Mrs Fawcett's Adelaide River Hotel, it was quite OK to borrow one of his several ramshackle dinghies, which we did. We loaded our basic supplies – a large can of "GOLDEN CIRCLE" FRUIT SALAD and a Browning ventilated rib, auto-loading 12- gauge shotgun, a selection of various grade, shot-size cartridges, and large, bullet- like, externally-vaned, purposeful, heavy Brenneke slugs – into the driest, safest- looking, battered plywood boat and rowed across the 50-yard-wide, crocodile-infested upper tidal reaches of the then nearly pristine Adelaide River.

****

Nowadays, in 2017 (as I was writing this), this stretch of the Adelaide River has become a well-known tourist attraction and is the natural river home of large, totally- wild, skyward-leaping saltwater crocodiles. That is, crocodiles leaping 15 or 20 feet up to the level of the tourists' safe, mast-mounted position high above the river in order to grab a fist-sized morsel of meat from the end of a hand-held, pointed, 10-foot long bamboo "chopstick".

****

We dragged the dinghy up high out of the water onto the East riverbank and utilised a handy, ready-made, up-sloping, slippery path above the bank, almost to the level of the overhanging plain, before embarking on our spontaneous, unplanned "Porky Pig" and "Magpie Goose"[24] hunting "expedition". WE LATER LEARNED THE SLIPPERY SLIDE WAS THE HOME LAUNCHING PAD FOR A HEALTHY, 15-FOOT PLUS CROCODILE who was usually close by, probably too close for comfort, and who no doubt silently, sneakily, witnessed our unwitting, unwelcome, unwanted, noisy trespass from beneath the concealment afforded by the opaque and murky waters.

---

[24] Cartoon characters

We then leisurely walked a few miles past the usual bandicoots, wallabies, Jabiru storks, goannas and raucous screeching cockatoos, and East onto the hot, dry Marraki Plain until about midday when our combined empty stomachs' gnawing, hollow, rumbling behaviour suggested it was lunch time.

****

After gently dislodging a passive, resident 12-foot, black-headed rock python from its castle, we used a low, bum-sized anthill as a comfortable seat next to an unusually contorted but very comfortable ready-made "regal throne"-shaped tree stump standing in among the cool and shading overhanging pandanus palms. AS DROOLING SALIVA PRE-MOISTENED OUR LIPS, we set about opening the inviting can of fruit salad when, to our great dismay – curses! shock!! horror!!! – we realised the TRUSTY CAN OPENER, our absolutely necessary old and vital friend, WAS MISSING!

Well, not wishing to be outsmarted by a brainless tin can, I immediately tried my trusty old Joseph Rogers bunny knife on the stubborn tin plate; a stubborn tin can still effectively protecting its contained fruit salad from us. I soon realised the old pocket knife was not made for opening tough contemporary fruit cans. So … NOW WHAT DO WE DO? Then EUREKA! I have it! The brilliant inventive thought hit me between the eyes like a bolt from the blue! If my ever-trusting companion G.L.B.H. would calmly hold the unopened can of fruit salad, very firmly, more or less over his vulnerable head and its unknown contents, but safely a little forward and to one side, then the open muzzle end of the large-diameter, lethal-looking, 12-gauge shotgun barrel could be placed easily and accurately in a direct-aimed, contacting "can't miss" attitude in a close and lightly touching relationship with the circular upper rim of the tough, until now pocket knife resistant tin can.

IF THE CAN WAS SOMEHOW PLACED IN A SUITABLE, STRATEGIC POSITION AND FIRMLY HELD MANUALLY IN PLACE, IT MIGHT EASILY ENABLE A JUST- PASSING, SLIGHTLY "GRAZING", FASTER THAN THE SPEED OF SOUND HEAVYWEIGHT BRENNEKE SLUG TO EVER SO GENTLY "SNICK" THE SHINY RIM'S BEADED EDGE, just sufficiently to maybe open it up slightly to enable, somehow, relatively easy practical thin wooden twig or sticky little-fingered, hungry human access to the otherwise unreachable, untouchable, forbidden, out of sight fruit salad.

Well, FOR REASONS BEST KNOWN ONLY TO HIM, G.L.B.H. EXPRESSED DOUBT; some alternate, inner, nagging voice or secret, hidden conscientious force was telling him it was NOT REALLY SUCH A GOOD IDEA. It was really difficult trying to get him to use a little common sense and come rationally around to my well- ordered, mentally-calculated way of thinking. I had to be firm! Though he was a few years older than me, I said to Geoffrey:

> "Be logical. There is absolutely nothing to be worried about. The Brenneke slug is just a great big, softish, big toe-sized lump of lead with a clear as daylight one track mind. When discharged, it's only going dead straight, safely one way, completely in the opposite direction, and that's absolutely 100 % safely AWAY FROM YOU! It's not going to turn around and come back, boomerang style, and bite you in the bum now, is it? Its inertia will carry it away safely in a straight parabolic curve, right away from us at 1,000 or more feet a second, while obeying all the concrete, set-in-stone, absolutely unchanging laws of physics. So for goodness sake, you're a 24-year-old adult. USE YOUR COMMON SENSE. WAKE UP MAN!"

Seemingly still very much against his better judgement, G.L.B.H. TENTATIVELY EXTENDED HIS ARMS, HANDS AND RELUCTANT TIN OF FRUIT SALAD generally upwards while meekly surrendering to the as-yet-uncertain, forthcoming, mysterious, yet-to-be-decided outcome. In spite of G.L.B.H.'s continually uttered verbal misgivings and protestations, I was eventually able to reassure him and place the innocent, wide open, great cavernous business end of the loaded 12-gauge shotgun barrel exactly in position next to, and in firm physical contact with, the upper tough-rimmed edge of the lightly hand-held, unopened can of fruit salad, all the while very responsibly, of course safely, pointing the single, one-track-mind gun in a position away from G.L.B.H.'s more-or-less secure physical position. After all, IT WOULD NOT BE IN MY BEST INTEREST IF HE WAS ACCIDENTLY SHOT AND INJURED because it would be quite difficult to properly explain to the various interested legal authorities, such as the Police, who may be excused for being sceptical about the strange, hopefully repeatable under oath, cover story I may have to tell. A cover story I may suddenly have to concoct somehow, awkwardly, for various and obscure reasons, if I ever found myself completely out of my depth, deep in the shit and legally on the spot!

Nevertheless, as the seconds slowly ticked by, G.L.B.H. did seem somehow, I think in his own mind, to have mentally gained by strange magical unorthodox means a little useful (I imagined) extra physical "length" to his arms, which to him, perhaps seemingly usefully extended ever so slightly his present, dangerously "short", minimal, manual safety margin or critical and safe distance from the dangerously very near, very close at hand, hand-held, pregnant, "tick, tock, ticking" can of fruit salad.

Well, FOR REASONS BEST KNOWN ONLY TO HIM, HE STILL SEEMED DEFIANTLY RELUCTANT, WAS CLEARLY NERVOUS, INCESSANTLY FIDGETING, AND WOULD NOT OR COULD NOT KEEP EITHER ROCK CALM OR DEAD STILL.

If I didn't really know absolutely for a fact just how brave he really was, I could have mistakenly thought for just a moment or two that he was actually in doubt! Anyway, after just a few nervous tense, premature, compulsive moments, his restless, endlessly-shaking, vibrating hand movements finally appeared to have settled down to about a steady ten shakes a second and I finally realised he was at last beginning to appreciate the genuine sincerity, the truth and the wisdom of my admittedly unorthodox and clever tin can opening procedure. He was finally coming to grips with the strange, different and unusual ins and outs of the rather odd present situation in which he seemed, for some reason, to still be uneasily physically and mentally squirming.

As the split seconds united, he reluctantly now, at last, ever so slowly, became finally and hopefully, I really thought, genuinely subdued and resigned. Well, it was midday, the sun was up over the yardarm and I for one wasn't going to wait all day. We were both hungry, we were both thirsty and we had to eat.

Firmly nursing the beautifully-crafted, mirror-polished, fine-grained European walnut stock of the Browning with its effective, soft-cushioning rubber recoil-protecting pad nestling comfortably in the crook of my shoulder, I carefully placed and aimed the long, ventilated blue'd[25] shotgun barrel at the very top metal-rimmed edge of the can at a very shallow, intersecting angle.

It was then at last that my sensitive, itchy trigger finger finally, ever so cautiously sought, touched, caressed and explosively hot-kissed the expectant, eagerly-waiting, light and readily-responding fine, delicate steel, precision-made "hair-trigger" of the patient shotgun's ready, willing and eager featherweight firing mechanism.

KA'BLAM!

---

[25] Bluing is a passivation process in which steel is partially protected against rust using a black oxide coating

I was struck first by the substantial and abrupt recoil of the shotgun as it instantly transferred enormous energy to my firmly padded shoulder and started a fresh and endless chain of unplanned, unorthodox events – events largely caused by the sharp, explosive "ballistite"-propelled departure of the great, single, solid, big-toe-sized, heavy-vaned and finned aerodynamic lump of lead, with its rear rivet-attached fibre composite gas seal, and the simultaneous, many coloured fantasia-like instant liquid- sprayed sunset vision, unveiled briefly as IT FLASHED IN THE SKY LIKE A 3D LIGHTNING-SPEED VAPORISED FRUITY, MILKY-WAY AURORA AUSTRALIS. A beautiful, instantaneous, crude harlequin vision of LUMPY, MULTI-COLOURED, AMORPHOUS, LIQUID FRUIT SALAD both magically sprayed and vaporised in a split millisecond before my dumbstruck eyes. And in the very same split millisecond, the laughable and comical, real-life chain of events, such as the sudden, MAGICAL, UNEXPECTED TRANSFORMATION OF G.L.B.H. INTO THE REALISTIC, UNMISTAKABLE, FRUIT SALAD-COATED COMICAL GUISE OF A CLOWN.

He just stood there, dazed, in a state of absolute and mindless awe. His face was covered in the main with yellow passionfruit and scattered, spotty black seeds and other blobs of completely pulped-on-his-face, amorphous banana, while a largish wedge of pineapple was somehow jammed between his rigidly-set, unsmiling teeth.

G.L.B.H. WAS NOT AMUSED …

Vestiges of something maybe apricot hung long and liquid, string-like from his eyebrows. From the end of his nose hung suspicious, yellow snot-like liquid strands of sticky sugar syrup. Through it all, his secret, underlying demeanour was not in any way the slightest help to his doubtful cause, for his cause had been well and truly lost. On top of this, his delicate situation was in no way helped by my loud, completely unrestrained, unthinking mirth as I spontaneously "LAUGHED MY HEAD OFF!"

****

A faded, long-lasting, indelible mental vision still remains feebly in the back reaches of my mind to this very day; G.L.B.H.'s instant chameleon-like black and yellow daubed skin contrasting with his dead and shifty eyes and his mentally-devoid, morbidly- absent, completely expressionless face, which thoughtfully occupied my gaze until moments later he roughly wiped his face half clean with the tail of his shirt.

****

A bright, shiny, sun-reflecting, flattened strip of tin plate 30 feet away really brightened the day up and revealed the brand new, precise ground coordinates of the heavily modified "ex can". While the steel can had contained sweet, sugar-syrup-immersed fruit salad, there was little left to be seen apart from colourful gooey syrup dripping from the freshly-wetted, brand new, magically-appeared TROPICAL FRUIT SALAD TREES overhead.

It was about this time the strength of our already-strained friendship seemed to nosedive. It deteriorated very suddenly to breaking point, though not a verbal word was spoken by the steadfastly lost-for-words, silent-as-a-lamb G.L.B.H. This was probably because he had really lost effective touch and control of his disoriented tongue. In fact, at this uncertain moment in time, he seemed surprisingly shocked, numbed and totally speechless, although on reflection he had never really had all that much to say anyway.

So, silently, we walked away from the fruit salad-spattered site of our minor misadventure, hot, sweaty, hungry and very, very thirsty, and

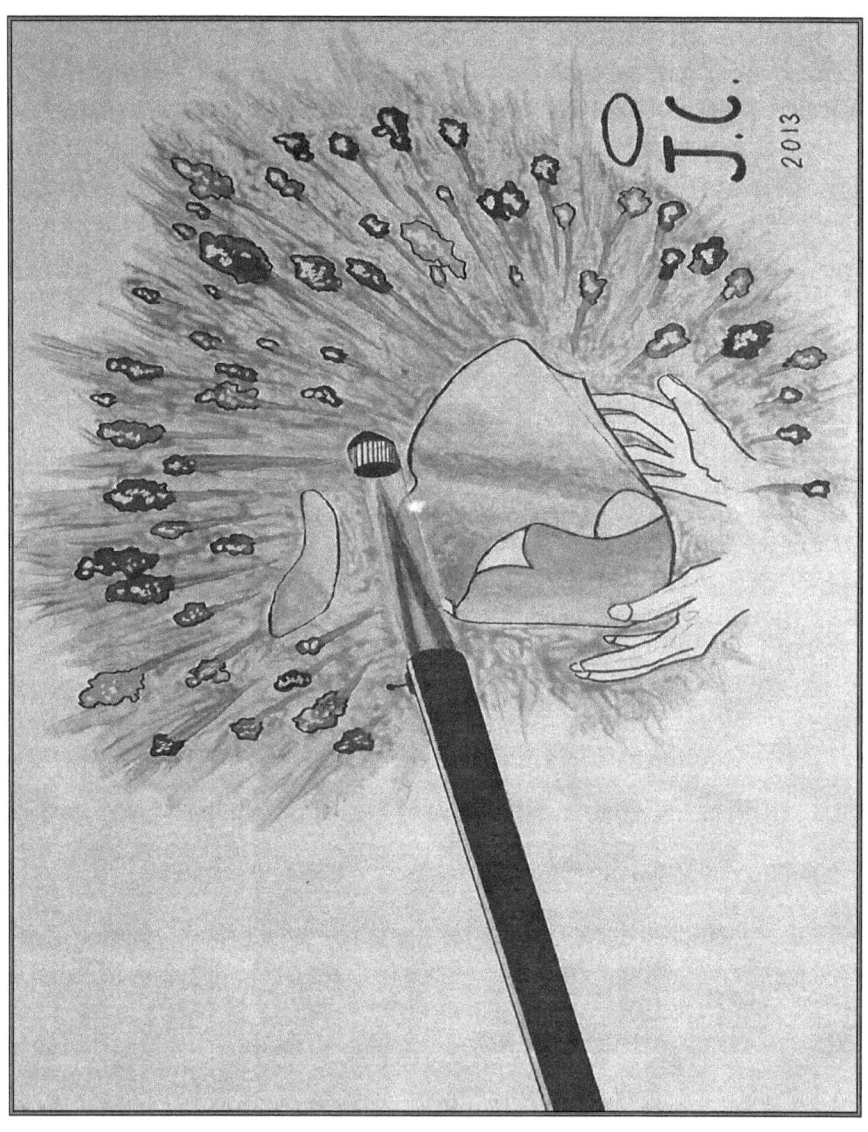
Fruit salad explosion

trudged grudgingly across the now ever-so-mentally unappealing flat miles of the forever-boring, uninviting, foreign-looking, expressionless black-soil Marraki Plain.

Judging by his constant vigorous, non-stop hand actions, IT WAS APPARENT G.L.B.H. WAS SILENTLY EXPERIENCING PERSONAL SOCIAL DEMONS OR PROBLEMS OF SOME KIND, WHILE THOUSANDS OF TINY EFFICIENT NIBBLING SUGAR ANTS AND DOZENS OF LARGE INCH-LONG, PROMINENT-MANDIBLED, MEAT-EATING, BITING BULL ANTS, WHICH HAD LITERALLY INVADED THE SACRED BODY OF HIS FLESHY PRIVATE PERSON, WERE ENDLESSLY CRAWLING ALL OVER HIM, everywhere, and were defiantly intent on exploring by any means the sweaty, innermost crevices of his not so sweet, unheavenly body.

Of course, the ants were not really trying to eat him. They were just after the copious oozing, congealing blood and pus slowly weeping from his numerous skin-deep cuts and scratches, or desiring to lick and slurp, in friendly ant fashion, the remaining sticky, drying fruit salad sugar syrup with which he had been instantly, freely and liberally anointed – indeed, spray painted head to toe – and of which he still had more than ample reserves at his immediate disposal for both the local ants and the whole world's ants' future sweet, sugar syrup supply. In any case, the total combined weight of all the ants present was really very tiny – miniscule – and, let's face it, any unwanted extra weight of their tens of thousands amounted to just a few ounces at the most; HARDLY MUCH OF A BURDEN for a brave, fit, strong, healthy, 12-stone, red--blooded Australian like G.L.B.H. to easily carry without noticing. At one time, he mumbled to himself something about "bloody ants", to which, I think, I outmumbled him, loud and clear enough for him to hear me whisper, "THEY AREN'T BLOODY WELL WORRYING ME!" I do remember, however, that as the shadows lengthened, the mosquitoes and sand flies did become troublesome.

****

And so, we slowly, slowly walked back, and as we did so, my aimless mind was beginning to wander randomly, unchecked, all over the place while I imagined a double malted vanilla milkshake sliding down my throat at Sigalas' milk bar in far-off Adelaide. I was actually beginning to have uneasy, unwanted, guilty pangs of conscience; flashes of memory, just-remembered visions, mental moments, memories of just-remembered school days, P.A.C. teachers, unholy cock-ups, canes, size 12 sandshoes, physics lessons, 100 lines, Isaac Newton and something suspiciously like "for every action, there's an equal and opposite reaction", which suddenly caused me to think laterally about a certain recently-exploded can of fruit salad … or was it Pythagoras? It then occurred to me that I really should have paid more attention to my dedicated, frustrated teachers when serving my hopelessly aimless time at P.A.C.!

Anyway, in 1955, which was now fully all of five years since I had left school, it was really too late to worry. Those almost-forgotten school days were now yesterday's past, and past is past, "gone with the wind", and so I quite wisely and discretely shut my mouth and said absolutely nothing to anyone about our recent, unholy "FAILED TIMES". After all, there's nothing to be gained after such a minor, un-newsworthy, unplanned, accidental, cock-up by needlessly telling the whole damn world about it, let alone "crying crocodile tears over long-lost, spilt milk" and "TWISTED FOLLIES".

****

You may be interested to know this is a true story. It's not fiction. It did happen in 1955, and for better or for worse I confess I was the 21-year-old thoughtless part of this thoroughly misguided event. In hindsight, having been uneasily under such a colourful exploding shower of fruit salad all those years ago …

>   I'D BELATEDLY LIKE TO APOLOGISE TO G.L.B.H. …

wherever he is now, for any small part I may have unconsciously played in relation to his somewhat dubious, past mental pain and suffering.

Meanwhile, I'll just mentally file this record of this particular event as ONE OF MY FAVOURITE, TOTALLY UNFORGETTABLE, "TWISTED FOLLIES" and leave it at that.

WHEREVER YOU ARE GEOFFREY, THE ICE CREAM'S ON ME!

46.
WHISTLECOCK 1955

About 1955, in the far North-West corner of South Australia, I noticed one of our fortyish, full-blooded, tribal Aboriginal helpers having a pee in the bush. There was something strange about the way he was standing and how he was doing it. It looked to me as though he had his left hand, middle finger inserted right up his hairy arse for some strange, unknown, innate reason, while at the same time he appeared to be piddling normally through his right-hand-held, long, black, snake-like penis.

****

A little later I mentioned this unusual happening to a red-haired Native Welfare Officer by the name of Mr. MacDougall who was employed by the "powers that be" in control of security for the Woomera rocket test range in northern South Australia. His job was to try to locate and relocate, if possible, small groups of spear- and woomera-armed hunter gatherers; sparse populations of still tribal nomadic Aboriginals roaming, aimlessly we thought, about the general desert rocket range and the Emu Field atomic bomb testing area. This area was bush, covering about 400 X 500 miles, so finding the Aboriginals was like "looking for a needle in a haystack". It has recently been revealed that an unknown number of Aboriginals, possibly as many as 30, had unwittingly been killed, maimed or blinded during some of the earlier 1950s-era British atmospheric atomic bomb tests at the Emu Field, Western Maralinga test site (see Story 49 for more details).

****

Regarding the strange piddling episode I had seen earlier, Mr. MacDougall explained to me that quite a few of the older Aboriginals had earlier been both "whistlecocked" and circumcised at puberty; an old traditional custom, he said, which by now had nearly died out because their tribal ways were fast disappearing with the encroachment of Western-type civilisation.

"Whistlecocking" was said to be a primitive, yet effective method of MALE BIRTH CONTROL. The procedure was said to use a small diameter needle-pointed bone, say one eighth of an inch in diameter, to penetrate the external underside of the penis in a position forward of the rear dangling testicles, the pointed bone being left in place until the new hole into the urethra remained permanently enlarged and open. This would therefore make it difficult to pass urine through the urethra, the hollow internal tube of the penis, unless the tip of a finger were used to simply block the small semen escape hole, causing the urine flow to pass normally through the full length of the penis.

On the face of it, when used as a birth control method, whistlecocking seems to be a very effective and simple method. At the moment of ejaculation, the whistlecocked, naked Aboriginal did nothing; he did not need to cover the open hole in the base of his penis because his ejaculating semen took a short cut straight out sideways through the handy semen escape hole to the underlying carpet of terra firma,[26] while at the same time he apparently achieved a satisfying sexual orgasm.

****

The name "whistlecock" came about because the male whistlecocked reproductive organs, when viewed from the side, are reminiscent of an old fashioned, ball-type umpire's whistle, with the urethra end of the shaft of the penis being the theoretical mouthpiece part, or body

---
[26] Earth

of the whistle, while the testicles represent the imagined round, ball-holding, noisemaking, important rattling part of the whistle.

47.
CAVENAGH WATERS 1955

A geologist and I were employed by Geosurveys of Australia to undertake nickel exploration activities in the extreme North-West corner of South Australia in 1955. We were operating just over the border from South Australia in the state of Western Australia (W.A.) and heading overland towards the Cavenagh Ranges, about 80 miles from our base camp at Mt. Davies, South Australia. We were travelling by Land Rover, sleeping under the stars and keeping in touch with base daily through Graham Pitts, operator of the Flying Doctor/ Alice Air Radio in Alice Springs. The desert scenery was magnificent, the winter skies were cloudless and we mainly navigated point-to-point through the bush by use of fine-grained aerial photos, a prismatic compass and 10X magnifying lenses. About 9:00 a.m. we arrived at the South-Eastern end of the Cavenagh Ranges; a small, rocky row of rugged hills about half a mile wide and maybe 15 miles long, where we were surprised to find a crystal-clear stream of running water emanating from a long, narrow valley, flowing maybe 30 yards out onto the surrounding desert floor, then soaking away and disappearing before our eyes. We tasted the water. It was good so we decided to camp there that night.

The geologist was busy mapping the geology of the area and doing his reports when about midday we noticed the stream had dried up! "Well", I thought, "we were just a bit lucky to have encountered the very last of the running waters just before they dried up once and for all. So be it"!

Next morning at 7:00 a.m. there was the stream, flowing past again, the same as yesterday. It is obviously a daily event; an event I have since seen a number of times, mainly in similar, dry, desert conditions, usually after recent rain. Perhaps the water- carrying capillaries in the rocks expand and close in the daytime, and relax open at night, releasing water? It's an unusual physical phenomenon, unseen by most urban Australians. Although a minor, rather uncanny, regular, natural, everyday event in the Cavenagh and other similar dry inland hills and ranges, it is definitely worth describing for the benefit of those who may never get the chance to witness it.

48.
A STALKING LESSON 1955

I was employed by Reg Sprigg's new company GeoSurveys of Australia in 1955 in his second year of operation. Previously, Reg had been senior geologist with the South Australian Government Mines Department and carried a varied bag of international mineral exploration experience as a hands-on, practicing geologist of steadily-growing international repute. His reputation had been enhanced by his earlier discovery of a pre-Cambrian geological sequence now known as the "Ediacaran Period" after he had discovered fossils of soft and jelly-fish-like ancient life forms at Ediacara in the Flinders Ranges; the first new geological age identified and subsequently confirmed internationally in about 130 years of geological history.

While still with the South Australian Government Mines Department, Reg had become aware of the presence of traces of nickel in the Mt. Davies area in the Tomkinson Ranges in the extreme North-West corner of South Australia. The government geologist H.Y.L. Brown, in his earlier records of the Minerals of South Australia, had confirmed the existence of nickel in 1908.

Reg had then resigned from the Mines Department and I believe he obtained some sort of prospecting authority over the area. He formed Geosurveys of Australia, then invited the world's largest nickel producer, the INTERNATIONAL NICKEL COMPANY of Sudbury, Ontario, CANADA, to jointly investigate the Tomkinson Ranges area with a view to ascertaining its nickel potential. Later, Reg was also instrumental in forming both Australian mining houses SANTOS and BEACH PETROLEUM (now BEACH ENERGY), which are still operational today

****

The International Nickel Company (I.N.C.O), with Geosurveys Associated in the field for ground support, set up camp not far from Mt. Davies. Access was direct by ground by sealed road for the first 200 miles to Port Augusta and another 600 miles of a dirt road of sorts to Kulgera near the Northern Territory border, followed by a set of wheel tracks West past the Ernabella Mission Station 300 miles to Mt. Davies. Or by air from Alice Springs, flown by my old employer Connellan Airways in their old De Havilland Rapide and Dragonfly wood-framed, canvas-covered, Gipsy Major-powered skin and bones aircraft.

Occasionally, we obtained supplies from the isolated desert store at Finke, and on one occasion when the truck from Finke was a day overdue, I flew as an observer in a Rapide about 150 miles East to find it. The truck had been held up with engine trouble and the driver was just about to resume his journey to us. As we circled overhead in the Rapide, he scratched a big "OK" in the red earth and arrived safely in our camp about four hours later. On another occasion, I had flown about halfway from the Alice to Mt. Davies in a Dragonfly when the weather closed in and we returned to the Alice. The very next day, the same aircraft did a flight 315 miles North to the gold mining town of Tennant Creek and due to a stuff-up when refuelling on a red-hot tarmac, the Dragonfly burst into flames and in minutes was destroyed on the airstrip !

****

The I.N.C.O geologist in charge of the camp at Mt. Davies was a white-skinned, blue- eyed, blonde-haired Canadian, Paddy Laine. The I.N.C.O geophysicist was John Dowsett, who had only been married a few months beforehand and now found he was marooned in the rather desolate (to him) Australian outback while his new bride waited despairingly (he hoped) in Canada. I well remember his occasional nightly antics, fuelled by Canadian Club whisky, as he wandered around our small, perhaps 10-person camp, mumbling to himself, over and over, "When the moon is like a pumpkin, that's the time for Dicky Dunking".

As a point of interest, when I was with the Western Mining Corporation in Kalgoorlie, W.A., nickel exploration in that state was in full swing and booming. About 11 years later in 1966, while cleansing my palette with a cold "Swan", I found myself looking at a fellow patron in the bar of Kalgoorlie's Palace Hotel. I asked one of the barmaids if she knew who he was. She said, "I think he's a geologist, Canadian I think". The penny dropped. I positioned myself about a foot behind him and clearly said, "When the moon is like a pumpkin!" He spun around like a top and said, "WHO SAID THAT?" It was John Dowsett. The memory of the rest of the night is nothing but a blur.

****

We also had an Aussie geophysicist, David Pegum, on site, and I well remember him for his bush-conceived salmon mornay. Geologists Ian Freytag, Bruce Wilson and Doug Scott were among the other Geosurveys staff I still remember operating at Mt. Davies. Not long after I had settled in at Mt. Davies, we got word that the Woomera-based, bush road constructing surveyor Lennie Beadell was planning to land a Bristol Freighter aircraft on our short bush airstrip to deliver a couple of new Land Rovers for use in constructing the Gunbarrell Highway, which was planned to pass our camp. So I was then instructed to remove hundreds of tough mulga trees by making holes between their roots with a crowbar, creating small pockets for explosives, then blasting the tap roots with a plug of gelignite in order to quickly lengthen and broaden our previously short airstrip.

****

We had some unusual visitors one day when a couple of the only remaining, truly nomadic, completely naked Aboriginals wandered into our camp with a semi-domesticated dingo at heel. She had a baby on the breast and carried a wooden bowl, a hard-pointed mulga digging stick and a smallish rolled up woven grass mat. He carried the multi-use wooden woomera (spear thrower) and a couple of long-barbed spears, and had a shoelace-like, pencil-thin, plaited hair belt around his waist. I tell their story in the next chapter.

At that time, the British were about to test fire another atomic bomb at the Emu Field test site about 300 miles South of Mt. Davies. The government of the day announced the test would only be conducted when the WINDS WERE NOT BLOWING SOUTH, on or over the "settled" lands of South Australia. We heard on the radio the test had gone off without a hitch, although we didn't hear a sound, see a flash, or even see the atomic mushroom cloud. The winds, we were told, had all gone safely our way, North, and there was nothing to worry about! WELL, THAT WAS OK FOR THEM. WHAT ABOUT US? AND THE NOMADIC ABORIGINALS? We had several times been visited by a Mr. McDougall, a red-haired Native Welfare Officer, whose job it was to locate isolated Aboriginal "human needles" in a 400 X 500 mile "haystack", and if or when found, somehow get them to move on somewhere. Our nomadic visitors were no doubt two of these needles.

In 2013, I heard a disquieting disclosure recently made under the Freedom of Information Act, where it was assumed a number of Aboriginals would not have been located at the time of the above-ground atomic bomb tests in the 1950s. It later turned out that while some unknowing Aboriginal people would have died instantly, others who may have survived, affected by atomic radiation sickness over a long period of time, subsequently perished unknown, undetected and out of sight in the timeless desert. Such is/ was the LEGACY OF THE THOROUGHLY IRRESPONSIBLE AUSTRALIAN AND BRITISH GOVERNMENTS OF THE TIME!

****

One of my various tasks was to clear a long straight line through the light mulga tree forest, maybe 10 miles long, across the flats and over hilly, rocky, 300-foot-high ridges in the vicinity of "Champ De Mars", named earlier in the days of Queen Victoria by the explorer Edward Giles. This is where we were camped and where, for a time, I SHARED MY TENT WITH REG SPRIGG'S ELDERLY FATHER, CLAUDE SPRIGG, who had only recently been widowed.

Until the last few weeks, I had as my BAREFOOT WORK MATE a tribal Aboriginal we named "HUGHIE", who only knew a few basic words of English, such as "p'flour", "t'chigarette", "ti" and "t'shugar". He wore an old pair of trousers which gradually removed themselves as torn tatters, shed bit by bit from his body over a long time.

I usually carried my new .22 Krico iron-sighted rifle in case I needed it and on a number of occasions we enjoyed quail and bronze-wing barbecued pigeons for lunch. My mate Hughie was good with the axe and held the survey staff more-or-less upright, and usually went where I pointed, when and as required. When the straight line ascended a rocky ridge, say at right angles, it was necessary to use an effective, simple device known as an OPTICAL SQUARE. This device enabled me to look down hill, both backward and forward at the same time, as I centred my position to achieve a dead straight line from, and over, the crest of an otherwise visually-blocking ridge.

On one occasion, we had reached the top of a rocky ridge, maybe 300 feet above "Champ De Mars", and had a bit of a rest while Hughie smoked a t'chigarette. We then saw a dingo investigating rabbit warrens 200 or 300 yards away from the base of our rocky perch. Hughie pointed at the dingo and holding an imaginary gun to his shoulder, pointed in its direction and with his tongue, verbally snapped his version of the "BANG" sound of a rifle shot. Well, I wasn't slow at taking his well-directed hint, but I thought to myself, "How could we ever scramble down the rocky ridge without alerting the dingo, let alone venture onto the wide open plain in full view of the dingo if or when he looked our way?" But Hughie was a barefoot hunter; a full blood, Australian bush-born and raised Aboriginal, with broad, wide-flaring nostrils and wavy black hair … though on this particular day HE WAS NOT WEARING HIS TRADITIONAL RED, PITJANTJATJARA TRIBAL HEAD BAND. In spite of this, he was today in his element.

****

Hughie knew what he was doing. He was in his home territory. He received free food, water and cigarettes from us. He had a full belly and he was "in the mood". I played my part reasonably well to start with, I thought, as we cautiously and silently, I hoped, scrambled down the loose rocky hillside and onto the verge of the plain, all the while keeping a weather eye on the dingo.

The dingo meanwhile had gone further out onto the open plain as we worked our way in his direction. This was the time my mate Hughie suddenly decided to assert some sort of authority over me and take over the unfolding situation. He just rudely, I thought, put himself right in front of me; so close I was having serious doubts about his intentions. Then he really got friendly and tried to clasp my hand in his, somewhere near his backside, and tried to get me to close my hands and make a "fist" firmly held in his overlapping, possessive hand. As fast as he clasped my hand together as a fist, I unclasped it. BOY, WAS HE GETTING FRIENDLY! I'll tell you what, I was really getting worried when suddenly the proverbial penny dropped and I finally woke up. …

It was only then, after overcoming my stupidity, that I finally made a closed, clenched fist, which he then held with my knuckles firmly pressing into the small of his back. By holding my wrist with his hands, firmly pressed against his body, HUGHIE HAD TURNED US INTO A ONE-PIECE, FULLY-UNITED OPERATIONAL PAIR. We now proceeded to effectively stalk the dingo. This was when the wisdom of his Stone Age stalking intentions really struck me and finally became obvious.

Whenever the dingo paused and briefly looked around, MY MATE INSTANTLY FROZE, and with my hand in the small of his back, AS AN UNOFFICIAL EXTENSION OF HIM, I ALSO AUTOMATICALLY, and INSTANTLY FROZE. It was uncanny. By these means, we gradually reduced the distance between the dingo and us.

After a while, we got to an awkward in-between position. We would close to about 200 yards then gradually drift out to about 300. We were getting nowhere and I guiltily thought we really should have been working, clearing lines for our Canadian masters, I.N.C.O, and their trusting shareholders back in Canada. So in the end I thought I would try and rest the Krico on Hughie's shoulders and have a long shot for an iron-sighted .22; about 200 yards. The dingo was looking away from us. His front legs were on a raised mound a few inches higher, making his shoulders the highest part of his body from our perspective, and he was still oblivious to our presence. Hughie made quite a steady resting post, and resting the rifle on his shoulder, I aimed the open iron sights at the dingo and fired. THE DINGO JUST DROPPED STONE DEAD ON THE SPOT. Wow!

Hughie was really, really impressed. So was I! He was making all the sounds necessary to say in any language, "GOOD SHOT!" Well, it was truly an "arsy shot." The bullet had luckily struck the spinal cord in the nape of the dingo's neck. Half an inch higher and the bullet would have gone harmlessly over his head. I WAS BLOODY LUCKY. The poor dingo was not! As a result of that truly arsy shot, I did not attempt to shoot anything in front of Hughie again; it was such a hard-to-repeat performance.

I preferred to mysteriously live henceforth on my "ARSY LAURELS"!

Barefoot Hughie, the unfortunate Dingo and Me 1955

49.
YATUNGKA AND WARRI 1955

At the time we were operating from our small bush camp near Mt. Davies, we occasionally received visits from Wongai tribal Elders from the Warburton Mission area in Western Australia, who sometimes overlapped with more frequent visits from Pitjantjatjara Aboriginals from the Eastern Ernabella region of South Australia. But we had never before had a visit from truly nomadic Aboriginals whose lives must have been greatly affected by the rapid expansion of the Woomera rocket testing range and the Emu Field atomic bomb testing site near Maralinga (not far from Mt. Davies). A great grid-work of bulldozed dirt access roads was being constructed mainly in flat, remote, desert-type terrain through the far outback of South Australia and Western Australia, extending thousands of miles to the comfortably warm tropical seas of the Indian Ocean along the Western Australian coastline.

The nomadic woman appeared to be 16 or 17 years old and of heavier build than her husband, without being fat. The small child was a boy of approximately one to two years old. The man was of wiry build, about five-feet-eight-inches tall and maybe 30 years old. He had a dead rabbit hanging from his hair waist belt. He also had a bloodied lacerated finger to which he trustingly allowed me to apply a bandage from our large metal Flying Doctor medical kit. He then accepted the unused balance of the bandage for later on. While I was looking at his finger, he pointed accusingly at his suspect dingo companion, which told us without a word the cause of his wound.

At this point in time we thought our guests may be some of the last surviving Pintubi, reputed, maybe, to still exist in the Western Deserts, but we had no means of knowing whether or not this was so. Initially seeing a naked Aboriginal wearing just a belt around his waist comes as a bit of a surprise, but is easily explained when, since he has no trousers, shirts or other forms of clothing with pockets, his woven hair belt is a very clever practical alternative to a Western man's taken-for-granted multiple useful pockets. His tight woven human hair belt enables him to carry dead lizards, snakes, marsupial rats or larger food items and the like, held firmly sandwiched between the belt and his body, leaving his hands free to carry his woomera and spears.

****

Wandering around our camp the next day, the man was not wearing yesterday's bandage on his finger but was wearing the balance of the unused bandage around his waist as a replacement for his somewhat grimy and rapidly-losing-its-hair plaited belt. Looking at his bitten finger, I could not see any sign of the laceration; it had healed without a trace within one day!

While in our company, his dingo companion wandered tentatively around the outskirts of the camp, cleverly observing, catching and eating dozens of fat juvenile locusts, swallowed as they descended momentarily from their short, fresh and sometimes first one and only flight. This was after watching their earlier short, 10–20-foot practice attempts at achieving outer space flight. Uncannily anticipating the locusts' next move, the dingo positioned himself at their next presumed landing point, which unfortunately for them happened to be right between his wide open, purposeful, pearly-white- toothed jaws … just like bears in the northern hemisphere catching salmon in chilly Arctic river waters.

Our geologist and I took some photos of our Aboriginal drop-ins and a day or two later they just simply disappeared overnight from our camp. As a 21-year-old back in 1955, I mentioned my unusual encounter with these naked, nomadic Aboriginals to a number of friends and strangers in pubs and other places, and I WAS TOLD I WAS TALKING 'BULLSHIT'. And so, THAT WAS THAT!

****

I was fascinated by the man's woomera, which I consider to be the Aboriginal equivalent of the Swiss army knife because it has many uses other than just being a spear launcher. The woomera is semi-hollowed hardwood, enabling the user to propel a spear twice as far as would otherwise be the case physically unaided. It is also a useful hollow plate, palette or bowl for mixing and carrying things, a woodworker's chisel, and in association with an endless supply of dry kangaroo dung, effectively an endless box of matches. Its hardwood edges may be rubbed under firm pressure hard and fast, saw-like on softer wood to induce fire lighting friction. Once the softer wood starts to smoke, it is sprinkled with dry, finger-crumbled kangaroo dung as tinder and gently blown upon, when after something like half a minute it usually puffs into flame. Using the very same hard edge of the woomera I had already seen used as a fire lighter and the same soft tinder-dry firewood kindling, THE BEST I COULD DO AFTER GREAT EFFORT WAS TO MAKE MYSELF INTERNALLY SUPERHEATED AND CLOSE TO A HEART ATTACK WHILE THE COOL, TINDER-DRY, UNIGNITED, UNIMPRESSED, INANIMATE, BARELY-SMOKING KINDLING SOMEHOW KNOWINGLY JUST CHUCKLED QUIETLY AWAY TO ITSELF and gave no signs of any forthcoming spontaneous ignition!

The lower-positioned, moulded woomera handle is usually glued and/or formed using a type of natural gum, such as that obtained from spiky spinifex bushes, or oozed from wattle or gum trees. The gum is heavily impregnated with fibre reinforcing tough dry grass, then fire heated, softened and hand moulded like plasticine, while still warm, to efficiently fit the thrower's spear launching hand. A hand-knapped, sharp, chisel-edged flint-like stone is then pressed into the still pliable gum handle, with the sharp end outermost, to act as an efficient, wooden-handled chiselling tool that is used to carve other wooden implements – more woomeras, spear points, bowls, boomerangs and the like.

The outermost spear-connecting end of the woomera is narrower than the handle, so the thinner, streamlined "swishing through the air" end is much more effective as a long-distance, levered spear thrower. The spear contacting end of the woomera is provided with a small inch-or-two-long pointed skewer-like protruding spike, usually bound to the business end of the woomera by strong long sinews from a kangaroo's leg, which, after being bound while wet, soon dries out tough, hard and very tensile. The woomera's spike is positively inserted or notched in a small, accommodating hollow or socket in the rear end of the spear.

When using the woomera as a spear thrower, an Aboriginal hunter on a treeless open plain and in full view can easily stalk solitary, up-wind, dim-witted kangaroos and emus, getting within 30 or 40 yards of his prey. It requires only a bit of time, perhaps 10 or 20 minutes, skill and patience to achieve positive results. Generally, the hunter never advances directly at the prey but moves left or right in short, sneaky, slow stages while getting closer, and maybe pauses to scratch himself under his armpits with his hands, imitating the everyday grooming actions of a daydreaming kangaroo, gradually lulling his prey into an ever-closer false feeling of security.

****

In the 1980s, I saw long-out-of-practice "civilised and detribalised" Wongai near the Warburton Ranges effectively spearing, with the aid of a woomera, an empty 24-pack cardboard beer carton about 30 or 40 yards distant, maybe 8 or 9 times out of 10.

****

A woomera-propelled spear can be thrown a very long distance, maybe as much as 80 or 90 yards, but without much accuracy. About the only time a woomera-propelled spear was useful at a long distance was in the tribal days of 30 or 40 years ago when warring groups of about 30-strong opponents per side, standing 60 or 70 yards apart, all threw their opposing massed spears at the very same moment to produce a GREAT, SIMULTANEOUS, OFTEN UNAVOIDABLE SHOWER OF SPEARS.

Occasionally, some of the unlucky combatants, friends or foes, were skewered, speared or clubbed, and died an agonising death on the blood-absorbing, porous desert sands, without a murmur.

Newly-fashioned, straightened spear shafts are usually about 10 feet long, tough and supple, and may be made from certain near-surface tree roots or other suitable thin, standing, tough saplings. If the shaft is not straight enough it may be wrapped in porous bark and wetted for a while, then fire steamed and carefully straightened out over a campfire. The business (sharp) end of the spear is fashioned from much harder wood such as mulga or ironbark, and wet-bound to the shaft with fresh, tensile kangaroo leg sinews. A short, wooden reverse barb is also fastened near the sharp end of the spear, also with kangaroo leg sinews. The barb is designed to keep the spear embedded in the body of the still kicking, struggling-to-survive animal, causing damage internally and effectively immobilising it. The soul of the downed animal is then clumsily despatched to the distant hereafter with the help of a few heavy blows to the back of the head from a heavy rock or "nulla nulla" (a club), then the animal is thrown UNSKINNED AND UNGUTTED directly on top of an open fire for a short, medium-rare barbecue cooking. I noticed that the whole animal was hardly ever turned over during cooking.

DINNER IS SERVED!

****

Fast forward from 1955 to 2016. I was talking to Peter Johnston, a nearby farmer at Gwabegar, New South Wales, and I showed him a photo of two naked Aboriginals and myself that I intended to use on the cover of my future book, *Failed Times and Twisted Follies*. (I have since decided against this and include the photo on the next two pages). His jaw dropped as he said, "I've actually got a book by a Doctor Bill Peasley entitled *The Last of the Nomads* and something about your photo really rings a bell!"

The very next day, Peter delivered his book to me and the bell rang loud and clear! Although my 1955 photo was taken 22 years earlier than those published in *The Last of the Nomads*, the resemblance, in spite of the considerable difference in time, is definitely there. I read the book from cover to cover in a couple of days and seriously wondered if there really was a connection between the naked Aboriginals in my 1955 photo and Bill Peasley's extensive collection of much more recent photos showing a pair of still-naked Aboriginals in 1977, now named individually as Yatungka (the woman) and Warri (the man).

Yatungka with child, Me, Warri with bandaged finger

Warrie hunting with a spear and woomera

Common sense suggests that the Aboriginals' contemporary period nakedness, general physical resemblance and known geographical circumstances made it possible, even probable, that they were one and the same couple.

If the piggy-backed child in my photo was Yatungka's first, say a one year old in 1955, then he may have been born some time in 1953, meaning that the probably pregnant young girl, who had already been promised to another older man, may have been forced to run away under a hail of barbed spears from Mudjon and the very hostile other members of the Mandildjara tribal group who were still at that time just existing in their tribal "twilight" in the lonely Gibson Desert.

Mt. Davies, where we had our camp, is only about 120 miles from the centre of the region known as the Gibson Desert, and a very pedestrian one or two-week sandy walk for a barefoot Aboriginal.

Having run away from Mandildjara law and their spear-throwing relations in the Gibson Desert, it is highly probable that Yatungka and Warri would have wanted to put as many miles between them, the Gibson Desert and their very recent unpleasant tribal family memories as they could. Conceivably, Yatungka and Warri may have headed off in a totally unexpected and different direction to avoid the real possibility of receiving a spear in back or a fatal tap on the head from a nulla nulla-wielding Aboriginal assassin silently doing his clandestine dirty work under the cover of darkness – a final solution generally delivered by a specialised, one-purpose, midnight, masked, blood and feather-footed, trackless "Kadaitcha Man", or from his irked and unforgiving friends or relations.

For whatever reason, with numerous sharp spears possibly still waiting behind them some time before 1955, it seems that the couple saw the Mt. Davies area or anywhere else well away from the Gibson Desert as a sensible direction to take. We were told by some of our locally-employed Pitjantjatjara Aboriginals at Mt. Davies, who generally understood Mandildjara language, that Yatungka and Warri had come from the general direction of the Gibson Desert.

****

I contacted Doctor Peasley in Broome, Western Australia, who has a copy of my single photograph of naked Aboriginals at Mt. Davies. He confirmed he could see the likeness but would like to look at other photos from other angles for further confirmation. At my suggestion, he got in touch with the geologist I had worked with at Mt. Davies, who confirmed he also had photos of our 1955 nomadic drop-ins, including one in which Warri was wearing the balance of the bandage I had put on his finger the day before as a new style white bandage belt, and had sent copies to Doctor Peasley for comment. Doctor Peasley, the geologist and I kept in contact for several weeks, communicating about the possibility that the 1955 drop-ins at Mt.Davies were/ are Bill's later-encountered Yatungka and Warri.

Based on the 1955 photos, Doctor Peasley's post-1977 photos, the vagaries of time and the unlikely discovery of any more than just two remaining fully naked Aboriginals still living in the Gibson Desert or anywhere else for that matter about 1977, and importantly none ever heard of since, it seems to suggest without doubt our drop-ins were Doctor Peasley's Yatungka and Warri.

****

Doctor Peasley later advised that he believed one of Warri and Yatungka's sons may still be alive. One had been a patient in the small bush hospital at Wiluna and the other had at some stage been receiving kidney dialysis treatment at the more distant Kalgoorlie Base Hospital. I asked Doctor Peasley if there was any way by which my 1955 photo could be shown to either of the two sons for identification purposes if they were contactable in or about Wiluna. Doctor Peasley later advised he had been in contact with the hospital in Wiluna and had sent copies to them, but unfortunately at that time there were no doctors at the hospital; they would not be back there for another month or so. Some months later, Doctor Peasley advised me that both doctors had been back to Wiluna and that both of Yatungka and Warri's sons had seen my 1955 photos. Not surprisingly, they had remarked that THE PHOTOS WERE DEFINITELY OF THEIR PARENTS, WARRI AND YATUNGKA.

EUREKA!!!

****

Surprisingly for me, both doctors at Wiluna Hospital came from Adelaide, South Australia – my home city – and alternated their services to the remote outback Western Australian hospital a few hundred kilometres South of the Gibson Desert. I must thank them both – Doctor Toby McLeay and Doctor Allan Maclean – for their part in unravelling the loose ends of this story. I have since spoken to Doctor McLeay, who confirmed the successful part he played, and I discovered he knew a friend of mine, Donald Holt of Delmore Downs Station via Alice Springs, where my sister Pamela was Donald's governess in 1948/ 49.

****

On Tuesday 14th January 2014, I received a visit from Doctor Peasley and his nephew David after his brother's 80th birthday in Forbes, New South Wales. We then caught up with Peter Johnston on his grazing property, after which I showed them the hot artesian baths at Pilliga and the massive radio astronomy telescopic installation near Narrabri.

I recommend W. J. Peasley's book *The Last of the Nomads*, published by Fremantle Press (ISBN 9780949206879), for the full factual story of the rediscovery of Warri and Yatungka, a rare, true and fascinating story.

****

Letter received from Doctor Beasley dated 19/7/2013 Dear John

On closer examination of the photos that you and [the geologist] took of the Aboriginal family in 1955 and those that I took in 1977, I believe that it is highly likely that the two adults in the photo were Warri and Yatungka.

Although it is difficult to estimate the age of Aboriginal people who have been leading a hard life in the desert country, I think the man would have been around 40 years of age and the woman in her thirties and the child would have been about 18 months to one year old although you considered that the man was about 25 to thirty and the woman about eighteen.

In 1997 when I retraced the route that I took during the search for the couple twenty years previously, I was accompanied by the two sons of Warri and Yatungka and I estimated that they were about 40 years old at that time and this would make one of them about one to two years old in 1955.

Warri died in 1978 and Yatungka a few weeks later and their age at that time was thought to be about 70 years, but this would have been purely guess work as there would not have been any records of when or where they were born.

You will see the two sons of Warri and Yatungka in the DVD of 'The Last of the Nomads' and you could estimate their ages at that time. Unfortunately they appeared to have lived a rather dissolute life after they came in from the desert several years before their parents were brought in. However, they were able to take me to some of the waterholes that they had visited with their parents and I was able to obtain the Aboriginal names of these and they will be shown on future maps of the area.

The "red-haired native patrol officer by the name of MacDougall" was with Len Beadell's survey party at times and Beadell gave his name to a small hill near the Canning Stock Route and it is shown on maps as MacDougall Knoll and I have climbed it on several occasions when I have been travelling on the CSR.

I hope that all this throws some light on the possible identity of the Aboriginal couple that you met although I suppose the only way that one could be certain would be through DNA but although it would be possible to get a sample from the two sons, it would not be possible to have a sample from either Warri or Yatungka.

Regards
Bill

50.
BANYAN BILLABONG 1955

I had been working underground at the Peko Gold Mine near Tennant Creek in the Northern Territory, which was now producing copper only, owing to the low U.S. $34 an ounce price of gold, which still existed in the upper levels of the mine. This is where I assisted the timber man, Bert Mander, as we hung from steel cable suspended "kibbles" (big iron buckets), one leg in, the other dangling out, and painstakingly lined the 600-foot main shaft with eight-inch-square oregon timber.

Oregon has a natural inbuilt audible safety feature useful in underground mines. When under extreme stress or dangerously excessive load conditions, and close to failure, Oregon can be heard literally "SQUEAKING"; and when you hear that ominous "SQUEAK", it's time to get out!

The mined copper ore was crushed, pulverised and acid leached on site to produce a sun-dried copper concentrate, which was then bagged and trucked 700 miles up to the port at Darwin for shipment to Japan.

****

In 2013, when I began updating this book, with the price of copper at thousands of dollars a ton and the price of gold at U.S. $1,775 an ounce, I couldn't help thinking back to those earlier times and remembering the many tons of pure NATIVE COPPER left hanging tantalisingly overhead in the upper level, gold-rich drives of the mine. But the mine had not been equipped to handle malleable native copper. If soft metallic copper had been fed into the crushers at the time they would simply just be "JAMMED UP", cause destruction of the crushers and block the flow. Native copper was a definite deterrent and not wanted in the Peko Copper Mine.

****

I became friendly with another worker at the mine, Geoffrey Lionel Banbury Hewetson (G.L.B.H.), from Warwick in South-East Queensland. WE WERE YOUNG, MOBILE AND STUPID. Life was just too easy. A young man could find work anywhere he chose to look. It was in the 1950s and there was FULL AND OVERFLOWING EMPLOYMENT in Australia at the time. We had then gone down to Adelaide where Geoffrey traded in his Vauxhall utility on a new Land Rover at Champions, and we worked our way North again to Darwin where we stayed with Frank and Gerry Favaro at Winnellie. We then found our way back to the thriving, purpose-built town of Batchelor and my friend Boyne Litchfield (manager of BANYAN FARM). The town was constructed to service the adjacent thriving uranium mines at Rum Jungle.

I think the area of Banyan Farm may have been a few thousand well-bushed acres in extent. On the South end of the property it was mostly virgin, uncleared scrub. The farm was no doubt named after a large BANYAN TREE on the property; a multi-trunked tree with maybe a hundred trunks of all sizes, up to say three feet in diameter, all earthed firmly in the ground. These trunks were connected as a single living entity by equally numerous criss-crossing horizontal branches about one or two feet in diameter, 30 or 40 feet above ground level. I suppose the whole Banyan tree and its many trunks would have been maybe 60 or 70 yards in overall diameter. These strange trees are native to the Indo-Pacific Australian region. ONE SINGLE TREE BY ITSELF MAY BE A ONE TREE, HUNDRED-TRUNK, PLUS OR MINUS A FEW, FOREST.

****

Armed with my 12-gauge Browning shotgun, Geoffrey and I battled our way through the now dry, 10-foot-high cane grass to the edge of an s-shaped crystal-clear lagoon or "BILLABONG", which was maybe a mile long, perhaps 50 yards wide and possibly 20 feet deep. It was hard to get to the bank without slipping into the unknown waters, as we were in large saltwater crocodile territory. A couple of hundred yards away we could see a horizontal, two-foot diameter gum tree trunk leaning out about 15 feet over a strategic bend in the billabong, and we worked our way through the high grass towards it. I climbed out on the trunk and looking down into the clear water I was able to see a great profusion of fish. I was surprised to see a dragonfly, hovering in front of my nose, shot down accurately by a squirt of water jetted from a sharp-shooting Archer fish. Pike-like, four-foot Long Toms drifted past in pairs, and I saw the swift swirl of a large Barramundi as it flashed by in hot pursuit of something or other.

We idly rested and contemplated our navels on the overhanging bough for a while, then saw a wallaby inching its way, kangaroo style, around the narrow, steep-sided edge of the water. The kangaroo family does not walk easily like us in a human bipedal fashion, one foot after the other; instead, they take their entire weight between their small forepaws and their strong tail, then swing their two now unencumbered, freely-dangling, awkward-looking long feet and legs forward jointly to efficiently contact the ground in a paired fashion.

At this point, the "beach" was narrowing and gradually being squeezed into the water, when we saw the wallaby, with nowhere else to go, just gently launch itself into the deep water, quite oblivious of danger, and swim quite well in our general direction.

We were still about 30 yards away when something caught my attention. And there, 20 feet behind the swimming marsupial, was a good-sized saltwater crocodile which had silently, sneakily surfaced and was just about to add the unsuspecting wallaby to its daily menu as it closed the gap.

Unknown to the crocodile, I had earlier exchanged my number 6 duck-shot for large, hard and fast, solid lead Brenneke slugs, which were absolute dynamite at such a close range. Hollywood couldn't have planned it better! The croc and the wallaby almost came together at a point just 10 feet below me. This was just as I almost lost my precarious balance on the over-water tree branch, and accidently pulled the trigger of the shotgun, followed by a great upheaval, commotion and disturbance in the water. Of the wallaby and the croc there was no sign, just a large area of disturbed water, numbers of stunned fish, lilies, leaves and dirty water.

AND SO ENDED IN DISASTER THE FIRST LESSON!

I had noted, however, that a well-used crocodile sunbaking slide was a few yards further along on the less steep bank, facing East, and reasoned that that would be where the crocodile would be lying at the next sunrise.

The next morning, I woke early; my conscience wouldn't let me sleep. I knocked off a can of peaches while Geoffrey was still snoring. I grabbed my Browning and walked a mile or so back to the billabong. I had also noted a couple of distinctive tallish trees in the vicinity of the "slide", and using them as clearly-visible landmarks, cautiously crept through the high cane grass in that general direction.

I crept inches at a time closer to the edge of the bank, gently parting the tall, 10-foot grass blade by blade. The very first time I actually saw the water, I saw the croc. He was just 10 feet from me, high and dry on his slide, eyes shut, though at a very shallow angle as he was looking (if his eyes had been open) straight up at me. There was not a moment to waste. He could open his eyes at any time, see me and be gone in a flash.

I aimed carefully and gently pulled the trigger.

BLAM!

The crocodile did not move. Not a sign of having been hit. From my position it looked as though he had not been hit. I couldn't see any signs of damage and I couldn't believe I had missed. No way! So I unleashed another Brenneke slug.

BLAM!

And it all became perfectly clear. He was dead the first time. I also noticed a fresh injury to the right side of his purpose-built snout, which would have been caused by yesterday's accidental near miss.

I had to skin the 13-foot crocodile right where he was because he was much too heavy for me to drag up the bank to a safer place. It took about an hour, while I also kept my eye cautiously on what else might have been in the deep water right beside me.

Leaving the croc skin near the carcass, I returned through the bush to G.L.B.H. and we drove the Land Rover tentatively through the bush to the billabong and recovered, then salted, the heavy crocodile skin.

****

A couple of months later I was in Perth, Western Australia, where I gave the skin to Dick Wiles, father of my friends Margaret and Helen, as a present. After all, he had earlier given me a World War 2 bullet (a .303) and said he would swap it for a crocodile skin.

****

Some time in 1955, Ron Boland, editor of Perth's *Sunday Times,* did an Editorial story about this "slightly interesting" event. And that was that.

Me with my prized crocodile, Banyan Billabong 1955

51.
CARRICKALINGA 1960

I was still in the spear fishing phase of my life, and I thought I would have a cursory look at Carrickalinga, a small beach-side weekend settlement on St Vincent's Gulf, about 45 miles South of Adelaide.

****

It was a nice summer's day, about 11:00 a.m. The sea was smooth and had an oily sheen on the surface. I was by myself. There was no one else around. I was not wearing a "wetsuit"; just bathers, a face mask, a snorkel and flippers, and had the place all to myself.

I entered the water at the North end of the beach under the overhanging shadow of the high cliff face and discovered within a few yards that the water depth increased quite suddenly. I found myself surprisingly in about 20 feet of water only about 30 feet from the sheer submerged wall of the high, vertical cliff. My aluminium-bodied speargun was a Lyle Davis model; a long-pull, single-rubber, bayonet-equipped type; powerful but very difficult to reload by hand in the water.

The water was quite noisy; incessant, sharp surrounding aquatic shrimp-like "clicking" sounds ringing in my ears, a rocky, clean-swept sea floor, and a distinct tidal current flowing North at perhaps 1 or 2 miles per hour. I don't remember exactly what had happened previously, whether I had shot at a fish or something, without success, as I do remember my gun was in its discharged state; but I had been down near the bottom, about 25 feet, for over a minute and was now in urgent need of a gulp of fresh air as I flipper-kicked my way back up to the surface.

AND THERE, RIGHT IN FRONT OF ME, WAS A VERY LARGE GREAT WHITE SHARK, maybe 15 feet long, with the GIRTH OF A VOLKSWAGEN BEETLE, just hanging suspended, seemingly motionless in space, it's GREAT BLACK RIGHT EYE LOOKING STRAIGHT THROUGH ME with x-ray vision, probably to see if I was worth eating; of that I have no doubt!

The shark was directly between me, the sea's surface and the shore, and I needed to breathe. I had no option but to power my way to the surface, TEMPTING FATE NO MATTER WHAT, straight past the SMILING JAWS and great black eye of the huge shark, when with bursting lungs I arrived at the surface, IN A SPLIT SECOND GULPED IN A BIG BREATH OF RELIEVING AIR, and instantly looked down again. Like magic, "abracadabra", without fanfare, the SHARK HAD JUST VANISHED! "PHEW!"

****

Now, years later, I realise what a fool I had been. But as they say, "it's no good crying over spilt milk", and it was, after all, a long 60 historical years ago.

A Great White "Smiling" S hark

52.
THE ALMANDA MINE 1960

In about 1960, I was going through an old copy of the 1908 records of the mines of South Australia, and was surprised to come across an old note, lying loosely in the pages. The note was from someone in Western Australia requesting further information about the Almanda Mine in the Adelaide Hills, which made me curious.

Later I visited the long-abandoned mine, tried to enter "Eys Tunnel", and looked around the old remnant buildings on the flat land near Scotts Creek. At the time an old hermit was camped among the workings and I didn't like to intrude on his unofficial space, but I did see, well embedded in the ground, what reminded me of a STEEL MERCURY FLASK, which caused me to wonder …

A couple of years later I revisited the mine. The old guy had long gone, and lo and behold, the flask-looking object was still lying there, partly buried, long captive and untouched. I attacked the hard clay soil with my geological pick and easily freed the object to discover it was indeed a mercury flask. It was as heavy as lead and in fact was FULL OF VALUABLE MERCURY. It weighed about 80 pounds.

When I got back to Ruthven Mansions, I drilled a small hole in the bottom of the cylinder and drained the mercury into a large aluminium saucepan. Then, feeling guilty, I wondered about the legality of my actions. Then I thought, "There's no one alive who could say whether or not the flask, lying there for perhaps 80 years, had actually recently contained mercury, so I'll just return the flask where I found it to its long-established resting place!"

As an afterthought, to give the empty cylinder a bit of weight, before returning it to its resting place, I poured beach sand through a funnel, as well as raw salt, and filled it with water, then sealed the hole externally with an epoxy cement and smoothed it down with a file. Mission achieved!

The next day I returned the flask to its former position at the Almanda Mine site, exactly as before, and rejoiced in the knowledge that not a soul on Earth would ever be aware of the strange, secretive story of THE SWAP.

****

About 30 years later, I was talking to an old friend, the Adelaide jazz trombonist John Pickering, when something came up about gold prospecting and "dolly pots". He said the best and lightest was obtained by use of AN ORIGINAL, SEAMLESS MERCURY FLASK WITH THE TOP CUT OFF, and "believe it or not, I ACTUALLY HAVE ONE!"

I said, "They're hard to find. Where did you get it?" He said, "Believe it or not, I found it at an old silver mine called the 'ALMANDA' in the hills near Scotts Creek".

I was both surprised and absolutely tickled pink to hear this. I said, "Did you get the mercury?" "No", he said, "it was full of RUSTY WATER". I said, "Did you see a drilled and epoxy-plugged, quarter-inch hole in the end?" He then asked me, "HOW DID YOU KNOW?"

I then told him that 30 years before, it was I who removed the mercury, replaced it with sand, salt and water to induce internal rusting, sealed it with epoxy cement, and, feeling slightly guilty, returned the flask to its original earth-embedded position at the old mine site.

IT'S A SMALL WORLD!

****

Sadly, John died about 12 years ago. His wife Jan thought the steel mercury flask/ dolly pot may still be loitering somewhere in the back of his old shed at Port Noarlunga!

53.
ROBBIE CHAPMAN 1960

In the late 1940s, my sister Pam was friendly with Robbie Chapman (S.P.S.C.), a university Engineering student and son of a senior South Australian Railways engineer. To supplement his finances at uni, and being an Engineering student, Robbie was very quick when any opportunity arose and he grabbed it by the throat when it did.

****

It was summer. Robbie was on holidays and someone, somewhere had some unused rolls of thin, plain, galvanised fencing wire for sale at a give-away price, and so Robbie bought the lot. He then hired a 240-volt spot welder from a machinery hire company for a couple of weeks and settled down in his garage to somehow straighten and cut the wire to length. Then, using a basic "JIG", painstakingly bent and made a large heap of wire COATHANGERS, which he sold for a very good profitable price to the various dry-cleaning companies.

****

The City of Adelaide, South Australia, has a range of good-sized hills bordering the Eastern suburbs, which at that time were largely steep, vacant slopes. The next thing, I was surprised to learn that Robbie had bought most of the slopes below Mount Osmond, and directly above the lowland suburb of Glen Osmond and the landmark Old Toll House.

One of the first things he did was to fill in with RUBBISH a still-sound, original, old silver-lead mine shaft just above the Old Toll house, which I find rather sad. I actually bought a block of land with an old silver-lead mine accessible tunnel in it directly above the home of Sir

Stanton Hicks, but I gave it back to Robbie without taking over the Torrens Title deeds.

Next, Robbie purchased a large area of hillside land above the grape-growing Stonyfell area, subdivided it and called it "SKYE". Today it is a proper suburb with a great view of Adelaide.

A few short years later, Robbie, now married, had me up to his house higher up in the hills, in the Crafers area, for dinner. He had a fine voice but I wasn't interested in anyone's private rendition of MACUSHLA over dinner. I never saw Robbie again. He died early, about 40 years ago, but I did hear some interesting tales of his later land sub-division fame regarding a sub-division he was trying to sell one hot, dry summer at Goolwa, near THE MOUTH OF THE MURRAY, AUSTRALIA'S BIGGEST RIVER (quite small by world standards).

The country was dry, parched and bare, so Robbie decided it needed a bit of colour, a bit of GREEN. He hired a crop spraying aircraft from "Robbie's Aircraft" (not our Robbie!) and HAD THE ENTIRE SUBDIVISION SPRAYED IRISH GREEN from the air.

All the grass ended up Irish green, as did the bare, painted, barren dirt itself, with not a blade of living grass between. When viewed at ground level, looking sideways over the scant painted grass, the sub-division did look a SORT OF DISHONEST GREEN, while the rest of the surrounding land, apart from Robbie's, was still natural bare brown and outback arid. Robbie's artificial green sub-division stood out like a sore thumb and raised many eyebrows. THIS, IN THE MINDS OF MANY, CONSTITUTED BRAZEN FALSE PRETENCES. It could not happen now but it certainly did then!

****

Anyway, I thought you may find a bit of interest in the story. Getting it off my chest and telling it is better than leaving it untold and forgotten, gathering dust in the mental mists of time …

54.
GREAT WHITES CEDUNA 1960

I grew up in my grandmother's house opposite Fernilee Lodge in Burnside, South Australia, the home of Tom Cooper. Tom was then the Managing Director of Coopers Brewery, while his mother was a close friend of my Grandmother directly across the street.

Tom was the member of the Game Fishing Club of South Australia who nominated me for membership of that august association when I was much older. Tom had caught a number of Great White Sharks, mainly in the Port Lincoln area of South Australia in the 1930s, and was also a friend of a Mildura orchardist, Alf Deane, who held, and still holds, the long-standing record for the HEAVIEST GREAT WHITE SHARK (2,664 pounds) CAUGHT WITH ROD AND REEL ANYWHERE ON EARTH. Alf had caught five of the six biggest White Pointers (weighing over a ton) ever hauled in on rod and line.

Tom Cooper had long before given me a large tooth from an 1,800-pound Great White Shark, which for years I used for flippantly cutting friends' ties off in the pub – sliced off in a split second, with one little "SNICK". Sharks' teeth really are as sharp or sharper than a razor, slicing holes painlessly in my trouser pockets, damaging them beyond repair, while lacerating my bleeding thighs!

****

As a young man, it was my desire to hook and land a fish of that magnitude, but I only had the basic gear; that is, a Penn 14.00 Senator reel, high-friction, tulip-tipped rod, about a mile of 24 thread or 80-pound braided nylon line, and almost no funds. I ALSO HAD NO GAME FISHING SEAT, NO GAFF, NO TRACES, NO HOOKS, NO MONEY,

NO EXPERIENCE and NO BOAT! I was, therefore, at a distinct disadvantage compared to my wealthy peers.

Not to be outdone by the mere absence of money, knowledge and materials, I got in contact with Ken Puckridge, the owner-operator of the 28-foot, two-masted fishing cutter named the "Victory", operating out of Ceduna near the head of the Great Australian Bight.

All of Alf Deane's giant, world record fish had been chummed, lured, sighted, hooked, successfully played to a standstill, then gaffed, roped and then towed into the weighing gallows port at Ceduna, on/ or from the Victory. Well ahead of his Australian competitors, Alf Deane had developed a special SWIVELLING GAME FISHING SEAT reminiscent of a barber's chair. It had an ADJUSTABLE FOOTREST and BOAT-MOUNTED, SWIVELLED ROD SOCKET and HARNESS, which was very securely BOLTED TO THE DECK OF THE VICTORY, which made fishing physically very much easier and less demanding, especially when fishing for large, 2,000 pounds-plus Great White Sharks.

Unfortunately, a lack of finances dictated that my own seat was an upturned, empty 4- gallon oil drum, loosely sitting, unrestrained, sliding around on the slippery deck, and an unsecured disposable cushion, held in place simply by my weight, good luck and gravity; a fishing rig less than ideal!

I arranged a deal with Ken Puckridge that allowed him free time to set and retrieve lobster pots at the St. Francis, twin Franklin and other islands off-shore from Ceduna while giving me less expensive game fishing time and allowing two of my friends, Robert Temme and Murray Weston, time to try and catch other non-game fish such as whiting.

****

We set out from Ceduna. The weather was fine, the seas were slight and we made it to the Isles of St. Francis by dark before dropping the lobster pots for retrieval the next morning. We then motored to the small, twin, sandbar-connected Franklin

Islands, arriving mid-morning. We baited the size 20.00 hook with a 20-pound piece of tuna and hung a small tin of sparsely dripping whale oil (about one drip per minute through a small nail hole in a tin can, semi-plugged with an adjustable match) over the side of the boat, which soon left a wide, oily slick on a smooth sea, way out of sight to the horizon. My friends meanwhile got among the large St. George Whiting for a while but then something strange appeared.

ENTER GREAT WHITE SHARK NUMBER ONE.

A large, dark mass or blob of something or other, about 200 yards distant, was unerringly coming our way directly under the shimmering oil slick. Ken said, "OK boys, get your lines out of the water and raise the tuna berley, it's about to happen!"

Before we raised the berley, however, the Great White slid slowly past the 28-foot Victory. It is important that I point out Ken is, or was, the only man alive, apart from Alf Deane, who had ever seen five of the largest Great Whites in the world, both in the sea and later on the weighbridge scales, and was the most experienced person alive to estimate a shark's size and weight both in and out of the water, and who said, in the present case, "It's a very good shark, about 14 feet and 2,000 pounds plus. GO FOR IT!"

In hindsight, my 15-foot heavy chain and 15-foot wire trace with wooden hand- gripping toggles was really far too heavy, cumbersome and an absolute overkill, but that's an unwanted, historical memory of this; MY FIRST "FAILED" INVOLVEMENT IN AUSTRALIAN BIG GAME FISHING HISTORY.

As I clipped my rod harness over my shoulders and fastened my groin-positioned and pressing rod-bucket belt while getting as comfortable as possible on the small cushion sitting on the empty 4-gallon drum, the boat suddenly shook as the shark bumped it and with one slicing bite and a momentary sideways shake of the head, ripped almost the entire 50 pounds of meat off a side-hanging, partly-immersed tuna berley bait.

Then, after circling the Victory, the shark rose up on the other side and took half of the other 50-pound tuna berley lure in another single side-slicing bite.

The second tuna had been forgotten and had carelessly been left hanging four feet above the water; an oversight on my part. THE SHARK THEN SWAM AWAY.

****

WHEN A GREAT WHITE SHARK BITES, IT SEIZES ITS PREY IN ITS JAWS AND BITES ONCE AND HARD WITH IMMENSE PRESSURE WHILE AT THE SAME TIME MOVING ITS WHOLE 2,000-POUND BODY POWERFULLY FROM SIDE TO SIDE, usually just a couple of times, ALLOWING ITS BREAD SAW-LIKE SERRATED TEETH TO CLEANLY SLICE EASILY THROUGH HEAVY BONE. THE SEVERED FLESH IS THEN SWALLOWED DOWN THE HATCH BEFORE THE SHARK TAKES ANOTHER BITE.

The bite of a Great White Shark is totally different from the dog-like, non-slicing, gulp, gulp of the crappy mechanical shark incorrectly portrayed in the movie "Jaws". The producer of that film had absolutely not the slightest idea of the slicing, side-to-side head shaking action of a Great White Shark.

****

In the absence of the disappeared Great White, Ken said, "Be patient, we'll just have to wait and see". Robert and Murray continued catching big whiting, Ken made the coffee and I waited with eager impatience. A few minutes later, the boat came back to life with a jolt after the returning shark gave it an unseen, very healthy nudge. I SPILT MY COFFEE. THE SHARK WAS BACK!

Then Ken started splashing the re-baited hook around in the water, like teasing a cat with a feather. Moments later, the Great White obligingly opened its cavernous mouth so wide you could see its tonsils, if it had any, which is when Ken dropped the size 20:00 baited hook and chain through CONCENTRIC RINGS OF LARGE, SHARP, PEARLY-WHITE, SERRATED TEETH. (As a point of interest, the gape of a size 20:00 shark hook fits easily around my 16-inch neck). It was all systems "GO". The shark shot off like a rocket for all of about 10 very short feet, then suddenly I was the meat in a sandwich. Unnoticed by me, a half-hitch type loop of braided 80-pound line had crossed tightly over itself near the outer shark-end tulip tip of the rod. Since the shark was pulling powerfully like the Queen Mary, the line would not, could not release itself in spite of me fully releasing the drag on the reel.

NO TIME FOR THINKING. THE FULL 80-POUND LOAD WAS ON ME AND THE ROD. If you can conceivably imagine what it would be like to lift an 80 -pound weight six feet away from you on the outer end of a six-foot pole or rod, then you know exactly what it was like. I held on for grim death to save my valuable rod and reel while I was dislodged from my tin can seat for a second or two. The rod was bending over the ship's rail when "CRACK"! THE 80-POUND BRAIDED LINE EXPLODED AND PARTED, AND I FELL BACKWARDS ONTO THE HARD WOODEN DECK. And that was the end of my first "FAILED" Great White game-fishing attempt.

EXIT GREAT WHITE NUMBER ONE.

****

Well, no good crying over spilt milk. Connect another size 20:00 hook, trace etc., rebait, check the whale-oil slick, sit back and wait. It was still only about 10:30 a.m. and the Victory was mine for a few more days yet. Ken repositioned the Victory near the now-submerged, usually-connecting sand spit over which the tide was flowing strongly. If we didn't have a deep keel I believe we may have been able to pass straight through the sandy passage between the islands without any trouble. Out of curiosity, I was tempted to land on the islands, but Ken said they really were quite heavily infested with hungry and unfriendly tiger snakes whose main spartan diet was penguin chicks and/ or each other!

ENTER GREAT WHITE NUMBER TWO.

We didn't have long to wait, half an hour at most, and in came a considerably bigger Great White Shark. At that time, we normally called them "White Pointers".

"Well", Ken said, "if you play your cards right there's a new world record". The Great White slowly slipped past the well-known shark comparison measuring marks helpfully painted on the side of the Victory. "Eighteen feet long and 3,500 pounds plus", said Ken.

At last! My second episode was straightforward. The giant shark was lured and hooked in copybook fashion. I kept the troublesome tulip tip clear and free of tangles and away went the line. In five minutes, the shark had taken off about 500 yards of line under a drag force of about 70 pounds before we raised the "pick" and started the motor! After about an hour of constant 70-pound drag fishing, we gradually retrieved about 200 yards of line from the shark and were now about five miles from the Franklin Islands and in deep water.

About this time, another Great White menacingly appeared, so I slackened the drag to about 20 pounds and allowed the hooked shark more latitude in case the other shark saw it as possibly wounded and therefore fair game for other similar-sized, fully-aware sharks. However, we didn't see any other sharks and resumed the battle. On one occasion, the shark was within 100 yards, straight down, but then it powered away again in seconds and was soon about 600 yards distant.

ALL THIS TIME I WAS VERY, VERY UNCOMFORTABLE. I HAD A SIMPLE SURF- ROD BUCKET PAINFULLY STUCK IN MY GROIN, AND THE CUSHION DID NOT WANT TO STAY ON THE UNATTACHED, SLIDING 4-GALLON TIN CAN SEAT, which was generally uncontrollable and fancy free on the deck.

****

At midday, Ken reported on the flying doctor schedule that "WE HAVE HOOKED A NEW WORLD RECORD GREAT WHITE SHARK and are busy fighting it!"

****

Well, by about 7:00 p.m. I WAS COMPLETELY BUGGERED, the shark was deep – straight down in 300 feet of water – while several times it had come up 20 or 30 feet, only to descend again, powering down like a runaway lead weight. As the sun set, we were now about 10 miles from the Franklins when an uncomfortable wind came up and the sea became very sloppy. I tightened the drag right up to the maximum, but to no avail. The shark stayed deep and I HAD BY NOW WELL AND TRULY HAD IT! I had completely lost interest, my tender groin was in absolute agony and I was determined to get off my loose tin can so I could to rest my weary body.

Finally, just to get rid of the Great White by any means, I leant the back of the rod over the ship's rail, held the rod tightly, and eventually, with the rocking of the boat, THE LINE FINALLY BROKE. At last! I was physically relieved.

****

I had been fighting a WORLD RECORD SHARK for over 7 hours while sitting on a small cushion loosely sitting on a loose tin can. THE SHARK, presuming it survived, HAD WON. I was instantly and unconditionally relieved. My rapidly-developed, very badly torn hernia was repaired successfully at St. Andrews hospital back in Adelaide the same week. And so ended another "FAILED" Great White Shark fishing attempt.

55.
THE VESPER CELESTE

The "Vesper" was a wooden-hulled motorboat, 55 feet long, with an 11-foot beam and a flattish bottom. It was seconded to the Royal Australian Navy during World War 2 and operated around the Southern Australian coast for the duration of the war.

Various motors and gearboxes had been fitted, tried with various amounts of success, and/ or removed over the years.

On one auspicious occasion, a thoroughly disgraced motor and gearbox, which had been a dismal failure, was deliberately dropped directly beneath the Vesper to use in port as its own heavy mooring. The Vesper had been owned by Ray Hannan at least twice, and Ray had twice motored it through the treacherous surf running at the mouth of the Murray River when the river still sometimes flowed out to sea. In 2010, I was told the Vesper was moored somewhere in the South Australian part of the Murray, possibly near Mannum or Blanchetown.

I'm not too sure of the date, but Ray had gathered a group of friends and fellow compatriots together for a weekend return trip from Port Adelaide across the Gulf St. Vincent to Port Vincent on Yorke Peninsula, with a return planned on Sunday. We assembled on the Vesper in the still, calm, protected, inner waters of Port Adelaide at "sparrow fart"[27] and cruised serenely down the smooth Port River while being politely advised by a fellow co-conspirator that he had heard a strong wind warning on the radio an hour or so before. Being a very careful, meticulous person, Ray slipped his digit finger into the moist, wet depths of his mouth and then inserted his freshly saliva- coated digit

---
[27] Dawn

scornfully up into the very lowest, bottom reaches of the sky to test the strength of the breeze. "She'll be right", said Ray confidently as we headed downstream.

As we motored past the rocky protective side walls of the Outer Harbor breakwater, things began to change. The offshore North-Easterly breeze was steady but as we were still close inshore the waves were little more than ripples. We had not gone far, however, when the upper deck superstructure of the Vesper started to catch the following Easterly breeze like a sail. Since the wind was blowing at maybe 30 knots and the Vesper was only doing 10, there was a tendency for the old boat to yaw as the stern kept trying to catch the bow as we motored dutifully West. The steady breeze gradually became a tailwind, the waves grew larger, higher and further apart, and the wind was approaching gale force of maybe 40 or 50 knots.

THE VESPER WAS BY NOW ROLLING FROM SIDE TO SIDE VERY UNCOMFORTABLY IN A HOPELESSLY CONFUSED SEA.

The previously happy, not-a-care-in-the-world passengers were by now frequently vomiting over the side and/ or tensely holding onto anything dry, fixed, solid or each other. About this time, a couple of inflated life jackets mysteriously appeared on deck, strategically placed it seems by the adjacent, presumably prospective user, in clear view and in easy reach, only to disappear then reappear sneakily close to another conniving passenger elsewhere on this most uncomfortable journey. The penny dropped when it became bleeding obvious; THE VESPER HAD MORE PASSENGERS THAN LIFE JACKETS, as the passengers played musical chairs at sea.

While all this was happening, "Herbie" was out of sight below decks in the smelly engine room looking after the engine and repeatedly transferring fuel from the main tank up to a smaller header tank, which would not have been much fun under the heaving sea conditions. This was about the time someone revived the OLD TALE ABOUT THE SEVENTH WAVE BEING A KILLER, which had the effect of causing us to count the crests of the waves up to six while the seventh, which was always latent, always lurking, never came, but was of course hiding somewhere discretely, just around the corner. It did seem at times the old Vesper was about to roll right over but at the very last instant recovered again in time to repeat the performance.

There were a lot of obvious, conspicuous, stressed, tight, white, firmly-gripping knuckles present for all to see. Through it all Leon Kirwin was steadfast, passive and seemingly unmoved, while Robert Temme was as passive as the Sphinx and kept his outside long chances bets completely to himself. Doug Sabey had a completely unemotional, poker-like, give-away-nothing countenance, while Ansett Airlines Captain Bob Thompson (Don Thompson's brother; see story 38, *Colt 45, 1951*) had confined himself to the cigarette smoke-filled cabin, and was looking with concern at the suspect, to him anyway, marine charts and compass.

Don Brown's thoughts were clearly on "Tobin Bronze" as it passed the winning post first in some far away terrestrial location, while at the same time HE WAS HEARD TO ENQUIRE WHETHER THE BRASSY "BINNACLE"[28] LOCATED BY THE BOAT'S "WHEEL" WAS A SET OF SALT AND PEPPER SHAKERS?

Then a large, reassuring floating beacon gradually came into view, which by its appearance gave our skilled navigators either the wrong impression, that we were not where we thought we were, or the beacon had been wrongly identified by us, and without a doubt, no doubt at all, WE WERE LOST AT SEA.

---

[28] Built-in protective housing for the boat's compass

It was then Bob Thompson, our experienced, Ansett Airlines Captain took our thoughts and us to one side and acquainted us "land lubbers" with certain, obscure, unknown magnetic compass facts. Bob said that under certain weather conditions, such as during powerful electrical thunderstorms, magnetic compass needles had been known to reverse their polarity; North became South and vice versa. It seemed to Bob, therefore, that we may have been on the receiving end of one of these rare occasions for reasons outside our control while out of sight of land in overcast conditions. We had probably unwittingly described a large arc and were now heading back due East; back to Port Adelaide from where we had started in the first place!

Then a further confusing, larger motor-car-sized beacon slowly came into view. This is when Don Brown was heard to loudly wonder to himself, for all of us to hear, whether it may be safer to take our chances clinging to the barnacle-covered though otherwise slippery sides of the BIG BLACK BUOY in the treacherous GREAT WHITE SHARK- INFESTED WATERS of St. Vincent's Gulf.

At this time a little common-sense raised its hidden head and it was decided to press on straight ahead on the off-chance we had actually been right all along. By now the cruel seas had moderated considerably. Those who were inclined to be seasick had already vomited a few times over the sides, "technicolour yawning" their hearts out, while the more relaxed, white-knuckled variety of passengers were no longer hanging on to each other like a bunch of castrated idiots!

And there, STRAIGHT AHEAD, SURPRISE, SURPRISE, WAS PORT VINCENT. WE HAD BEEN RIGHT ON COURSE ALL ALONG. So how about that! We had been from one side of the gulf to the other of a "mini storm in a teacup".

****

Thankfully, we motored in over the sandbar to the dredged safety of Port Vincent and greatly relieved, moored tightly to the positive, solid security of the high wharf.

Meanwhile, our still-subdued, slowly-relaxing co-conspirators gathered in silence as they felt the reassuring, solid, down-to-earth terra firma solidly under their jelly-like seasick legs as they considered thoughtfully their next illusory move. We remained moored securely to the wharf that night, while some of our compatriots were already on the phone to Adelaide seeking another way out, while a few brave souls plucked up enough courage to have a drink or two at the Port Vincent pub.

I actually had a fishing rod with strong nylon, a large hook and an even bigger bait in the water, unattended until early in the morning when I was woken up by the squeal of the reel as a stingray or something big took hook, line and sinker, and a couple of hundred yards of nylon line. I went back to my bunk and slept like a log until dawn.

Sunday mid-morning we prepared to sail. IT WAS OBVIOUS DON BROWN WAS NOT RETURNING ON THE GOOD SHIP VESPER, since he stayed high and dry in a superior laughing position up on the wharf and waited patiently for his father's arrival and his rescue via Rolls Royce.

With Don up in his high, completely off-the-Vesper vantage point, we started the engine, cast off our mooring lines and turned the Vesper around 180 degrees on the spot by clever forward, reverse, forward, reverse movements in a tight turning circle. Then, facing the direction of far-off Adelaide, we slowly proceeded about a hundred yards into the mid-morning sun in the East. As we pulled away from the wharf, a farmer friend of Ray's up on the wharf called out to warn Ray of a shallow sandbar which he could plainly see was directly ahead of the Vesper but was quite difficult to see under the direct glare of the morning sun. Not wishing to be outdone by his mate's timely, gratuitous advice, given from a much better vantage point (a position at least 10 feet superior to Ray's much inferior position), Ray raised himself up another six inches on his toes, which was still more than nine feet inferior, looked directly into the dazzling sun without sunglasses, and once again said, as he motored ever so smoothly straight ahead,

"SHE'LL BE RIGHT".

No sooner had the Vesper moved ahead than it started slowing down again as it gently buried its long hull in the sexy, all-embracing, gentle folds of the retentive sandbar and slid to a complete halt on a fast-falling tide. Not wishing to be fazed by these new unwanted circumstances, Ray immediately engaged reverse gear in the Vesper and gave it the gun. "VROOM, VROOM". Strange noises we had not heard before followed the "vrooms".

KER-BANG, KER-FLUNK, KAPUT!!!

All alone and unassisted, RAY SINGLE-HANDEDLY DESTROYED THE GEARBOX and its strange and mysterious inner workings.

****

We were stuffed, the gearbox was stuffed and our chances of early salvation were stuffed. We were high and dry in the harbour 100 yards from the wharf; marooned, isolated and going nowhere. At this point, some of our fellow passengers demonstrated a certain amount of unease as the obvious hopelessness of our situation dawned. On board the Vesper, Ray had a small, 11-foot-long fiberglass "Haydon" runabout with a powerful (for the size of the small boat) 40 horsepower "Evinrude" outboard motor.

Panic stations and despair descended on us like a ton of bricks when, after a moment's thought and slow hesitation, we quickly lowered the empty hull over the side of the Vesper dextrously by hand. Captain Bob then climbed aboard the Haydon as we lowered the motor directly, with some difficulty, onto the transom while Bob quickly fastened the control cables, the fuel line to the fuel tank, and the engine clamps. A short tow rope was then passed down from the Vesper to Bob in the Haydon, where Bob passed the rope over the transom, past his rear seating position and carefully tied it by an unbreakable "Gordian knot" around the only possible hitching point; the solid, central cross seat in front of Bob's rear operating position.

All matters being equal, confirmed and correct, Bob gave the Evinrude the gun, "BRM, BRM", and the loose tow rope tightened, tighter, tight and taut. It strained its heart out and I think the grounded Vesper almost moved, when right on time our old friend and foe, DISASTER, struck again. The tow rope to the Haydon passed directly under the Evinrude outboard motor and unwittingly BOB HAD ONLY LOOSELY HUNG THE MOTOR ON THE TRANSOM WITHOUT TIGHTENING THE CLAMPS!

The flat-out running motor lifted straight up and off the transom, leapt momentarily out of the water with a howling scream of water-frothing protest, then succumbed to a moment of complete surrender as it let out one expensive low howl followed by a last "GLUG, GLUG, PHWTT" as it drowned on its way down to join Davy Jones in his underwater locker.

****

The good news was the now lifeless, submerged motor was still tenuously attached to the Haydon by its strong control cables and neoprene fuel line, and was not quite a total loss. Surprisingly, Herbie and Leon were later able to rinse the seawater out, dry, then successfully restart the motor, but I was unaware of this for many years afterwards.

****

Being a man of action, and maybe because of a feeling of guilt on seeing the shallow sandbar right next to him, Captain Bob, without looking, confidently jumped into the water on the opposite side and disappeared totally from view. A moment later Captain Bob's Ansett Airlines pilot's cap popped up like a cork from Davy's locker, followed by a spluttering Bob, clutching his shirt pocket and his drowned, soggy cigarettes. At this point in time, there was not really much that could be said politely in public.

Meanwhile, RAY'S FARMER FRIEND AND DON BROWN PERCHED HIGH UP ON THE WHARF IN THE GALLERY WERE STILL WATCHING AND THOROUGHLY ENJOYING THE AMATEUR PANTOMIME being presented before their very bemused eyes. Ray, having witnessed Bob's unfortunate string of soggy events, wisely said absolutely nothing but called on his farmer mate to ask if he could secure a rope from the Vesper to his Ford V-8 Customline and pull the dead Vesper off the sandbar from his superior towing position.

Well, by the time the tow rope had been connected to the Vesper, the tide had fallen further and the Vesper was more of a dead weight than ever. This is when the V-8 Customline really started burning rubber up on the wharf's tarmac. Great clouds of stinking rubber rose from sticky melted bitumen, but stubbornly the good ship, spontaneously renamed the "Vesper Celeste", stayed put. With a buggered gearbox, the Vesper Celeste wasn't going anywhere. She was destined to stay put right there until repaired and refloated (before hopefully being operational again), and once the necessary high tide came back in.

****

This was about the time Don Brown's father Walter arrived on the scene as a knight in shining armour in his Rolls Royce, and Don swiftly departed Port Vincent together with Captain Bob, who in fact was flying somewhere that night, while Doug Sabey, whose wife Jan may worry if he was late home, also contrived to leave the sticky, still- unfinished situation.

The rest of us got home to Adelaide by various means, each of us remembering over the following years his own version of the weekend's events, while trying very hard to remember the good bits. Ray, Herbie and I returned to Port Vincent the next weekend with spare parts. Herbie fixed the gearbox and we returned to Adelaide on the good ship Vesper Celeste on a calm, dead-flat, millpond-like sea.

56.
THE BUTCHERS' PICNIC 1960

In 1959 I was employed by Hannan Bros, in Adelaide, as manager of their Evinrude Outboard Motor marine division, and was present one evening at a general get-together of like-minded outboard motor enthusiasts and dealers who proposed restarting the long defunct Adelaide Outboard Motor Boat Club.

At that time we had not realised that the Adelaide Outboard Motor Boat Club had existed before the 1939 war and had ceased operating with the onset of hostilities. But now in 1959, 20 years later, as import trade restrictions were finally relaxed and previous luxury items, including outboard motors, were finally coming in, things had changed for the better.

An elderly gentleman was present at the get-together who introduced himself as the former, pre-1939 Secretary of the Old Adelaide Outboard Motor Boat Club, and in his hands he held, as he had done for the previous 20 plus years, the long-unseen records of the long non-operational club; records that included what was originally a small, but still ongoing, bank account, which, with peppercorn interest unconsciously accumulating during the past 20 years, now amounted to quite a tidy sum. And so, in 1959, the Adelaide Outboard Motor Boat Club was re-formed with a very tidy balance sheet, thanks to the old, honest, former secretary, who is entitled, wherever he is, to rest on his still-going hidden laurels. The club restarted operations; barbecues, picnics, time-trials and out-and-out racing, mainly off Snowden's Beach on Adelaide's Port River.

The boats and motors were mostly off-the-shelf models, loosely classified by horsepower, boat type, length, weight, etc., which worked fairly well before the competition got serious as business slowly horned its ugly way in.

Initially, the day's program was mainly devoted to controlled racing by class, with the final difficult-to-categorise last race of the day being for mixed and difficult-to-classify awkward big boats, small boats, rubber dinghies, etc., and was called "THE BUTCHERS' PICNIC". Never having raced before or since, I decided spontaneously to give it a go and entered Frank Hannan's heavy, slow "Bell-Boy" runabout, fitted with a 70 H.P. Evinrude O.B. Motor, with my friend Robert Temme as my tentative passenger. As far as I remember, life vests and helmets were not legally required at that time and were rarely worn.

I knew the underpowered Bell-Boy was a slow boat, but its shallow broad hull enabled it to turn like a top, on the spot, and its low propeller pitch angle gave it low speed but a high, immediate grip on the water and very fast acceleration, but only up to lower speeds. At racing speeds it was naturally too heavy, too slow and not meant to be a winner. I therefore reasoned that if I turned very close to each marker buoy, I could actually spin the Bell-Boy to a dead stop and turn 180 degrees in less time than the others travelling a longer high-speed course, then instantly accelerate from scratch to an admittedly lower speed while the opposition hurtled flat-out around a much longer distance, at higher speed, giving us an outside chance of not being disgraced in the race; a bit like THE TORTOISE AND THE HARE.

So away we went. I think we led the race for the first hundred yards but were quickly overtaken by most of the others. We arrived at the first buoy in about the middle of the field. We then SPUN LIKE A TOP, ON THE SPOT AND RAPIDLY ACCELERATED,

AGAIN WITH OUR LOW-PITCH, LOW-GEAR-LIKE PROP, and were again initially in front as we pulled quickly away from the buoy. We maintained our position throughout the whole race, being AMONG

Failed Times and Twisted Follies

THE FIRST AWAY FROM THE BUOY after each turn but falling behind as the race proceeded, and alas, CAME A COMPLETE AND FINAL CROPPER AT THE FINAL BUOY. This was as we again spin-turned on the spot, when a BOTTOMLESS-TYPE, UNFRIENDLY HOLE TO THE CENTRE OF THE

EARTH APPEARED ON THE SURFACE OF THE SEA, right where the water had just been. It was at precisely the wrong instant and in the wrong place for us when the hard-edged chine of the hull "positively bit" the concrete-like edge of the temporary hole in the water, without fanfare, as WE FLIPPED UPSIDE DOWN in an instant.

The upturned Bell-Boy clearly had no intention of righting itself, so I ducked down underwater and out into daylight to look for Robert, but I couldn't see him. So I ducked down and back under, inside the inverted boat to find him, again without success.

Robert meanwhile was doing precisely what I was doing but at different times, and out of phase with me, as I was later told by others who, beer cans in hand, were enjoying the ongoing spectacle from the dry security of the riverbank.

> SO ENDED MY FIRST, AND LAST, OUTBOARD MOTOR
> "BUTCHERS' PICNIC" POWER BOAT RACE.

****

Yet "ANOTHER FAILED TIME" for my historical, mentally-engraved, dubious record.

57.
GREAT WHITES, SUBURBAN ADELAIDE 1962

I was having a beer or two in Tony Mathews' "Feathers Hotel" in Burnside, South Australia and talking to Allan Turner, a wholesale meat provider and friend of my old mate John Engel (S.P.S.C.). Allan had recently taken delivery of a 23-foot fibreglass- hulled "Bertram" boat powered by a 180 H.P. Mercruiser and was singing its praises while talking about fishing in general. During conversation, I had mentioned my previous dubious episodes with Great White Sharks out from Ceduna on the West coast of South Australia, which immediately aroused Allan's interest.

I said I still had the basics, that is, a Penn 14.00 game fishing reel with over 1,000 yards of 24 thread, 80-pound breaking strain braided nylon line, a large tulip-tipped game fishing rod, a light, grossly-undersized surf fishing rod harness, an old 4-gallon drum as a seat, a daggy cushion for my bum, and hard earned, limited Great White Shark fishing experience.

****

I had grown up in Adelaide where the 1926 death of Primrose White, taken by a Great White just after she dived off the suburban Brighton jetty, still lingered in older memories, and 41 years later was still latent and fixed firmly in my mind. As a young teenager, I also remembered Don Shepley's father Vivian and his several episodes with a 15-foot Great White in the 1940s directly out from the old beach shacks at Marino Rocks. These exploits were undertaken from his relatively unsafe position in a wooden, clinker-hulled, single cylinder, inboard-powered 12-foot boat. The large shark was generally known as "Fred", while his usual area of activity was known locally as "Fred's Patch".

Over the years, various reports of Great Whites near Adelaide appeared in the local dailies and on the radio. The reports registered unconsciously on my mind. I then remembered my own very close encounter under water with a Great White, 50 miles South of Adelaide in 1960 in a noteworthy episode I have named after the vicinity, "Carrickalinga" (see Story 51).

About two years later, in 1962, Rodney Fox very luckily survived a Great White attack at Snapper Point, Aldinga; the same place where

**Me, my rubber powered speargun and an unfortunate eagle ray, minus tail.
Snapper Point, South Australia**

I had myself earlier in 1951 been the winner of the Under 18 South Australian spear fishing title. All this confirmed in me the fact that Great Whites were right under our noses and patiently waiting for you and me to enter the deeper offshore waters right on Adelaide's doorstep.

A couple of weeks later a call from Allan informed me he had acquired a lot of suspect beef and some fish remnants from George Raptis, a commercial prawn fisherman usually operating a fishing prawn fleet in Queensland's Gulf of Carpentaria but currently at home back in Adelaide. So, Saturday morning, away we went. Allan launched his 19-foot Bertram at Seacliff and we anchored about 2 miles South of the long-gone shacks of Marino Rocks, and only a couple of hundred yards off-shore. We hung string bags of our meat and fish offal berley over the side while I set up a match in an identical sized hole in a treacle tin containing a small amount of whale oil to slowly drip enticingly into the clean waters of St. Vincent's Gulf.

Shortly after, a small boat anchored about 100 yards away. I remembered the face of one of the occupants from about 1946, when, as a returned soldier, he had operated a kiosk on the foreshore at Port Noarlunga. He seemed to remember me and gave me a friendly wave. Not long afterwards, A HEFTY BUMP UNDER THE BERTRAM SUDDENLY ANNOUNCED THE ARRIVAL OF MY GREAT WHITE NUMBER THREE as we regained our feet to take stock of the newly-unfolding situation.

Then the shark side-sliced a football-sized chunk of well and truly "off" pork from a lifeless, dangling pig's leg and moved slowly forwards toward the bow. It then came back towards the stern. When Allan dropped a chunk of something large and edible straight down its wide open, cavernous gullet, it was time to positively hook and engage the large 14-foot, 2,000 pound plus shark. The Great White then rose up, its nose momentarily about five feet above the water, and opened its great, serrated, ivory-toothed jaws as Allan dropped a size 20:00

fishhook, a shoe box-sized chunk of meat and 15 feet of strong chain followed by a 15-foot wire leader straight down it's waiting throat.

At this point in time, my old World War 2 mate from Port Noarlunga in his small boat seems to have strategically up-anchored and disappeared. I haven't seen him since.

The shark with the baited hook in its mouth acted as though nothing had happened until Allan, taking the heavy trace in hand, suddenly jerked one of the hand-gripping toggles on the chain, setting the hook deep in the shark's jaws and setting the shark off explosively in an equal and opposite direction. It shot off past the bows like a torpedo and in order to save my Penn reel and rod, I clambered dangerously along the narrow, six-inch-wide deck alongside the half cabin with my heavy rod in hand as the great tail of the shark swept right alongside and just ahead of me. I then became urgently aware that the weight of the shark was all on the tip of my rod, and unnoticed by me, the 80-pound line had once again crossed over itself and become positively locked – exactly as had happened before at the Franklin Islands – as I tried desperately hard not to fall into the already shark-occupied water.

In a further second, as I balanced precariously on the slippery, narrow deck, I backed the star drag of the reel right off, but it was all too little and much too late. In a moment, I HAD THE FULL WEIGHT OF THE GREAT WHITE ON MY HEAVY HAND-HELD FISHING ROD while I was fortunately retained on the boat only by the strong hand safety rail and a bollard at the bow as THE LINE SNAPPED, thankfully in my favour.

****

This event goes down as ANOTHER OF MY "FAILED TIMES AND TWISTED FOLLIES" of which I have successfully accumulated a disproportionate number by this my 80th year! On reflection, I realise countless large sharks, rays, sailfish, swordfish and marlins and the like, once hooked and broken free, were forever condemned to a tragic downhill existence as they trailed heavy, all-encumbering, tangling metal traces, hooks or chains around while they attempted to somehow survive in spite of these ongoing hindrances. HEAVY TACKLE THAT REMAINS ATTACHED AND HINDERS A FISH OR SHARK ONCE IT HAS BROKEN FREE SHOULD BE BANNED FOREVER!

But, at this late stage in my life, having finally woken up, WHO AM I TO TALK?

58.
NOTORYCTES TYPHLOPS 1962

About 1962, we were driving off-road in a French Petroleum Company (I worked for them in the early 1960s) Land Rover through dry, loose, sparse, scrubby, red, sandy outback station (ranch) country near Curtin Springs, about 250 km South-West of Central Australia's Alice Springs, and about 100 km East of the giant Ayers Rock/ Uluru monolith. We were slowly following a pair of indistinct, sandy wheel tracks through low loose dunes when a very small, eyeless, short stubby-tailed, light golden- coloured, rat-sized, silky-coated animal was chanced upon in the act of crossing the red sandy track after inscribing its unmistakeable signature – a "ZIG-ZAG" TAIL DRAG VISIBLE MARK – in the sand just a few feet ahead.

I stopped the Land Rover and was able to grasp the tiny blind animal just a moment before it could disappear completely from sight by literally swimming, fish-like, down through the dry, loose, liquid-like sand by using its horny spade-like feet as DESERT SAND SWIM FLIPPERS and so on down into the relative safety of its cool, dark, earthy underground environment.

Returning to the Land Rover, I was proud to announce to my companion, Claude Couppey, a French Petroleum geologist, that he/ we were extremely fortunate to have just encountered and witnessed the very rare, elusive, hardly-ever-found above ground level, AUSTRALIAN "MARSUPIAL MOLE".

Claude casually made certain undecipherable, non-sensible foreign language utterances which sounded something like "UH HUH, NOTORYCTES TYPHLOPS", as a result of which it was immediately apparent to me he had not understood a single word of what I had just said to him in plain-as-day spoken English! Seemingly, he was blissfully, totally unaware of the undoubted importance of the earth-shattering, "Gaullist" type pronouncement I had just made, or the great international importance of our very, very lucky, needle-in-a-haystack, one-in-a-million, chance encounter with the rare Australian marsupial mole.

As a result of Claude's quite obvious ignorant, totally unpronounceable mumbo-jumbo utterances, I took great pains to point out to this very much away-from-home Frenchman that this strange little creature was the very secretive AUSTRALIAN "MARSUPIAL" MOLE, and that "MARSUPIAL MOLE" was, is and always would be this rare animal's correct and proper "AUSSIE" name.

Besides which, I had not the slightest idea of knowing what Claude was actually trying to say anyway! Well, what could I say? Claude again repeated the foreign, French or Hindustani words, "UH HUH, NOTORYCTES TYPHLOPS". I was simply astounded at his continuing, ongoing, pragmatic, one-track ignorance, and his inbuilt Gallic misunderstanding both of me and the English language, and so at this point I diplomatically said nothing, deciding in my undoubtedly superior French/ Australian wisdom to simply let the matter rest, out of sight and mentally filed in the too-hard basket.

However, a few days later as a result of certain unsatisfied feelings which would not go away and were ceaselessly gnawing at my conscience, or out of simple curiosity, boredom or whatever, I hesitatingly opened the INDEX PAGES OF THE REFERENCE BOOK "AUSTRALIAN MAMMALS"; a book I had owned for years, looked up "Marsupial Mole", and was confronted face-to-face with its scientific Latin name, "NOTORYCTES TYPHLOPS".

I was astounded. My mind was instantly blown away. How the hell could a French Petroleum geologist working on the other side of the world in Central Australia's outback ever be expected to know the actual scientific, Latin name of the very rare, subterranean, presumably completely out-of-context to him, Australian marsupial mole?!

It was then the penny finally dropped and I realised I had shot myself in the foot. I was in an instant rudely surprised and woke up arriving headfirst in the sea of reality. My face was crimson red! I then tried to regroup and regather seamlessly the broken pieces of my shattered composure. I apologised to Claude profusely for my own previous personal stupidity and the brief doubts and misgivings which I had earlier had about him! What else could I do? And from the limited safety of my broken shell, I timidly asked Claude how he knew the scientific name of Australia's marsupial mole, "Notoryctes Typhlops".

Claude then informed me that during his geological studies at university in France, as a totally non-related interest, he had also studied the various diversified yet converging habits of the European, Asian, African, American and Australian underground mole-like creatures of the world, for no particular reason, and of course wrote a thesis as a part of his studies, which included the rare, generally unknown, unique Australian marsupial "Notoryctes Typhlops". An old but still familiar scientific name to him, which even now, years later, remained dormant yet ready for instant utterance at the very slightest provocation on the smooth tip of his until now discreetly silent French tongue, showing in a way it really is a very small world!

****

P.S. There are about 65 million people in France. It is highly likely that Claude Couppey is the only one who has actually seen a rare, living, Australian marsupial mole, and still has its scientific Latin name, "Notoryctes Typhlops", dormant but ready for action on the tip of his Gallic tongue.

****

THIS BACK-FIRING EXPERIENCE WILL BE FILED AS ONE OF MY TOO NUMEROUS TO MENTION "TWISTED FOLLIES".

Notoryctes Typhlops and its zig zag tail marked trail in the red desert sand

59.
TUMBLING TURDS 1962

Our French Petroleum sister company, Compagnie Générale de Géophysique (C.G.G.), had recently finished bulldozing and grading a dead straight line through the spiky spinifex and East-West across the width of the Simpson Desert. The line had started near a railway siding, Pedirka, which was about 60 miles North of Oodnadatta and about 700 miles North of Adelaide, the South Australian capital.

Graders and bulldozers had headed off in an Easterly direction, about 400 miles across the Simpson and past Poepel's Peg, which stood at the junction of three states (South Australia, the Northern Territory and Queensland), then on towards the small outback settlement of Birdsville in Queensland's far South-Western outback.

The North-South oriented sand dunes on the Western side of the desert were little more than knee high parallel ridges, about 30 yards apart, gently sloping on the side facing the prevailing Westerly wind and short and steeper on the Eastern down side. As the bulldozed track proceeded East, the height of the dunes gradually increased, so by the time they were near Birdsville, 350 miles further East, the larger dunes may have been over 100 feet high above the intervening, well-grassed flat lands between, and about half a mile apart.

On the Western side, there were natural artesian springs marking the Western extremity of the Great Artesian Basin, not far from Pedirka on a station or ranch called Mt. Dare, owned by Rex Lowe. These HOT WATERS were known as the "DALHOUSIE SPRINGS" and consisted of a few small tepid ponds, the largest being about 30 yards wide, crystal clear and about 20 feet deep. They contained numerous small fishes that were fully acclimatised to the hot water. I swam in the largest pond but after a while I found the waters a little TOO HOT FOR COMFORT and swam ashore, short of breath. The ponds were surrounded by dense beds of bullrushes and only the largest pond was readily accessible for swimming. Rex had built a lockable, galvanised steel shed alongside the big pond, which was called the "Springs Hut". I had informed my South Australian Museum herpetologist friend John Mitchell of the Dalhousie Springs. He was always intent on paying the area an official visit but never made it before he died prematurely.

Old stone ruins marked the remains of an earlier station house a few yards away, shaded by several still-surviving unkempt, tattered date palms struggling to make a living. A few miles further along, the French Petroleum Company engaged a North African Drilling Company, "FORASOL", to drill our first deep hole called "Dalhousie".

A Petabilt prime mover and other large trucks pulled a lot of heavy air-conditioned caravans, a large laboratory, diesel fuel tanks and several thousand yards of drill rods etc. – more than 500 tons of drilling equipment – into our desert site. Plus 30 or 40 swarthy FORASOL personnel, mostly Algerians and Moroccans who arrived on site as experienced drill-rig workers.

Using a National 80B drill rig, it took a few weeks to reach full depth. Claude Couppey and I gathered our data and moved on. Once we started drilling on the next site, I was employed in the drill-rig laboratory, carrying out routine calcimetry testing as the hole deepened to its programmed cut-off depth. There were no signs of commercial oil, so we moved on about 30 miles further East into the true desert and the increasingly higher sand dunes. We started our second deep hole at a dot on the map called "Purni", well and truly in the desert. Our nearest water was about 30 miles behind us back at Dalhousie Springs and rainfall was a scant three or four inches a year. It was summer and daily shade temperatures probably averaged about 115 -120 degrees Fahrenheit. At the time we were there, Australia's highest temperature was recorded at nearby Oodnadatta. I don't remember exactly but I think it was over 150 degrees Fahrenheit and would have been hotter in our desert location among the sun- reflecting sand dunes.

The North Africans were quite indisposed when it came to hygiene. If the sands were cool enough to walk on in their bare feet they always stepped outside for a "pee". If the sand was too hot, they just stood in the doorway of their air-conditioned caravan and peed anyway from the cooler underfoot step, which was more or less acceptable in a men's camp at the time, but when it came to doing a "number two", it made no difference. They just squatted on their heels and did it anyway, leaving the sausage- shaped lump uncovered, although usually deposited a few more strategic yards away from their air-conditioned sleeping quarters!

With daytime "sun temperatures" probably well over 200 degrees Fahrenheit, a solid "turd" completely dehydrated in less than an hour and became just a featherweight, whitish cotton wool-like dehydrated rolly polly, which blew away anywhere the wind was blowing; an AIMLESS, MINDLESS "TUMBLING TURD". A very off-putting side effect meant that used, very second-hand, technicolour-smeared toilet paper was blowing around the camp accommodation huts and the operating drill rig, and sooner or later got caught up on anything it may wrap itself around, such as your legs.

One day, one of the Moroccans arrived back at the drill rig with a brumby/ wild horse/ mustang he had managed to capture somewhere. Somehow, it had a very badly swollen right shoulder, twice the size of the other shoulder, and found it difficult to even hobble on its three non-swollen legs. There was not a blade of grass where we were and we fed the poor animal the choicest French Petroleum vegetables from the refrigerated cold store, bread, fruit and water by the bucket. After several days, the horse had wandered off into the surrounding desert and no one cared. So with half a bucket of water in one hand

and a Browning shotgun with Brenneke slugs in the other, I tracked the passive, thirsty, hungry horse half a mile overland, watered it and fed it the choicest French Petroleum Company's Greens, let it rest awhile, and after a few minutes I blew its brains out.

I then performed an autopsy on the poor, long-suffering animal, removed the grossly swollen leg and found it completely shattered in the shoulder. I could see the broken ends and splinters of the upper leg bones, shattered, chipped and worn as they rubbed painfully together each time the poor brumby took a single agonising step. I took the shattered heavy leg back to camp to show the Moroccans why the leg would not heal itself. The Moroccans were more interested in the actual location of the dead horse, so I told them where it was. The next I knew, much of the euthanised horse had been retrieved and the North Africans, who preferred horse meat to beef steak, were barbecuing the edible meat back in camp.

By this time, unofficial word had reached the medical authorities in Oodnadatta regarding the generally unclean state of affairs at the Purni drill site, and we received an unannounced, unexpected visit by 4WD vehicle from a couple of Nursing Sisters from the small hospital at Oodnadatta. The nurses tentatively tip-toed among the plentiful festooned, colourful, used toilet paper streamers hanging here and there, just as an errant, full-sized, wind-blown, dehydrated TUMBLING TURD TUMBLED GLEEFULLY PAST, propelled by the scented breeze!

THE NURSES' MAIN CONCERN AT OUR PURNI DRILL SITE INITIALLY HAD BEEN TO INVESTIGATE WHETHER THE DRILLERS WERE BEING FORCE-FED HORSE MEAT! Now they had more to worry about. In a few days there was a fair bit in the newspapers down South.

****

Heads almost rolled, and attitudes and prospects at our next drill site called "Poonarunna" were actually greatly improved as a result of the "VERY BAD PRESS THE PURNI SITE HAD RECEIVED ON TV 700 MILES DOWN SOUTH".

****

We also had on site a six-foot stack of seismic gelignite explosive, about a ton, which, owing to the extremely high baking temperatures in the sun, was dangerously "weeping" its main explosive ingredient, nitroglycerine, into the desert sands. It was a situation where the slightest bump could set it off, and as it was now surplus to requirements and situated safely about 500 yards from the drill rig , it was primed and wired for electronic detonation.

We all sat expectantly on a sand ridge about 200 yards away while I, feeling very much like Lawrence of Arabia, took up a strategic position next to the remote firing plunger device and handed my movie camera to a fellow member. I asked him to start filming the moment the powder monkey started his count down, and not surprisingly he obtained first class results of capturing the massive explosion.

At the same time, I used my Canon Pelix 35 mm reflex camera and clicked the shutter seemingly too early, but also obtained first class explosive results. We walked up to the devastated, wiped-clean landscape and I picked up a small marsupial, a bandicoot, which we had seen hopping around straight after the big bang. The small animal briefly "shivered" for a second, then expired in my hands. In due course, it went frozen to the Adelaide Museum, where I was later told it was a new sub-species.

****

We encountered deep seams of black coal at Purni and not much else. We left Purni as a fully-flowing, unlined running bore, gushing tens of thousands of gallons of artesian water wastefully into the desert each day.

From the moment Purni first gushed water, it also gushed rocks the size of the internal bore hole. Every few seconds, six-inch rocks were shot out. French Petroleum offered to fully case the bore, with the cost to be borne by Rex Lowe, the station owner, but he declined the offer and the bore ran wastefully wild for maybe 30 years (some time in the early 2000-plus period the government stepped in, took over and cemented the flowing bore shut).

****

Leaving Purni, we went DOWN FROM OODNADATTA TO THE OLD AFGHAN CAMEL DRIVERS' TOWN OF MARREE, THEN NORTH again up the Birdsville Track TO COWARIE STATION, AND IN TOWARDS THE NORTH-EASTERN CORNER OF THAT VERY LARGE SALTPAN, LAKE EYRE, near Coopers Creek, and set up the Poonarunna drill site. Apart from my French Petroleum duties, I wandered about a mile or so around the drill site looking for tektites, meteorites, gold and whatever, without success, but soon realised the ground was generously covered by fossils. Tektites are usually glassy and greenish-black in colour. Good specimens are usually mushroom-like in appearance, presumed to have become mushroom-shaped after travelling through the atmosphere at supersonic speed while in a semi-molten state. Different types of tektites occur in different regions of the world and are currently not classed as genuine meteorites from outer space, but rather as emanating from an UNKNOWN TERRESTRIAL SOURCE.

I gathered a number of fossils and made thin-sliced mounted specimens in the laboratory with the aid of our diamond saw, diamond laps, glass slides and balsam cement. About half a mile from the Poonarunna drill site, I made the important find of a crocodilian-like skull about three feet long, removed a single large tooth, and left the skull right where I had found it. To remove it, it seemed necessary to remove a whole big heavy chunk of sand and soil in one piece. So I left it! (I later mentioned this find to Tim Flannery when he was the Director of the South Australian Museum but I don't know if he ever followed it up).

****

After Poonarunna, I was flown in a De Havilland Dove to Sandringham Station, about 200 miles North of Birdsville in far Western Queensland, as French Petroleum's on- site representative. Here we used a smaller Mayhew 1000 drill rig and I remained on site to confirm that all had gone according to plan. Then it was BACK TO ADELAIDE FOR AN OVERDUE BIT OF REST AND RECREATION, AND THE GREEN, GREEN GRASS OF HOME WITH NO TUMBLING TURDS!

60.
POEPEL'S PEG 1962

Before we drilled the French Petroleum Company's Witcherie, Purni and Poonarunna deep-drilled investigative bore holes, I was in the first motorised crossing of the Simpson Desert by the French Petroleum Geological staff. The "French Line", generally heading towards Birdsville, had actually been constructed on our behalf by another French company, Compagnie Générale de Géophysique (C.G.G.) during 1963 and '64. Their personnel had built the track and of course used it many times while it was being constructed. However, since the track had been conceived, planned and paid for by the French Petroleum Company, it was correctly called the "French Line". And so, Claude Couppey and I had left the yet-to-be-drilled Witcherie and Purni drill sites and headed East along the newly finished French Line towards Poepel's Peg.

The State Premier of South Australia, Thomas Playford, and his Queensland counterpart Frank Nicklin, were in a party following the next day. Boldly painted on fuel drums for their attention was the graffiti,

"FUCK SOUTH AUSTRALIA, WACKO QUEENSLAND".

But after we passed this Simpson Desert graffiti, looking back on the other side of the same drums, for persons going West, were the words,

"FUCK QUEENSLAND, WACKO SOUTH AUSTRALIA!"

In 1879, Poepel's Peg had been placed glaringly in the wrong position – "missed it by that much" – by the previous South Australian Surveyor Augustus Poepel. The mislaid Peg marked the important junction of the South Australian, Northern Territory and Queensland State borders.

I didn't see the actual "Peg", wherever it was hiding, but we had a couple of beers and were now in Queensland. We kept charging East over the higher and higher sand dunes towards Birdsville, sometimes making several attempts to get over the high dunes.

After cresting one 90-foot-high windblown sand dune, the front part of the forward control Land Rover I was driving hung tentatively balanced in inner space and was on the point of tipping sideways as the dry, loose sand fell away from under it. To keep the Land Rover upright, I slid over from my seat to the passenger's side with Claude, and we dropped down into the loose, treacherous sand beneath the vehicle and quickly dug under the wheels with our bare hands while the vehicle slowly settled back onto a more even keel.

We arrived in Birdsville when it was quiet. We were not there during the popular Birdsville Cup. The settlement was virtually empty and we stayed at the Birdsville Hotel while our forward control Land Rover stayed peacefully outside.

Unknown to me, a thief entered the canvas-enclosed back of the vehicle and stole my Abu fishing reel and Trigger Grip type fishing rod, and disappeared into the night. It was only weeks later when we returned to Oodnadatta that I realised my rod and reel had gone missing in Birdsville. I phoned Sergeant Eric Salmon of the one-man-strong, Birdsville Police and told him of my interstate predicament.

A week later, my fishing rod and reel arrived at Oodnadatta, delivered at no charge by Trans Australian Airways (T.A.A.) airfreight with a covering note from ERIC SALMON. Apart from being the Birdsville policeman, Eric was responsible to the Department of Meteorology for his routine weather reports, looked after Births, Deaths and Marriages, was a Justice of the Peace, a Life Insurance agent and for all I knew, probably held Tupperware parties in the desert. To top things off, he was also the Birdsville agent for T.A.A. and could sell you an airline ticket to anywhere! And so, IN BETWEEN ALL OF HIS OTHER ACTIVITIES, ALL ALONE AND UNASSISTED, HE HAD SOMEHOW TRACKED DOWN THE BASTARD WHO HAD STOLEN MY ROD AND REEL AND RETURNED IT TO ME ON THE OTHER SIDE OF THE SIMPSON DESERT. The miscreant was probably lucky lynching was illegal.

****

We were in Birdsville for a few days when the regular DOUGLAS D.C. 3 ARRIVED. IT PULLED OFF THE DIRT AIRSTRIP AND TAXIED OVER AND PULLED UP RIGHT OUTSIDE THE PUB. It was an overnight stay for the aircrew and the hostesses were choosy as to which room they would stay in because a few walls were cracked rather badly, and some of the local ringers (cowboys) had been caught peeking through the mile-wide, open, peepshow-like cracks.

The owner publican at the time was LEN GAFFNEY, a local, who was badly in need of a haircut. One of our guys dobbed me in, saying I had some hair clippers in my possession. SO, THERE I WAS, NEVER HAVING CUT A PERSON'S HAIR BEFORE, EXPERIMENTALLY CUTTING THE PUBLICAN'S HAIR IN THE BAR OF HIS HOTEL WHILE HIS PATRONS LOOKED ON. Len Gaffney at the time was related to Colleen Clancy, who later married my old friend Tony Mathews (S.P.S.C.) of Adelaide's Feathers, Largs Pier and Buckingham Arms hotels fame.

61.
DONALD CAMPBELL 1962

About 1962 I wandered into S.A. Sportsgoods in Pirie Street, Adelaide, since I was passing. I saw Donald Campbell and his attractive Belgian wife talking to Don Fleetwood, the proprietor. Being a bit of an extrovert and a friend of Don's, I got myself introduced to Donald Campbell and joined them for a cup of coffee out the back. At the time, Donald Campbell was setting up a world, wheel-driven attempt on the land speed record on South Australia's inland giant salt pan, LAKE EYRE.

Not long after meeting Donald Campbell, I was in Northern South Australia (500 miles North of Adelaide) with the French Petroleum Company, camped in a wide, dry, riverbed; a tributary of the normally dry Neales River. On this particular Saturday we were 60 miles north of our camp in the small outback town of Oodnadatta for the annual race meeting, the Oodnadatta Cup. While the race meeting unfolded at Oodnadatta, back at our camp the black skies above the Neales River also literally unfolded. We had no idea of the deteriorating weather picture down there.

Late in the afternoon, we saw the skies in the South looking ominous and thought it prudent to leave the outback race meeting and drive back to our vulnerable camp. As we drove South, the skies ahead blackened and not long after large, sparse drops of heavy tropical-type rain began to SPLASH down on us. BY THE TIME WE GOT BACK TO OUR CAMP IN THE MIDDLE OF THE NORMALLY WIDE, DRY RIVERBED, THE RAIN WAS PISSING DOWN AND OUR CAMP WAS IN TROUBLE.

We were slipping and sliding all over the place as we churned and splashed our way in our 4WD across the high open ground to the edge of the river. The quarter-mile wide river course was normally a number of dry, intertwining, sandy channels and gravelly, sandy islets. Our senior French geological staff had decided a flat, sandy, hundred-yards-wide, weed-free section of the riverbed was the ideal place to set up camp. With an annual rainfall of something like three inches, flooding was considered most unlikely. Now, however, in the downpour, the dry, sandy riverbed was not so dry.

Water was already coursing its way underground through the surface sands but was still unseen on the surface.

Leaving my forward control Land Rover up on the relative safety of the higher bank, I scrambled down to my tent in the flooding river, dropped it to the ground, gathered it, my bed and bedding, carried it up the slippery slope and tossed it into the Land Rover.

One of our other five or six Land Rovers was not so lucky. It was stuck in the riverbed. I managed to snap a steel tow cable as I tried unsuccessfully to pull it out of the already wetting riverbed and harm's way. A couple of hours later we could still see the tropical-white-painted aluminium roof of the submerged vehicle sticking up defiantly above the flooded river. We also lost a refrigerator, large gas bottles, tents and a number of 44-gallon drums of petrol as we stood in the torrential rain and watched our world submerge.

****

There was "good" news, however, a few months later. Long after we had left the scene of our disaster, the French Petroleum Company in Adelaide received a thank you note from Donald Campbell and his team "for the petrol". They had found drums of petrol, plainly marked "The French Petroleum Company", littered along the North-Western shoreline of a flooded Lake Eyre, about 100 miles or so downstream from Nilpinna.

There was, of course, "bad" news. The same flooded Lake Eyre put paid to Donald Campbell's attempt on the World Land Speed Record that year. Two years later, on July 27, 1964, he returned to a dry Lake Eyre and BROKE THE WORLD WHEEL- DRIVEN LAND SPEED RECORD at 403.10 miles per hour.

Later that same year on December 31st, Donald Campbell returned to Lake Dumbleyung in Western Australia in his jet-propelled "BLUEBIRD K 7" boat. He set a NEW WORLD WATER SPEED RECORD of 276.33 miles per hour. Two years later, on January 4th 1967, back in England's Lakes District at Coniston Water, he made an attempt to reach an average speed above 300 miles per hour. His first run went well and he achieved an average speed of 297.6 miles per hour. Sadly, his record attempt and his life came to a sudden stop towards the end of his return run when his boat became airborne, somersaulted, then plunged nose first deep into Coniston Water.

The remains of the "BLUEBIRD K 7" were found a few weeks later, while what was left of Donald Campbell's mortal remains were not found until long after, only being recovered in May 2001.

****

As a point of interest, on October 8th 1978, an Australian inventor, KEN WARBY, driving his home-made "SPIRIT OF AUSTRALIA" on the Blowering Dam in the Snowy Mountains in New South Wales, was the first and still only person to drive a boat past 300 miles per hour at an average speed of 317.6; A WORLD RECORD which he still holds today (2019), 41 years later! It is the longest-standing World Water Speed Record in history.

Various other international record-breaking attempts since 1978 have resulted either in mechanical or financial problems, and/ or tragedy.

The "SPIRIT of AUSTRALIA" is still on display in the Maritime Museum in Sydney.

Ken Warby setting a new world record on Blowering Dam 1978

62.
BILBIES 1966

Halfway between Alice Springs in Australia's Northern Territory and Kalgoorlie in Western Australia's outback lie the Warburton Ranges; a low, isolated, rather insignificant collection of desert hills. Most of the area is designated tribal Aboriginal land where about 100-200 remaining original Wongai and Pitjantjatjara Indigenous tribal members continued their uncertain, twilight existence under the umbrella protection of a foreign-sourced and financed Christian church group. Local Aborigines had previously found a small outcrop of rocks with copper carbonate stains, which, after digging down a few feet below ground level, had revealed chalcocite; a valuable, high grade sulphide ore of copper. A few tens of tons were mined and sold.

The Western Mining Corporation (W.M.C.) at Kalgoorlie was invited to come in and generally investigate the mineral resources of the area on behalf of the Indigenous locals, which is about the time I came into the picture. As a result of the locals' invitation, W.M.C. had placed on site, at Warburton, a number of 40 -foot, air- conditioned, aluminium-clad caravans and transportable cabins. We also used smaller caravans for longer individual bush exploration trips. We employed about 15 W.M.C. members and a variable number of local Aborigines on a day-to-day basis at our Warburton base.

A diamond drilling contracting company conducted an extensive appraisal of the area and a Bell helicopter was used for investigating small, isolated outcrops up to 120 miles away, far out in the uninhabited, unfriendly terrain of the Gibson, Sandy and Great Victoria deserts.

****

Events In Oz

It is at this point the story deviates, for as a non-related, personal sideline, I have been associated with the South Australian Museum for a long time as an honorary collector. In my travels, at different times to different places, I have always had my eyes, and ears, open for items of museum interest. I was mindful that the Nail Tail Wallaby had formerly been collected in the area and may still, hopefully, exist somewhere.

It was ONE OF THE LOCAL ABORIGINAL ELDERS, PETER FRASER, WHO STILL SPENT A LOT OF TIME TRACKING AND HUNTING IN THE BUSH, who presented me with living examples of the Crest Tailed Mulgara (Dasycercus Cristicauda), a small, rat-like animal with a pouch for its young, like a kangaroo, a body about the size and weight of a hen's egg, a big head, and fearsome teeth and large jaws in comparison to its tiny size.

I placed one in a small cage with other Native non-marsupial mice, and when I looked in later, I discovered the other mice were all dead and some of the heads had been completely eaten by the Crest Tailed Mulgara. He was a tough little bugger!

I had been in touch with the Western Australian Native Welfare authorities who had no problem with me collecting animals for the museum, as long as the local Aborigines were paid a cash equivalent in relation to the size and perceived food worth of the collected animal.

Peter later surprised me by describing an animal that sounded suspiciously like a Bilby or Rabbit Eared Bandicoot as being present somewhere in the area. It was described as being "rabbit-sized with long, grey, silky fur, a long, thin, white-tipped tail and a marsupial pouch, and it lived in deep, excavated, rabbit-like burrows"!

****

One weekend, I set out with Peter, crowbars, picks and shovels on our quest for the "YEEDARRADOO"; the local Aboriginal name for the mystery creature. About 10 miles away, Peter started digging at a deep, well-used, animal burrow and half an hour later, about five feet down, a beautiful silky fur coat was just visible hiding in the dirt on the floor of his burrow, which is when Peter handed me a LIVING, SUPPOSEDLY "EXTINCT" at that time, Bilby, or Rabbit Eared Bandicoot!

Over the next few months, Peter collected about five or six more, for which I paid him $10 each, an amount well in excess of their food value by weight. This was in the early '60s and I believe, according to the museum, these were the first living examples rediscovered in Australia until more recently.

In captivity, the Bilby took a great liking to thick kangaroo tail soup and surprised me by easily crunching the sizeable, cooked tail bones in the bottom of the large soup container! In the first instance, when I only had one Bilby to look after, I kept it in a plywood tea-chest with a heavy wood panel on top. During the first night, the Bilby managed to dislodge the timber weight without waking me and surprised me later on in the night by my discovery of him in my bed, snuggled up between my legs just like a house cat; he was between the sheets, no begs or pardons!

I was, for a time, concerned about certain of my vulnerable, unprotected private parts after seeing the way he crunched the large bones in the cooked kangaroo tail soup! However, I soon learnt the Bilby bore no malice. It liked to cuddle up in the sweater I was wearing, and was as placid and tame as you like, right from the start. I took the first Bilby with me to Adelaide by plane and delivered it personally to the South Australian Museum. The following five were later sent by air and the group then formed the basis of a breeding colony at the museum.

****

I then went to Africa for just on 10 years and have no idea what eventually happened to "MY" Bilbies in the care of the museum. I had originally been led to believe the museum's intention was to breed from the first of the few I had delivered but I have never seen any evidence that this happened. It is still an unknown situation to me.

Me holding the elusive YEEDARRADOO (Bilby/ Rabbit Eared Bandicoot)

63.
A GOOD BIG BLOKE 1966

My Danish friend Christian and I were both working for Town and Country Homes as "carpenters" (HE WAS ONE, I WASN'T), mainly squaring door frames from bulk- packed, individual components. We had just eaten a meal at the "Greasy Spoon" restaurant in Port Hedland, a large iron ore export port about 750 miles North of Perth, Western Australia, about 1966.

After consuming a cup of thick black coffee, we headed over the road to the pub to have a beer or two and watch the passing parade. After a while, we couldn't help but notice a shortish, nuggety, argumentative Welshman seemingly intent on picking a fight over nothing with all and sundry.

A little later we heard raised voices at the other end of the bar and realised "Taffy" was involved in the disturbance. This is when a fellow we had just met said, referring to the person "Taffy" was obviously trying to antagonise, "This could be interesting. That fellow looks as though he might be able to handle himself".

Our new-found mate at the bar briefly explained Taffy was very good, very cocky and due for a fall, and perhaps this could be it! Taffy was living on his nearly unbeaten, unofficial record as a hotel bar fighter. Virtually everyone he picked fights with, fought and beat was bigger than him. He had a very good fight record for his weight.

We watched a while in anticipation as "the kettle came to the boil" and an over- confident Taffy raised his fists and looked red hot and ready to strike.

BANG! WALLOP!! THUMP!!!

TAFFY WAS DOWN AND OUT as the other fellow calmly went back to his beer.

After being splashed with water from the ice bucket, Taffy slowly revived and came to his muddled senses. The mystery pugilist then ordered a fresh beer for the dismayed "Taffy" and when handing it to the reviving Welshman, was heard to say, "Listen you cocky little bastard, I was warned about you. You're good, but not that good. For what it's worth, I'll tell you something you may, in a crisis, choose to remember. A GOOD BIG BLOKE WILL USUALLY BEAT A GOOD LITTLE BLOKE!"

64.
MARBLE BAR 1966

I boarded a "Mickey Mouse Airlines" (M.M.A.; Macrobertson Miller Airlines) D.C. 3 in Perth and was destined for the small, hot, inland town of Marble Bar, about 800 miles North, to work at the large, alluvial, MOOLYELLA TIN MINES near Bamboo Creek.

The D.C. 3 only carried 21 passengers in three rows of seats. The left row seated 14 and by removing the forward front row seat, room had been made for a large, refrigerator-sized electronic device to be carried up front, the back of which was in plain view of the passengers.

A couple of weeks after settling in at Moolyella, my Danish friend Christian and I paid our first visit to the town of Marble Bar and entered the one and only local café where we had a surprisingly good meal. It was then we noticed a brand-new juke box in the most prominent position in the café, and I realised it was my former electronic travel companion from the flight two weeks before.

We were still eating when we were surprised to see a full-blooded Aboriginal couple enter the café, both bare footed. He was, nonetheless, neatly dressed in shirt and trousers, and she wore a white, home-sewn dress, made from clean washed and ironed, still readable, "LAURA" BRAND SELF-RAISING FLOUR SACKS.

The year was about 1966. We were even more surprised, and very amused, when, after placing money in the juke box machine, it belted out Rolfe Harris singing his recent hit song, "MY BOOMERANG WON'T COME BACK".

65.
GOLD TO BE GOT

In 1966, I was operating a Caldwell rotary bucket drilling rig not far from Australia's hottest town, Marble Bar, with a record of 163 consecutive days over 100 degrees Fahrenheit in the shade. THE GOOD NEWS IS IT WAS WINTER!

The drill rig was used to quickly bore a three-foot diameter hole down through rough, rocky, alluvial earth, rocks and gravel to a maximum depth of about 50 feet, to hopefully find concentrations of valuable alluvial TIN, TANTALITE, DIAMONDS and low-priced U.S. $34 an ounce GOLD, and/ or any other heavy economic minerals.

The gold recovery system in operation at the time utilised "CONES", which were good on the minus one-inch material but inefficient on larger material, which would require other expensive, gold recovery means and apparatus. For reasons of economy, it had been established that most of the recoverable tin was less than about an inch in diameter, so the plant was designed to reject and divert straight to waste all minerals, rocks (including cassiterite) and gold nuggets greater than one inch in diameter.

Quite a lot of smaller alluvial gold was also recovered along with the tin, but because of its low price, gold was only of minor and secondary interest. Nonetheless, they did recover a steady stream of fine gold and small nuggets up to the TIN CUT-OFF SIZE OF EVERYTHING MINUS ONE INCH, which, even at U.S. $34 an ounce, helped the mine's economy.

From time to time, large nuggets of gold commonly called "slugs" in Western Australia were sometimes noticed and RECOVERED

BEFORE BEING BURIED, out of sight, once and for all on the huge, high-heaped mullock dumps. I've seen SLUGS OF GOLD NEARLY AS BIG AS MY FIST, which is when the foreman would stand by the conveyor belt for a few hours or days and snatch them up on the compan y's behalf (and HIS???) before allowing them once again to be buried on the dead-end mullock heap. Today, metal-detected gold is plucked off the belt, day and night, automatically.

But we are not talking about today, we are talking about the past, and past is past----but it's also STILL PRESENT, LATENT and WAITING!

****

There were no electronic gold detector devices available or other mechanical methods employed at the time to somehow trap this oversize gold or oversize cassiterite. Metal detectors were in their infancy, and it is therefore patently obvious, unfortunately, that a LOT OF THAT HEAVY YELLOW STUFF, AND TIN, PLUS RARE COLUMBITE AND TANTALITE, HAD GONE SILENTLY TO THE MULLOCK HEAP OVER THE YEARS, BURIED OUT OF SIGHT, UNSEEN AND UNDETECTED, MAYBE FOREVER.

****

Years later, I had my own gold mine in Rhodesia and in 1973 paid a fleeting visit home to South Australia as a result of the 3rd prize in the Plum Tree draw of the Rhodesian Lottery. Because I knew GOLD NUGGETS HAD BEEN PICKED UP OFF THE GROUND IN THE PAST NEAR MY INGUBO GOLD MINE IN RHODESIA, I

decided to obtain an electronic metal detector and I knew there was a person at the Australian Mineral Development Laboratories (AMDEL) in Adelaide who was making them. I paid a visit to AMDEL, bought a detector, and returned to Rhodesia via Hong Kong and England, then set to work on the INGUBO with my new toy. The very first day I set out to make money with my metal detector, on my first attempt I picked up a lot of bullet cases and horseshoes etc. while sweeping the head of the detector from side to side, when lo and behold, six feet in front of me I SAW A GOLDEN GLEAM. I leant down and picked up a nice gold nugget that weighed three quarters of an ounce, worth about $1,330 in today's money (2021).

THE TYRANNY OF TIME!

The trouble was it happened in 1973 when the gold price was still pegged at U.S. $34 an ounce, and so there was nothing to get excited about. It was only worth about $25 Australian then. I'd really love to talk here about my old INGUBO mine in what is now Zimbabwe but it MAKES ME CRY (see stories 13, 17, 74 and 78). I had in sight $200,000,000 worth of gold at 2013 prices, identified in the first 20 feet of a large outcrop, ready, willing and able to be treated by the simplest means, but I lost the lot to Mr Mugabe and his henchmen.

****

After the gold price went suddenly up to a heady U.S. $800 per ounce in the space of a day in 1977, my thoughts turned to the gold nuggets we had turned up every day at the OPEN CUT MOOLYELLA TIN MINE in W.A. I've often wondered in my later years about identifying the old, auriferous dumps containing these "SLUGS" (those which had been dumped and sent to waste). In 2011, when I published my first rough version of this book, the price per ounce had more than doubled again to U.S. $1,900. Now, in 2021, it would be worth U.S. $1870. This means that those pre-1977 already mined, oversized, plus one-inch material SURFACE SITTING DUMPS, if still intact, untouched and unmolested, are waiting to be PLUCKED. Knowledge of the huge leap in gold prices and where to find "unwanted" gold would still be in the memory of, and shared by, OTHER OF MY ELDERLY CONTEMPORARIES, who one way or another may have already taken advantage of this POT OF GOLD SITUATION.

The dumps, from memory, were something like 500 yards long by 50 yards wide at the base, by about 50 feet high, and by simple scraping and detecting, might take several months each to treat fairly cheaply, I would think, for a very large profit! If they are still there, it's a matter of RE-PEGGING the dumps and just scraping the top couple of inches of old waste material off over the side of the slightly lowered dump, then detecting the small nuggets and slugs with a metal detector. Then doing the same thing over and over, level by level, as the height of the dump gets lower and lower, RECOVERING THESE PLUS-ONE-INCH SLUGS AND LAUGHING OUR WAY TO THE BANK.

****

I also identified a large area of shallow alluvium around the old copper/gold mine of Mt Morgan, near Rockhampton in Queensland, containing a lot of gold dust, but it was still held as a mining lease so I won't talk about that; it's out of bounds.

****

IT'S UP TO YOU, the cashed-up investigative entrepreneur, TO SEEK AND FIND THE REMAINING GOLD!

66.
CIRCUMCISIONS AND A DESERT CHOPPER 1966

Halfway between Kalgoorlie in Western Australia and Alice Springs in the Northern Territory, about 600 miles either way, lie the obscure, low, dry, non-descript hills called the Warburton Ranges. The area generally is home to the Western Wongai and the overlapping Eastern centralised Pitjantjatjara tribal Aboriginal groups. These people were drawn here because of the strategically positioned Christian Mission Station, Jesus Christ, the missionaries and its small shop.

A few months before my arrival, the Aboriginals had brought the mission staff heavy grey rocks covered in mainly blue and green crystalline coatings, identified as chalcocite, a rich copper ore. As I related in Story 62 (Bilbies), the Kalgoorlie-based Western Mining Corporation (W.M.C.) had been invited into the Warburton area to evaluate the possible value of the chalcocite to the Aborigines.

In the 1960s, Aborigines still existed in a day-to-day kind of twilight land, semi-civilised to a degree by colonial standards, mostly wearing trousers at the mission, while a few stayed naked in the bush and carried on their happy, though primitive ways by our standards, regardless. They were traditional hunter-gatherers with meticulous, keen eyesight, and fully observant.

If we were standing in their place and looking around, we would only see an empty, lifeless landscape, but if they stood in the same place, they were in a wide-open Pandora's Box with a thousand untold interesting tales all visible to them, begging to be told. If they ran out of store-bought matches when in the bush, they still made fire in a minute or two by "sawing" softer firewood with the hardwood edge of a Woomera (spear thrower). This caused dry, crumbled, sprinkled kangaroo dung, applied to the friction-heated junction of the tinder-hot softer wood, to smoulder and after a gentle puff of air by the Aboriginal exponent, slowly smoke then flame into fire.

The men still hunted kangaroos and emus with woomera-propelled spears and killing sticks (clubs), and the women gathered grass seeds and ground them to flour on large, flattish, semi-recessed, well-worn rocks (Nardoo stones), and/ or dug for yams, honey ants and the like with wooden digging tools (sticks).

Both men's and women's secret ceremonies continued to be observed as always, and teenage youths were circumcised at that painful older age with razor sharp, freshly- flaked, very hard stones such as flint, agate, quartz or chalcedony.

****

NO ANAESTHETICS, NO ANTISEPTIC, NO PAINKILLERS

****

When in the Warburton Ranges as a member of W.M.C., I was twice invited to sit in on a circumcision ceremony out in the bush. One evening, a younger white W.M.C. member was also invited, but as a token of respect he had to lie on one side with one elbow on the ground in a sub-servile position. The Elder tribal circumcision exponent then napped a piece of clean-looking chalcedony with a piece of other hard rock, and after a few attempts flaked a RAZOR-SHARP STONE SCALPEL from the core of the rock. While this was going on, the Aborigines maintained a repetitive chant, over and over, with rhythmic clapping of hard pieces of wood together, "click, click, click, click", in a vocal/ instrumental Warburton Range "hit parade".

The circumcising "Witch Doctor" then went to work and pulled the nervous youth's loose surplus foreskin just over the head of the penis, then with one stroke of the razor-like rock, sliced the foreskin off as clean as a whistle! The youth briefly bled like a stuck pig, then in seconds he looked as pale as a white man's ghost!

This is when I SAW ONE OF THE CAMP MONGREL DOGS SCOFF DOWN THE SURPLUS FORESKIN.

****

W.M.C. had earlier set up a substantial base camp and drilled a sub-artesian water bore hole fitted with a windmill-powered water pump, which drained into a tank with a tap. The Aborigines from the mission walked past our camp every day and soon discovered the virtue of this water tap, which we allowed them to use whenever they wanted. Unfortunately, they did not always turn the tap off fully, often leaving it dripping or even running, and on two occasions our 200-gallon water tank had fully emptied overnight; and this at a time with no wind! So we ordered lockable taps and padlocks from W.M.C. Kalgoorlie, and fitted and locked the taps securely in position as soon as they arrived.

The next day, the passing pedestrian Aborigines discovered their access to our water supply denied, which was when a number of upset tribal Elder grey-beards appeared on the scene, stating that W.M.C. had cut off their access to their TRADITIONAL WATER SUPPLY. Traditional my foot! It hadn't been there until we came and installed it, several months before. What were they talking about?

Well, the mission staff intervened, and W.M.C., doing the right thing, ordered and installed a petrol-driven "jet" pump, which resolved the issue. When the tank ran empty as a result of "THEM", we just expensively pumped it full again!

****

There were about a dozen 40-foot-long, air-conditioned caravans forming the camp, each provided with hot and cold running water, shower, kitchen sink, full-sized refrigerator, electric stove and a closed-system, long-drop toilet. W.M.C. had pre- drilled about six 30-foot-deep, closely-spaced, long-drop pit toilet holes per caravan, in a straight line, so that when one was full, the caravan was pulled forward a foot and reconnected to the next long drop without any hassle.

The very large 40-foot caravans were issued at one per person and there were absolutely no complaints about the standard of accommodation in the Warburton Ranges. Another 40-foot caravan housed a full-sized geological laboratory, with an Australian-conceived Atomic Absorption Spectrometer, which was used to assay thousands of grid and stream-minus-400 mesh soil samples.

We also had on site some diamond drillers from A.D.D., a company I would later work with in Melbourne and Kalgoorlie. I well remember BARRY WARD, who answered day and night to his fitting nickname "SKUNGEE!" I still remember his usual war cry at the end of a long hot tiring day; "GET A CARTON!"[29]

We had a number of 4WD Toyotas, which were generally replacing Land Rovers in the bush at the time, and our supplies came up 600 miles from Kalgoorlie on an infrequent basis, carried by cartage contractors. Our main area of interest was quite large; several hundred miles in any direction, and a fair bit was desert sand dune country, North-West in the Gibson Desert and South-East in the Great Victoria and Great Sandy deserts. To visit much of the outlying desert country overland by 4WD would take a very long time, so we had a Bell helicopter on site, flown by a personable English ex-R.A.F. pilot. When he wasn't trying to land the "skids" of his helicopter directly on the small roof of a Toyota station wagon, he was delivering fresh strings of "air-dangled"

---

[29] A carton of 24 bottles of beer

bags of eggs from the head geologist Bob Hewitt to the missionaries, as a gift.

****

The missionary in charge at the mission was also a qualified pilot and on one occasion he had borrowed a Cessna from Jan Beers, the owner/operator of an air charter business, "NOESKA" (Norseman Esperance Kalgoorlie Aviation), for an overnight trip from our Warburton base camp to Ayers Rock, about 300 miles away to the East, and I went along for the ride. It was the evening of April 24th, about 1966, and there were a number of R.S.L. (Returned Services League) ex-military members present as tourists at Ayers Rock. Since my pilot was a religious person, he made a popular decision among the ex-servicemen and agreed to hold an impromptu ANZAC DAY DAWN SERVICE CEREMONY AT THE ROCK.

Next morning, up before dawn, a very moving ceremony, and a mention of our impromptu Anzac service on Alice Air Radio, then 300 miles back to Warburton.

****

Much of the time I rode a small 90 c.c. capacity Honda motor bike as I sampled outlying stream sediments, which involved consulting fine-grained aerial photos with a 10 X magnifying lens and taking sediment samples every so often along the length of the usually-dry outback gutters and stream beds while noting and mapping the results.

Out in the desert 100 or more miles away were situated a number of small ridges, hills and stony outcrops, some a mile or two long, others just isolated mounds in the bush. They all shared one feature in common; they were slightly elevated high points from where flooding waters years apart sometimes ran. And these waters ran in crevices, trickles, gutters and larger streams, and sometimes carried traces of solid or dissolved minerals in their path. This is why W.M.C. was invited there.

To sample those isolated, outlying stream beds, I was flown out daily in the chopper up to 100 miles from base with my Honda motorcycle tied to one skid, a gerry can of petrol tied to the other, and a packed lunch. I was dropped off for a day's sampling and collected at the end of the day with my stream samples well before nightfall while leaving the Honda in the field overnight to gaze at the stars in solitude. Needless to say, it was very interesting flying low and slow over that rarely seen terrain. We sometimes saw large numbers of feral camels in mobs well in excess of 100, plus kangaroos, emus, mallee-fowl, dingoes, a few rabbits, and bush turkeys or bustards, and were sometimes well and truly upstaged in flight by the large-wingspan wedge tailed eagles.

****

I picked up a few glassy, greenish-black "tektites" from the ground but not a speck of gold. For tens of thousands of years in Australia's long human settled history, over the ages, most of these isolated grassy sites had been associated with well-worn, flat, mortar-board-like Nardoo stones lying around and occasionally used; and/ or lying latent for scores of years, some with their smaller, hand-held, grinding pestle and mortar-like stones still sitting on top of their large, related Nardoo grinding stones, belatedly, expectantly waiting, ready for grinding flour-making action from vanishing tribal Aborigines who most likely will never come again.

Reminds me of the prophetic words of Bob Dylan's song, better sung by Burl Ives:
"THE TIMES THEY ARE A'CHANGING"

67.
METEORITES

Nickel-iron metallic meteorites and gold generally have one thing in common; both are easily detectable by modern, electronic metal detectors.

As a boy in the '40s, I was a regular visitor to the South Australian Museum in Adelaide's spacious, tree-lined North Terrace, and passed by the large, one ton, refrigerator-sized HUCKITTA METEORITE, displayed in the open display area on the way in through the external foyer. The museum had a very large collection of metaliferous and stony meteorites on display, and as I found out later, a lot more out the back in storage.

****

Arid outback South Australia was an easy place to find meteorites. They stuck out in the sparse vegetation like a sore toe; you couldn't miss them if you luckily happened to be there before anyone else. As I grew older and became known at the museum as a regular visitor, sometime donator of various specimens, and also known to F.J. (John) Mitchell the herpetologist (reptiles) and Paul Lawson (taxidermist), I discovered they had tons of undisplayed, twisted meteorite metal shards, just like exploded, expanded bomb casings from World War 2. Some of the twisted metal pieces were three or four feet long and probably weighed in excess of 100 pounds, and these were just the fragments, bent in amorphous shapes like art gallery art, scrambled like twisted atomic hoop iron fragments from Hiroshima.[30]

****

---

[30] Site of the first American World War 2 atom-bomb attack on Japan in 1945

Probably about 1960, Bruce Wilson, a geologist I used to know (and worked with previously at Reg Sprigg's Geosurveys of Australia in the Mt. Davies area of North-West South Australia), was working on the flat, treeless Nullarbor Plain, South of Mt. Davies, and realised the only large rock in the area, which was known and used by one and all as a high land-mark in the otherwise absolutely flat area, was in fact a large motor-car-sized meteorite, which I believe is now in the South Australian Museum precisely where the Huckitta Meteorite used to stand, and which, I have been told, now bears the name of Bruce Wilson.

****

Later, in 1980/ 81, I was travelling around the country selling my barbecue concept, known and sold as the "CARR-B-Q/ Bush Barbecue", to country and outback shops and stores (see Story 78). I was killing time in Alice Springs while waiting for further long-overdue barbecues to arrive from Melbourne via the Ghan. I was talking to BRUCE CHALMERS, owner of the Stuart Arms Hotel, and he told me he had a Whites 5000 metal detector and said I could borrow it any time.

Well, Alice Springs is in meteorite country. The big BOX HOLE CRATER, a hundred yards wide, was situated about 130 miles North-East on DNEIPER STATION (which Bruce, at that time, happened to own), and tons of large meteoric fragments had been recovered and removed over time.

One day while about to enter his house in the Alice, I recognised a nickel-iron meteorite lying on the ground on the public, gravel footpath. It weighed about half a pound. I had it for years but misplaced it. It was most certainly from Box Hole.

Closer to the Alice, only about 60 miles South, lay the HENBURY METEORITE CRATERS, a cluster of craters up to about 50 yards across. They were more convenient for me to visit at the time. I borrowed the Whites 5000 detector from Bruce and paid a visit to Henbury. One of the first things that caught my attention was a business card lying on the floor of a crater, bearing the name of an internationally known American authority on meteorites on one side and his grocery list on the other, which included "SPAM".[31]

During the course of the night, I collected about a hundred small meteorites, thumb- sized and smaller, and wondered if perhaps larger meteorites could somehow still be lodged in the cracks and crevices either between, or in, some of the large motor-car- sized boulders. After dancing around precariously from rock top to rock top like a ballerina, waving the detector like a fairy's wand, I eventually got a signal from a large crevice about five feet above the ground, looked in sideways and pulled out a fist- sized meteorite, still sitting there at eye level in clear view if anybody had looked; still wedged loosely in place, presumably from the moment of its earth impact tens of thousands of years ago.

When I had been working in the Mt. Davies S.A. and Warburton Ranges W.A. areas, I had actually found a few blackish-green, glassy tektites, originally thought to be meteorites, sitting on terra firma, and traded and/ or swapped them. Now considered "terrestrial" and NOT METEORITES, they are not of much value unless you are collecting them.

****

I have heard that some time later, the government banned the collection of meteorites from known Australian craters, or anywhere else for that matter, but really, they just closed the door after the horse had long since bolted. Australia's meteorites are still for sale overseas on the internet.

Makes you wonder what the fuss was/ is all about?

---

[31] Canned ham

68.
LASSETER'S REEF 1968

I must mention an interesting occurrence in the tribal Warburton Ranges of W.A., which occurred one day in the late 1960s; a day unfortunately when I was away from base.

I was told A 4WD LAND ROVER HAD ARRIVED IN OUR CAMP, about three miles East of the Warburton Aboriginal Mission, WITH AN ARMCHAIR SOMEHOW ROPED TO THE ROOF. SITTING UP "LIKE JACKY" IN THE COMFORTABLE ARMCHAIR

WAS THE SON OF HAROLD BELL LASSETER of Lasseter's gold reef fame, leading a team of financial backers or get rich quick entrepreneurs, looking of course for his father's fabled, already twice found and twice lost "gold reef".

He advised that since his father's original topographical, geographical description had been made and recorded while sitting at an unusual, elevated eye level, maybe 12- feet high, on the back of a belching camel, the present contemporary view from normal motor car level would be quite different.

"True", I thought, but without reference to the fact his father would not have been travelling on the present surveyed and sometimes graded roads now being traversed years later by the younger Lasseter. He would most probably have been tens of miles away in any direction on a topographic plan … if the story were true in any way.

****

In the 1960s I had met and socialised with a few ancient gold miners, still around from the 1920s and '30s, in the "STAR AND GARTER" hotel in Kalgoorlie, by the fabulous "GOLDEN MILE", which has produced well over 150 million ounces of gold and is still producing. These old miners told me a different story. I was told it was common knowledge that Lasseter worked underground as a young man, probably under an assumed name, at one of the rich Kalgoorlie gold mines in the late 1890s, and would have seen very rich specimen gold from time to time passing temptingly under his nose. Whereas most gold mined at Kalgoorlie was fairly fine and hard to see in the ore, or rock, sometimes coarse, lumpy gold was encountered. When such a rich occurrence was found, it was called a "Jeweller's Shop" or an "Aladdin's Cave", with rich gold specimens, rare crystal gold, mustard gold, wire gold, sheet gold, and in particular locations, hard-to-smelt gold tellurides.

Unsurprisingly, from time to time, a fair bit went both East and West. I was told most of the miners and ex-miners either had, or had had in the past, rich gold specimens from their occasional face-to-face confrontation with very rich specimen gold – GOLD HURRIEDLY SHOVED OUT OF SIGHT, ANYWHERE, IN A SOCK, THERMOS FLASK, LUNCH BAG OR CLEFT IN THE SIDE OF THE TUNNEL FOR LATER, DISCREET REMOVAL. It was a common, universal, and unstoppable occurrence.

This then serves to remind me of my own, similar in a way, occurrence as a 12 -year- old boy in Adelaide, South Australia, about 1946.

****

MY PATERNAL ENGLISH GRANDFATHER, JOHN WELCH, had died in 1921, 13 years before my birth. A number of his old collected bits and pieces were still around in a back "junk room", and more in the woodshed on top of the old piano packing case, in company with a brush tailed possum, sleeping daily in an old, black, enamelled cast iron saucepan.

While exploring in the depths of the shed one day, I came across some rocks in an old Treacle tin; a few pieces of copper ore, chunks of silver-lead and a piece of worn alluvial quartz, with a match head-sized piece of gold exposed. A few years later my Uncle Dick was visiting and saw the gold specimen on a shelf in my room and asked where I got it. NOT WISHING TO SAY I HAD FOUND IT IN A TIN BELONGING TO MY LONG-DECEASED GRANDFATHER, HIS FATHER, QUICK AS A FLASH I SAID,

"FROM A WATERHOLE IN DUNSTAN GULLY" on Adelaide's outskirts. And from that time onward I WAS STUCK WITH MY LIE.

To my great surprise, a few weeks later Uncle Dick arrived with my Great Uncle Steve Golding, my Grandmother's 75-plus years old brother-in-law (an old gold miner from Echunga in the Adelaide Hills), on a NEW GOLD HUNTING EXPEDITION. So I then had to scramble my gold hungry uncles about a thousand feet down a steep and slippery billy goat track, through the prickly blackberries to the bottom of Dunstan Gully, and the SECRET, so-called SOURCE OF MY ALLUVIAL GOLD SPECIMEN. They looked around and agreed it LOOKED LIKE GOLD COUNTRY but had never heard of it being found in this gully before. Reassuringly Uncle Steve wisely remarked, "There's always a first time".

****

The point I am making is that about 65 years before my own forgettable event, it is highly probable a young Harold Bell Lasseter, working underground in a Kalgoorlie gold mine, could much earlier have been in a SIMILAR SITUATION to the one in which I had later found myself in my own misguided youth.

If a young HAROLD had been flaunting purloined gold around, as a young man would be prone to do, and was then seen by a person potentially unfriendly to his cause, if asked where the gold came from, he CERTAINLY WOULD NOT, COULD NOT SAY, "FROM THE MINE I WORKED IN", now could he? It is more likely he would have instantly dreamed up his COVERING LIE, "I FOUND IT IN THE BUSH, HUNDREDS OF MILES AWAY, AND ITS POSITION IS MY SECRET!"

And like me, this is the STORY HE WOULD HAVE BEEN STUCK WITH, to repeat parrot fashion, over and over for ever and ever! The end result being he now had to embark on a number of expensive expeditions paid for by greedy entrepreneurs, confidence men and hangers-on, and maintain a flow of promising stories, and more and more excuses for his continued ongoing failure – made up stories to simply justify to various gold hungry delusionists to PUT UP THEIR MONEY to PERPETUATE HIS SMALL AND DECREASING INCOME, and his EVER-EXPANDING LIE.

Common sense tells me that if you, or I, ever found such a virgin, rich gold reef in the easily accessible, wide open Australian bush, even without navigation aids, you, and I, would take great pains to record its geographical location. There is NO WAY YOU WOULD LOSE IT, re-discover it three years later in company with the "bush surveyor Harding", then lose it again, a second time; ABSOLUTELY NO WAY!

****

Harold Bell Lasseter was clearly the dead-end victim of his own self-perpetuated lie. His body was dug up from the floor of a cave near the Petermann Ranges and reburied in the Alice Springs cemetery on December 14th 1957.

> His son's Land Rover, with the armchair on the roof, is now on display in the Transport Museum in "the Alice".

69.
STAN BRIDGMAN 1968

Stan Bridgman was a Western Australian State Government Native Welfare Officer based at Laverton in about the 1955-1980 period. He performed a wide range of duties in an area sparsely populated by mainly Wongai and to a lesser extent Pitjantjatjara semi-civilised, semi-tribal Aborigines in a large amorphous area about 400 miles North to South, and 500 miles West to East, as far East as South Australia's Western border. Stan travelled daily overland by Land Rover, sleeping under the stars among the still stone-age minded natives, handing out rations of tea and sugar, flour, salt, matches and tobacco, sometimes water and other necessary basic items on an irregular basis.[32]

While the Aborigines hunted or gathered food items such as traditional kangaroo, emu, wallaby, possum, goannas (large seven-foot lizards) as well as stone ground grass seed flour, ground between Nardoo Stones, not to mention introduced rabbits, a staple diet at the time, they also received a small regular cash payment. But since they mostly didn't own or wear trousers, they had no pockets in which to keep their loose money, although some wisely kept some money in an old tobacco tin or the like. Nevertheless, they were in occasional receipt of the LEGAL COIN OF THE REALM, such as £2 for a dingo scalp, and were sometimes cashed-up by their standards.

****

Stan was sometimes called on to settle arguments, using white man logic and/or justice, or sometimes stood right in the background, allowing the combatants to settle their differences the time-honoured

---

[32] From a colonial viewpoint

way by being speared right through the thigh with their oiled, heat-hardened, mulga wood barbed spears, which sometimes allowed the odd not so happy recipient to bleed to death, or slowly die in agony later from infection.

If invited, Stan sometimes attended traditional circumcision ceremonies, as I did twice. Youths about 14 or 15 had their foreskins stretched tightly forward beyond the end of the glans penis by the circumciser's fingers. A freshly-flaked, razor-sharp agate or chalcedony blade then severed the stretched foreskin in the fashion of a surgeon's scalpel. I noticed some of these youths were almost Scandinavian in complexion after their unpleasant ordeal, yet I never once saw a single sign of pain. After sitting in for a circumcision in the Warburton Ranges about 1967, I carried a few loose, sharp chalcedony flakes around in my pocket for a couple of days as souvenirs before I discovered my own thighs had been painlessly lacerated. My legs were bleeding, my own trouser pockets were now empty and my beer money had gone, so it was then I discontinued the new habit.

****

In their daily wanderings, the hunting natives' keen, observant eyesight enabled them to see and find many things apart from game. They identified valuable sandalwood trees for later on, sugar ants and their honey, edible underground yam-like roots, small damp water holding crevices and pools, long, straight surface-exposed roots for spear making, grass trees for glue and conspicuous ground surface-strewn items such as tektites and gold specks, or large heavy nuggets weighing many ounces, usually called "SLUGS" in Western Australia.

Occasionally the Wongai did collect GENUINE METEORITES from the ground, usually the nickel-iron type, which because of their weight stood out exactly like a sore thumb. As for gold, Government of the U.S.A. had frozen the price at U.S.$34 an ounce in about 1934, coincidentally the year of my birth, and gold was no longer such a valuable, high-priced metal. Nevertheless, when just picked up off the ground, it had considerable value to the lucky finder, and Aborigines found a great deal in the W.A. bush but had very few outlets or opportunities in which to sell it.

****

Stan Bridgman was in the right place at the right time. He was not overpaid by the government and managed to subsidise his income by any fortuitous means that came his way; he bought gold cheaply from the Aborigines whenever it was offered.

****

When I was employed by Reg Sprigg's Geosurveys of Australia, in 1955, while operating over the state border in the Bell Rock or Blackstone Ranges area of W.A., I do remember seeing the name S. Bridgman scratched in the overhanging rock face of various caves and thought no more of it. Then, in about 1966, while with the Western Mining Corporation (W.M.C.) in the Warburton Ranges about halfway between Kalgoorlie W.A. and Alice Springs in the N.T., we received a visit in our base camp from Stan Bridgman, which was when I eventually made his acquaintance.

A year or two later when passing the small town of Laverton, I called at Stan's house and luckily found him home. When he made me a cup of tea and produced some very nice fresh scones and cream it made my day. I told Stan of the recent visit to the Warburton Ranges by the son of Harold Bell Lasseter of LOST GOLD REEF fame, and our conversation turned to the still lowly-priced, special metal GOLD. This was when Stan excused himself for a minute and returned with a NOMINAL ONE-POUND WEIGHT GOLDEN SYRUP CAN and placed it on the table. The over-full can contained gold nuggets, some weighing tens of ounces, heaped an inch or two higher than the rim of the can. IT WOULD HAVE WEIGHED ABOUT 40 POUNDS, OR ABOUT 640 OUNCES OF GOLD, which at this time of writing (2013) was selling at U.S. $1775 an ounce, making the contents of the can WORTH MORE THAN U.S. $1,000,000.

This of course is the price of the gold metal itself. The specimen value of the smaller minus-10-ounce nuggets would add at least another 25 percent to the contained gold metal value. But this story relates back to 1966, or thereabouts, and the price was still U.S. $42 U.S. an ounce, and the future, sadly, was not at that time ours to see. So, as well as giving me afternoon tea, Stan grabbed a very small nugget from the tin and gave it to me as a souvenir. To me it was a generous gift. It weighed a little less than half an ounce, WORTH ABOUT $20 THEN, OR ABOUT $885 NOW (2021).

I never saw Stan again as I was in Africa and operating my own gold operation, but later, about 1977 after Mr. Mugabe's takeover of Rhodesia, I once again found myself back in Kalgoorlie, where I learned Stan's "HIDDEN NEST-EGG", +/- 640-ounce tin of gold, had quietly DISAPPEARED FROM BENEATH HIS BED while he trustingly left it always unguarded and the house open.

In light of the new gold price, if Stan was still alive today, memories of this very sad affair would undoubtedly break his heart!

70.
DISSUASION 1968

About 1966 I was working for the Western Mining Corporation in the Warburton Ranges, W.A., in an Aboriginal reserve about 600 miles North-East of the 100 plus years old gold mining town of Kalgoorlie, W.A., or 400 miles West-South-West of Alice Springs in the N.T. Ours was a mining exploration camp; a small collection of air- conditioned caravans, a laboratory, Toyota 4WDs, motorbikes, a truck or two, and a Bell helicopter and pilot, usually based on site. It was a camp of about 20 men – geologists, draftsmen, drillers, mechanics, samplers – looking at a number of small outcropping copper occurrences while mapping and looking for possible mineral extensions to the small, valuable ore bodies so far defined. We had on site a lockable shed, about 30 feet x 10 feet, used as our store, which held our various supplies of food, hardware, beer and the like, replenished by our monthly supply truck coming up the dirt track 600 miles from Kalgoorlie.

As a condition of our restricted entry into these Aboriginal lands, we employed maybe a dozen local Aborigines as casual labour, and all was well for a time. One morning, however, we were surprised to discover that OUR ABORIGINAL HELPERS HAD DESERTED US. Not a local man could be seen. It was a mystery until it was discovered that the galvanised iron cladding had been removed from the back of the shed and our beer supply, about 20 cartons, had "vanished overnight". That morning, one of the usual local suspects appeared, barely able to stand, let alone talk. He innocently asked, incoherently, what we would like him to do. I forget our answer …

The result – a full day intoxicated holiday for the locals and ZILCH for W.M.C.! However, we had a few lengths of 6-x-4-inch steel arc-mesh lying about, and I decided to learn how to weld to make a large, lockable enclosure to house our next beer supply, and padlock the beer cartons securely in the repaired shed when they next arrived. Mission completed, we waited for the truck from "Kal".[33] It was delayed a couple more days and was a delight to see when it finally arrived. We then unloaded the very important beer straight into the newly constructed, weldmesh cage and padlocked it after first side tracking and refrigerating our immediate needs. We then clasped two strong Chubb padlocks together and retired to the mess for an eagerly awaited, long overdue, cold beer.

We slept soundly that night, as did the busy Indigenous locals after they had once again broken into the shed, and, threading their supple arms easily through the weldmesh, proceeded to cut up and dismantle the newly-arrived beer cartons, dextrously, one by one, while still enclosed inside the weld-mesh cage. They then DISAPPEARED WITH OUR CANS OF BEER, ONE BY ONE, OVER THE BLACK HORIZON AFTER MIDNIGHT, with most of our remaining beer supplies tucked illegally under their arms.

This was a serious event: THE FINAL STRAW!

It called for serious action on our part if we wanted to secure the ongoing future safety of our limited monthly beer supply. We badly needed an audible warning system of some sort to safeguard our beer, and I had a bright idea. I took a SINGLE STICK OF SEISMIC GELIGNITE from the explosives' magazine, inserted an electric detonator in the softish material and an electric firing wire into the detonator, added a few turns of string to hold it together, and HUNG IT VISIBLY AS A DETERRENT from the upper branches of a mulga tree, about 20 feet high and 10 feet from the shed. I then connected the wires to a Heath Robinson type circuit breaker, intricately made from delicate no. 8 agricultural fencing wire.

---

[33] Colloquial term for "Kalgoorlie"

Then came the final sticky, tricky part ... safely joining the wires to a 12-volt car battery while at the same time doing nothing stupid and not touching the delicate hair trigger mechanism I had just cleverly constructed from fencing wire. It was now JUST A SIMPLE MATTER OF CONNECTING THE WIRES TO THE BATTERY TERMINALS

TO MAKE THE APPARATUS IDIOT PROOF, when the system would effectively be up and running, with all systems ready, live and set to go. I was securely fitting the clearly red coloured wire to the positive terminal, to be followed by the negative, when MY ELBOW ACCIDENTLY BRUSHED THE INTRICATE CLOCKWORK-LIKE APPARATUS.

KA,BLAM

"Bloody hell!"

The gelignite exploded in the mulga tree just 25 short feet away, thankfully on the outside of the shed. My plans were thwarted. I had obviously stuffed-up. Things had obviously NOT GONE QUITE ACCORDING TO PLAN, and had momentarily frightened the ++++ out of me!

I was of course deeply embarrassed, and momentarily stumped for words. Needless to say, however, the basic idea had worked well, though a little prematurely. We now had a common talking point. The healthy explosion was heard three miles away by the heavenly fathers at the Warburton Mission. It was effective. IT DREW THE INTENDED ATTENTION TO ITSELF, AND THEREFORE UNCONSCIOUSLY, ONE WAY OR THE OTHER, ACHIEVED ITS INTENDED PURPOSE!

A couple of hours later we had a visit from a few of the Pitjantjatjara and Wongai tribal grey-beards, wearing their red tribal headbands, who were concerned their young men would be killed by our audible, visible, explosive devices when next they came to steal our beer. We pointed out that if their young men did not come to steal our beer, they could not possibly be hurt in any way. The grey-beards then reiterated the young men would, sooner or later, be back, and that was their ongoing, ever-ready stated threat and perpetual worry!

The good news is we had no further beer theft.

OUR AUDIBLE DISSUASION DEVICE HAD PROVED ITSELF, IN THE END, QUITE CLEARLY, LOUDLY EFFECTIVE.

71.
TASMANIAN BUSH 1977

We left Victoria's Moorabbin Airport in a Cessna light aircraft and flew south over Port Phillip Bay, Geelong and across the 140-mile-wide "Roaring Forties" latitude of the Bass Strait, down along the West coast of Tasmania, and landed unofficially on a narrow ocean beach West of the old copper/ gold mining town of Zeehan.

I was, at this time in 1977, the newly appointed manager of Mindrill Limited's Western Australian branch in the old gold mining town of Kalgoorlie, in the Eastern Goldfields. Things had changed at "Kal". Nickel was booming, gold was stagnating and diamond drilling was re-emerging as the industrial flavour of the month.

Associated Diamond Drillers (A.D.D.), Mindrill's sister company, were just about to start DIAMOND DRILLING FOR TIN IN A VERY REMOTE, DIFFICULT-TO-ACCESS CORNER OF TASMANIA on the wet West coast, North of the Pieman River and South of the Savage River. It was felt my presence, and the extra experience gained as a hands-on driller and observer while on loan from Mindrill for a few short weeks, would be invaluable to me as the forthcoming manager at Kalgoorlie.

We had landed on the beach to deliver some diamond drill bits to some of our isolated A.D.D. drillers working in the dense terrain not far from Zeehan, which was separated from the actual coastal bush by heavy swamp. We had then flown all of 10 short minutes to the official town airstrip at Zeehan.

I remained in Zeehan for a few days while the drillers dismantled a Mindrill drill rig to manageable bite-sized pieces and loaded fuel drums, drill rods, provisions and tents painstakingly into quarter ton "slings" for about 40 helicopter flights into our drill site in virgin Tasmanian forest.

I was about the last person in to the one-acre drill site, a felled clearing among very tall swamp gums, or mountain ash, of which a few would have been approaching 300 feet in height, and two large Huon pines, one of which was in our way and had been felled, the other luckily still standing proud and tall. I'm told the highly valuable, slow-growing Huon pine can lie on the floor of a forest for many, many years and still produce perfect cabinet making and boat building timber when finally milled. I just hope I can remember the actual ground relocation co-ordinates!

****

There were about a dozen of us in the party. We slept in tents with an extra fly, not for the heat but a little extra protection from the rain. The cook earned my displeasure by clubbing a nuisance Tasmanian Devil to death for frequently raiding our garbage bin.

It was summer, the days were warm, the place was wet, and we were in the midst of thousands of frogs of all shapes and sizes, high up in the trees, underfoot, and under every ground-based supply box, bag of potatoes or private bed. Giant earthworms, some over five-feet long and as thick as my little finger, were also everywhere as they came up for air in the mostly almost-drowned terrain. On top of that, in several weeks we probably killed about 30 smallish TIGER SNAKES up to three feet long within 20 yards of our camp, OBVIOUSLY DRAWN TO OUR CAMP BY OUR INFECTIOUS

PERSONALITY AND AN ENDLESS SUPPLY OF FROGS. Luckily, we didn't have to resort to our snake-bite antivenin medicine. There were several small tannin-stained, running, permanent-type streams in the nearby forest and sardine-sized galaxias, or whitebait fish, were present in quite large numbers. When the whitebait were absent, we invariably noticed a good-sized brown trout in the immediate vicinity. I was told the giant Tasmanian freshwater lobster, weighing up to 2 or 3 pounds, was also in the general area but I was not lucky enough to see one.

****

The interesting part of the HELICOPTER-BORNE EXERCISE was in getting the reassembled drill rig, now mounted on large metal skids, from the landing assembly point into the soggy, rotting floor of the forest under "its own steam". This was achieved by using the drill's own engine, its gearbox and winch to gradually pull itself, stop-start, into the dark forest of standing giants and fallen memories, decaying timbers, multi-coloured toadstools and rotting wood. This was a very slow, tedious and sometimes hazardous process.

In the first instance, the strongest member of our party took the end of the steel winch cable and scrambled into the forest over the fallen logs of all shapes and sizes, frequently resorting to the chain saw, while pulling the cable and unrolling it from its heavy drum, sometimes climbing over occasional fallen tree trunks, a couple up to 12 feet in diameter. When the drill cable had been pulled out 100 yards, the distant end was shackled to a tree or trees and the drill winch then employed to pull itself on its large metal skid, powerfully and slowly, INCH-BY-INCH, FOOT-BY-FOOT, DEEP INTO THE FOREST. It took a whole day to get the skid-mounted diamond drill into its first drill site position just a couple of hundred yards into the forest. The ground was mostly soft and swampy. LEACHES WERE HERE AND THERE AND EVERYWHERE, DROPPING INVITINGLY, DELIBERATELY ONTO OUR RED-BLOODED BODIES, or brushing off on us from the wet undergrowth as we unwittingly played an important, vital part of their life cycle reproductive process.

I found myself in trouble, as the best way to make a leech see daylight and let go was to tickle its bum with a lighted cigarette, and draw in. Unfortunately, I didn't, and still don't smoke, so I was frequently in need of the friendly "smokers" in our midst, as I TEMPORARILY ENCOURAGED SMOKING!

Getting our other drilling equipment into the bush was as painstaking as unrolling the drill's cable in the first instance. Wheeled devices were out of the question. Drill rods, 12-gallon drums of diesel and core barrels were all carried into the wet, rough terrain by "Shank's pony", and/ or on the back of our old Spanish mate "MANUEL LABOUR".

****

We were drilling for reef tin in very old shallow alluvial workings, last worked nearly 100 years ago. I found an old Cornish-type green, heavily mildewed, WOODEN WHEELBARROW, still intact and standing, 100 yards into the dark forest. I JUST TOUCHED IT AND IT SIMPLY COLLAPSED IN A HEAP OF AMORPHOUS ROT.

About three weeks went by quickly, and with our drilling program complete, I was helicoptered out of the forest to Zeehan, took a light piston-engined aircraft to Hobart, a jet to Melbourne, had an overnight stay, then a jet to Perth and finally a jet back to Kalgoorlie and my new Mindrill position, all accomplished in under 48 hours.

72.
ECHIDNA VENGEANCE 1978

It was about 10:00 p.m. one night in 1978. I was driving a Holden Kingswood station wagon from Kalgoorlie, Western Australia, to Melbourne, Victoria. It was my third long day at the wheel and I guess I was a little tired. I was approaching the town of Stawell in Western Victoria. Too late to avoid it, I saw a solid looking "SOMETHING" moving on the road. I hit it hard, braked, brought the car to a halt 50 yards further on and walked back with a torch to investigate and see what I had run over.

It was an unlucky Australian ant-eating, pouched, egg-laying ECHIDNA – a solid mammal – a 10-pound bundle of TOUGH SIX-INCH HOLLOW SPIKES and MUSCLE. The echidna was mercifully dead, with no external signs of injury, and I thought a university in Melbourne may like the body for science, so I wrapped it in an old towel and placed it in the back of the station wagon.

Approaching Ballarat about midnight, I was getting tired and decided to stop at a motel if I found one open. Luckily, five minutes later, I was being signed into a very nice, landscaped-garden motel.

In the meantime, the strong, natural odour of the echidna had permeated the interior of the wagon and I certainly could not leave it in the car overnight; the car would most certainly stink to high heaven come morning. So I REMOVED THE DEAD ECHIDNA FROM THE BACK OF THE WAGON AND PLACED IT GENTLY ON THE LAWN BY

THE FISHPOND. But for some innate reason, without thinking, I COULDN'T STOP MYSELF FROM POSING IT, comfortably spread-eagled, in a more natural, lifelike fashion before innocently going to bed, where I slept like a log until woken up about 7:00 a.m. by voices outside my window.

An old man and an elderly lady were standing by the deceased echidna. He looked like a World War 1 veteran and she reminded me of the Victorian-era Daisy Bates. He had an expensive silver-handled, gnarled walking stick, and was still a fine upstanding figure of a man in the twilight of his life. While I secretly looked on, he prodded the SPIKY, EXPIRED ECHIDNA ever so gently with his rubber-tip of his walking stick several times, and I heard him say to his lady:

"THEY HIBERNATE YOU KNOW".

Realising he was greatly mistaken, I didn't want to spoil the present, enjoyable-for- me, illusion. I just said nothing and drove off with maybe a slight smile on my lips.

The next morning in Melbourne, I found two steel radial tyres of the station wagon were completely flat. The tyre repair people found a number of not-quite-penetrated, sharp, tough, hollow, broken ECHIDNA QUILLS, still hiding, threateningly embedded in the tyres …

LATENT AND READY FOR ANOTHER ROUND OF PAYBACK ECHIDNA VENGEANCE.

73.
THE SUNSHINE KID 1981

It would have been 1981, the year after I had won the "WHAT'LL THEY THINK OF NEXT" inventors show on Channel 9 T.V. for MY BUSH CAMPFIRE, SOLID- FUELLED BARBECUE APPARATUS.

I was in Darwin waiting anxiously for a further 100 "CARR-B-Q" barbecues to arrive to further my tenuous selling activities. Tenuous because I had more-or-less painted myself into a corner, caused by a chronic shortage of cash, caused by the tyranny of time and distance, and not much wholesaling experience.

The good part was CARR-B-Qs were easy to sell to the retailers but being forever short of working capital, I was leading a hand-to-mouth existence. I would sell 100, then snail mail funds to my Melbourne-based manufacturers, on receipt of which they would rail 100 more CARR-B-Qs to me in Darwin. That is 1,500 miles over 3 different rail gauges by rail via Adelaide to Alice Springs, plus road freight a further 1,000 miles on to Darwin, which took about a month per batch. The trouble was I had started my new venture on the smell of an oily rag, I was grossly under resourced and it was too late to back out. I was stuck fast solidly between a rock and a hard place. Whereas I had initially stayed at motels, I now found myself sleeping anywhere I could at the cheaper end of the bed market, and on the day in question I was domiciled at the Y.W.C.A. hostel in Darwin.

I was surprised when the hostel manager informed me he had a phone call waiting for me from someone in Sydney, N.S.W. It was my old mate Ian Murray who, having heard I was up in Darwin, had asked his secretary to phone the hotels and other providers of accommodation in an attempt to track me down. Well, he succeeded!

****

"Carr you bastard, what the hell are you doing in Darwin? NO, don't tell me. I'll be arriving tonight. Book us both into a good hotel, meet me at the airport at 7".

Well, I had been doing precisely nothing except waiting for CARR-B-Qs to arrive and time was on my hands.

IAN MURRAY, in earlier days as an Engineering student, had obtained a degree at the Adelaide University which had unerringly set him on an opposite and unrelated equine path straight into the ups and downs of horse racing, the undoubted sport of kings.

Ian managed somehow to repeatedly outwit the bookies at their own game and was grudgingly Knighted by them "THE SUNSHINE KID". By his successful betting forays at the racetrack as the RED HOT MASTER PUNTER, Ian became a real and pressing thorn in their collective iron-sided backsides. A leading rails bookmaker at the time is on record as having written to the Sunshine Kid imploring him to "please bet with the other more needy bookies and NOT ME" owing to his parlous financial state and his dicky heart.

Ian is on record as winning more than $1,000,000 as a punter from the unhappy bookies in a few short months in the seventies. His photo appeared on the front cover of the weekly magazine "THE BULLETIN", emblazoning an article entitled something like "THE MAN WHO'S KILLING THE BOOKIES".

****

At another moment in time, Ian had travelled to England for a change of scenery and reappeared back in Sydney a year later as Jim Slater's right-hand man to set up Slater Walker Securities Australian Merchant Banking Operation. Ian was a shrewd and clever operator in the cutthroat world of finance as well as being accepted as an established Merchant Banker.

****

Anyway, back in Darwin we hired an aluminium dinghy with an outboard motor, lashed it upside down on the roof of my Toyota Hi-Lux 4WD, drove 300 miles South-West to the Victoria River and unsuccessfully tried our hand at fishing for giant barramundi in the murky, crocodile-infested river. We didn't see a single crocodile though they without a doubt saw us. We also saw a number of their well-used slides or launching pads leading to the deep water's edge. On one occasion we were startled by a sudden large belch of underwater bubbles a couple of yards from our present position, which told us unerringly we were not alone. The crocs were obviously busy, probably gobbling up the very last barramundi. Empty handed, we drove back to Darwin.

****

That night we dressed informally for the casino. While Ian settled down for a little action on the roulette wheel, I looked over his shoulder to hopefully improve my sadly lacking gambling know-how.

After a few fruitless ups and downs, Ian's situation changed for the better as he settled on a profitable one-track path involving the suit of Diamonds. He deliberately left his money on Diamonds all alone and unassisted for about 9 throws of the dice while the money just rolled in. With not a penny of my own on the table, I was close to gnawing my fingers to the bone and wondered hopefully when Ian would call it a day. Then came relief as Ian simply said, "We'd better collect". With pockets bulging and hands full, we took Ian's chips to the cashier and in return received a couple of reinforced paper bags about the size of two shoe boxes full of $50 notes; ABOUT $40,000 AUD FOR IAN'S READY-TO-RECEIVE COFFERS.

That night we left the money rolled up in the centre of my swag (bedding roll), safely under lock and key in the padlocked rear compartment of my Toyota Hi-Lux. We checked out of our expensive hotel in the morning and looked for my Hi-Lux in the street but couldn't find it where we thought I had left it. Panic stations!

First logical move, see the Police, where I was politely asked whether the vehicle was perhaps under a hire purchase contract and if so, perhaps I should contact the finance company concerned. This was when the penny dropped. The Hi-Lux was under an arrangement with Custom Credit and yes, I was in arrears. I was battling to make a living in Darwin on the Top Side of Down Under sinking deeper and deeper into the SHIT while my mail, including final notices, was being delivered to my vacant Tasmanian address on the underside of Australia.

Fortunately for me, Ian knew the current head of Custom Credit in Sydney. The only real obstacle stubbornly in the way was that the only immediate money theoretically at Ian's disposal was already, although unknown to them, in the hands of Custom Credit. All monies owed plus a lot more were concealed in the back of the secured rear of the Hi-Lux. First we would need access to the vehicle itself simply to get at Ian's missing LOOT! It was still secured, we hoped, in the back of the still missing Hi-Lux impounded out of sight in a holding complex somewhere in Darwin.

A rather STRANGE AND UNUSUAL SITUATION WHICH, IN THE END, WAS SEEN AS EASILY SURMOUNTABLE in view of the pot of gold at the end of the rainbow, a thankful Custom Credit Corporation and ME!

****

THANKS IAN.

****

Ian Murray in front of a Boab tree at Timber Creek, on the Victoria River, Northern Territory 1981

Ian burning rubbish in his garden at Mittagong about 2005

74.
THE SAME QUESTION 1981

When I was living in Rhodesia and operating my Down-Under Mining Company, the Rhodesian Mines Department inspector who used to visit me was Peter Garland. He would occasionally come out to the INGUBO MINE I was attempting to re-open while the price of gold remained at U.S. $34 an ounce. It was an uphill battle. Rhodesia had painted itself into a corner and was ostracised by the outside world. Petrol was rationed while mining machinery was hard to get and expensive. And behind the scenes a certain Mr Robert Mugabe and his African henchmen were trying to take over the country by terror and/ or military means. In the end, I could not make ends meet. A number of my friends and associates had been butchered by the Mugabe gang and it was time to go.

****

Safely ensconced back home in Australia, I had been employed in managerial positions by Mindrill, who manufactured diamond drill "CORING BITS" and equipment. As manager of their Western Australian operations I was based in Kalgoorlie. Later, I was employed as manager of Ingersol-Rand in Hobart, Tasmania, from where I had won the "Inventors" program on T.V. in June 1980 for my CARR-B-Q. I then resigned from Ingersol-Rand and started making and selling my barbecues, and travelled over most of Australia wholesaling them to retail stores.

When in central Australia, in Todd Street, Alice Springs, I entered a general goods retailer and, speaking to the lady behind the counter, couldn't help but notice her South African type accent. She told me she was from Zimbabwe, Mr Mugabe's new name for the now African-controlled former Rhodesia. "Whereabouts?" I asked, and she said "Bulawayo", which is when I told her I had also been in "Byo" for five years until three years ago. She said her husband had been in the Mines Department as an inspector. I then told her I had operated the still exploratory INGUBO GOLD MINE in the Umzingwane tribal trust lands until events forced me out. "What's his name?" I asked. "Peter Garland", she said. "He's now a Northern Territory Mines Department inspector here in the Alice. He'll be here in 5 minutes. Stay and have a cuppa!".[34]

A minute later Peter walked in the door, looked at me with a very, very surprised look, as though he'd seen a ghost, and said, "What the hell are you doing here?"

I looked at Peter and said to him,

> "I WAS GOING TO ASK YOU THE SAME QUESTION!"

---

[34] Cup of tea

75.
THE MUTT (circa 2000)

About the year 2000 I was having a drink with Ian Murray, the "Sunshine Kid", in a hotel in Bowral, N.S.W. This is the town where the cricket legend Sir Donald Bradman had grown up in the late 1920s.

While having a beer at the bar, Ian had put his finger randomly on a list of racehorses warming up, ready to go, and racing somewhere in a minute or two. Without a moment's thought Ian spontaneously backed a horse of unknown background, breeding or form on the pub's T.A.B.[35] to the tune of $20 as a light-hearted speculation. Moments later after Ian put his rose-tinted glasses on and looked further afield, in this case backwards to the previous pages of the betting form guide, he realised with a rude shock HE HAD ACTUALLY BACKED A HOUND IN A DOG RACE BY MISTAKE.

This sort of stuff-up was totally foreign to Ian! There is no way Ian would ever be seen betting on tadpoles, greyhounds, dogs or bitches, and he asked the barmaid to cancel the bet.

"Too late", she said, "they're racing!"

> THE "MUTT" WON AT ABOUT 30 to 1!!!

---

[35] TAB is the Totalisator Agency Board. Organized betting system in Australia

76.
VAN DE MERWE 2010

When I lived in the Republic of South Africa (RSA) from 1969 to 1972, the humour of the day, as often as not, revolved around a FICTITIOUS CHARACTER BY THE NAME OF VAN DE MERWE. The name was a very old and very common Afrikaans surname, about as popular as Smith is in the English tongue. Van De Merwe could be anyone; a NIECE, a GRANDFATHER, a PRIEST, a LAYABOUT. He/ she appeared in every guise known to South African man.

I left the RSA in '72 and have not been back. Thirty-eight years later, on New Year's Eve 2010, I was buying petrol at a garage in Coonabarabran, northern N.S.W., Australia when a 4WD with South Australian number plates pulled up behind my car. The driver and I came face to face at the petrol pump and me, being an ex-South Australian, asked where he was from. "I'm from Adelaide", he said in a HEAVY AFRIKAANS ACCENT which I was quite surprised to hear after many, many years. And so, to get his undivided attention, I simply said "Voetsak!", the common expletive of my earlier impressionable years in the RSA, which means more or less "PISS OFF",[36] or worse, to which he instantly asked how I knew the everyday expression of his homeland.

I explained I had lived in Johannesburg for about three and a half years, during which time I had sold new cars, including Lotus Sports Cars and Alfa Romeos, but the real money had been in Toyotas; and he was driving one. He said he was just returning to Adelaide in a roundabout way via Sydney, as he had just crossed the Simpson Desert in his 4WD. I was a little surprised to hear this and I told him I

---

[36] Go away! Get lost!

had been working for the French Petroleum Company between 1962-1964 when we actually constructed the track he had just passed over – about 360 miles and 400+- fixed red sand dunes, which got higher and further apart as we went East. And I had subsequently been on site when we rotary drilled three deep exploratory oil investigation wells, two of them alongside the French Line, leaving the Purni hole as a water bore, running free, but it has since stopped and been capped.

Then we shook hands and he said:

"BY THE WAY, MY NAME IS VAN DE MERWE".

****

AND SO ENDS MY TELLING OF MY FAILED TIMES AND TWISTED FOLLIES IN 'OZ'

Me with my painting of OZ

77.
WHIMSICAL: A POEM OF SORTS FOR DREAMERS 2010

Did you ever gaze and wonder on a starlit starry night, at distant blazing crystal stars, at stellar chandeliers?

Have you ever once imagined, in the twinkle of an eye, did your wildest fancy lead you, light years to the stars?

Tell me, if and when you went there, did you dance a dance fantastic, a lunar dance, a solar dance, a stellar dance galactic?

A madcap fling in outer space, and did you see a "HORSE'S HEAD", a silhouette against a cloud, a nebulae at large?

And did you see the Zodiac, its signs are all about, did you meet those Gods of old? Tell now if you did.

And tell me now those Gods of old, if indeed you met them, are they wiser now than then; with hindsight is there wisdom?

Are things today just as before, do changes follow changes, do you believe we're standing still, is the universe expansive?

And if you in your fancy roam those starry skies, do you see strange satellites, orbiting their stars?

Are you captivated by events so far away, do you dream occasionally, of giant rocks of Asteroids, scattered in the sky?

Do you find yourself a'wishing you could really see a black hole's inner secrets, its secrets from inside?

Did you "crack a whip" in vacuum space, yet never hear a sound? Or pull the cork on starlit wine and toast in space your maker?

Did you ever catch a Comet, did you ride astride its head, and leave a tail of scattered light, a million miles behind?

Are your inner thoughts, your private thoughts, beyond our outer reaches? Did your X-ray mind, your probing mind, see an X-ray source beyond it?

Were your radar ears in any way, tested to their limit, were solar flares, odd Quarks and Quirks, by any means detected?

Did your pioneering orbit ever lead you by the nose? Did your closest circuit take you, past inner solar planets?

Past Venus dead before our time, a shrouded sphere of searing gas, beyond its secret hidden past, Kaput and gone before us.

Did you flash through space at light-speed plus, while in your fleeting fancy, through space it seems without an end, unbounded by restriction?

Did you catch a glimpse yet brief in time, of vastly different stars and things, specks in space so far apart, but thin and random scattered?

And speeding on without a pause, while in your fleeting fancy, pursuing light at breakneck speed, with light-speed as your measure.

Do you believe at sub-light speed, we're ever going to get there, should Earthly Gods, and Cosmic Gods, unite in space join forces?

For do you believe in a moment of time, while travelling every direction, criss-crossing space everywhere at once, in a mini micro-second?

To Galaxies far beyond our scope, outside our local region, could we hope to count those teeming lights? They're numbered by the Trillion.

For common-sense itself demands, in a frigid frozen instant, you'll all but miss those far-flung stars, each lonely star to eternity.

A scent of life occasionally, distant planets here and there, lonely planets far apart, yet numbered by the Zillion.

No doubt you'll find on planets far, waterfalls and rivers, sunsets vivid, coloured skies, thunderclouds and rainbows.

A shipwrecked sailor cast ashore, another planet's ocean, praying to the God he knows, his God at last may find him.

For its plain you'll see in different parts, planets now existing, with life in strange and different forms, beyond our comprehension.

Yet here and there it's nice to know, exists our mirror image, on par with us no doubt at all, with a plus maybe or minus.

They do their thing, they live and die; they love and kill each other, their muscle men they muscle on, it's war and peace eternal.

Foreign wars in outer space, in normal Earthly cycles, for history repeats itself, no matter where it's standing.

So life goes on in different realms, at different rates of progress, some behind and some ahead, and some the same around us.

Failed Times and Twisted Follies

A finely balanced bark canoe, a thinker on a mountain top, a ROBOT flying STARSHIP ONE, and Dragons far below us.

Yet if you propose to visit some time, beyond our Solar System, pause a while, re- think your cause, re-plan your destination.

For if, in spite of warnings free, you still decide to go, you'd better leave now at the speed of Light and cancel Light's resistance.

For it's plain to see you first must solve, one or two minor problems; to simply equal the speed of Light, you'll have to get a move on.

Twenty-five thousand times as fast as present rockets travel, to reach that planet of your dreams, within your generation.

And furthermore, to visit or phone, your cousin in Andro'meda, it'll take some time to get results, you'll need a lot of patience.

FOUR MILLION YEARS or thereabouts, at the speed of Light to have a talk; plus three minutes of course for a metered call, for a two-way conversation.

A telephone call without a doubt, no man could ever pay for, including you my Earthly friend, if it's charged at first by metered time.

With costs imposed for passing by, by countless generations, or like a length of endless string, simply by the distance.

Since time is brief you do not have, within your mortal span, time on Earth to make mistakes, a second chance you'll never get if you dial your number out of turn.

For out of turn is ETERNITY, should you select unwittingly, an OUTER SPACE WRONG NUMBER.

78.
THE "CARR-B-Q" BUSH BARBECUE APPARATUS: BACKGROUND OF THE ALMOST ENDED STORY

For persons interested in a long lasting, all stainless steel, outback, wood-fuelled campfire cooking apparatus for use "way beyond the Black Stump".

This is the whole unfolded story of the "CARR-B-Q" as it slowly materialised in Australia and Africa in intermittent spurts over a longish 21-year period.

****

About 1958, my friend Neville Thomas, an old Prince Alfred College pupil, showed me a simple "NATTY barbecue grill cooking device" he had purchased new from Sven Kallins, general outdoor retailers and "Vincent" brand motorcycle distributors in South Australia. The NATTY B.B.Q.[37] became the starting point of the germ of an idea behind the eventual CARR-B-Q design as it subconsciously evolved.

The NATTY B.B.Q. model consisted of five parts, the largest being a 30-inch long, pointed at one end, half-inch diameter galvanised mild steel ROD, which was driven into the earth with the back of a hammer or tomahawk and used as THE MAIN VERTICAL, LOAD-CARRYING COMPONENT. During cooking, the round horizontal grill could easily be rotated in the horizontal plane for more even cooking, while at the same time the whole food-laden horizontal arm, with its wire grill,

---
[37] Slang Australian term for "barbecue"

could be swung 180 degrees away from the central vertical rod for USER FINGER COMFORT AWAY FROM THE FIRE and into the cool, ambient air. This B.B.Q. was, and still is, OK in theory, but using it showed it had a number of PROBLEMS STILL OUTSTANDING. At the time, I thought it was acceptable.

****

In 1979 I sailed from Port Melbourne on the R.M.S. ORONSAY to England. John and Jenny Engel (S.P.S.C.) saw me off at the pier and away I went overnight to Adelaide, then a day bus tour of the Barossa Valley, Seppeltsfield wine tasting and the Seppelts family mausoleum, then on, as the paper streamers unrolled at the Port Adelaide pier, into the Great Australian Bight.

Crossing the Indian Ocean shortly after leaving Perth, a STOWAWAY was discovered on board. Unluckily for the freeloader, we were due to encounter a "sister" ship, the ORSOVA, the same day, which was returning to Perth back the way we had come.

We halted mid-ocean to transfer the culprit to the ORSOVA. With the sea like a mill pond, the two 28,000-ton liners hove to, 1,000 yards apart, while the crew practiced lifeboat drill using a big, motor-driven lifeboat to convey the unhappy stowaway back to Perth.

About this time I fell into conversation with TERRY ALDERTON and his wife from Melbourne, who were travelling to South Africa to join Terry's brother Danny at Alderton Motors, the Lotus Sports car distributors for Southern Africa. They were also metropolitan Alfa Romeo, Renault and Toyota dealers, operating at Craighall Park, Blairgowrie and Randburg in affluent-at-the-time Johannesburg. Terry had the feeling I might make a useful car salesman for his brother's new car business and assured me that if I changed my plans and disembarked at Durban, a job would be waiting for me in Johannesburg, 300 miles inland. So I disembarked in South Africa and after a couple of days in humid Durban, thought, "Why-not check out the sincerity of the offer?" I made my way inland, past large Aussie blue gum trees, much of the way North-West to Johannesburg. I had always thought Jo'burg was in dry, desert surroundings because of the great sand dunes endlessly perpetuated in the South African travel brochures. But it was obvious that I, and countless others, had been misled. They were not desert sand dunes, JUST GREAT WINDBLOWN, SANDY MINE DUMPS, and JO'BURG WAS CERTAINLY NOT IN A DESERT.

Arriving in Jo'burg, Danny gave me a job at his Alderton Motors, a BRAND NEW ALFA ROMEO SUPER, and the keys to an apartment at the SUMMIT CLUB in HILLBROW near the C.B.D.[38] until I could make my own accommodation arrangements.

It later appeared Danny had enticed a number of wealthy South African backers to invest in "HIS" Alderton motors, and things were not as good as they seemed. I had only been with Alderton's about six months when, immediately after winning the "Formula Ford" car race at the Kylami Racetrack and being the overnight flavour of the month, DANNY VANISHED FROM SOUTH AFRICA TO INSTANTLY REAPPEAR, large as life and out of easy legal touch, IN ENGLAND.

Luckily, I had previously received offers from other dealers in the new car retail business, including Toyota dealers Lawsons and Dan Perkins, and a quick phone call to Ted Moore at Lawsons gave me an immediate start with them. I started selling Toyotas at retail level, then was quickly employed as Lawsons' TOYOTA FLEET SALES MANAGER and was doing very well. Lawsons were also Mazda and Renault dealers, and had been offered the inviting, sole Mazda Assembly and Distribution

---

[38] Central Business District

rights for South Africa, so long as they dropped the competing Toyota franchise.

At that precise time, I was unfortunately in the middle of negotiations with the South African General Electric (G.E.) Company and close to finalising a deal for 52 Toyota Hi Ace panel vans and 2 Dyna light trucks, with generous sales commissions I would lose if, and when, Lawsons lost the Toyota dealership. I made contact with Dan Perkins, Toyota dealers, out at suburban Springs, Brakpan and Benoni. Dan said I could start with him immediately as fleet sales rep, but to forget about the G.E. deal, as he already had that particular deal tied up and "IN THE BAG". I then learned that IMPERIAL MOTORS, just around the corner from Lawsons in Commissioner Street, Jo'burg, had been appointed the new Toyota dealers to replace Lawsons. Having a vested interest, Percy Abelkop invited me to join Imperial Motors and deliver the G.E. Toyotas from their sales floor, FOR WHICH I, not Dan Perkins, who had told me earlier that they had the G.E. deal "in the bag", RECEIVED THE FULL COMMISSION!

Importantly, at that time, I also sold six Toyota 4WD Land Cruisers to the UNITED STATES STEEL COMPANY (U.S. Steel) for use in mineral exploration work in BOTSWANA, an adjoining independent African nation (formerly the Bechuanaland Protectorate, or "B.P."), just across the border and North-West of South Africa. During conversations with U.S. Steel exploration personnel, I mentioned I had been involved in similar extensive projects in mining and exploration work in Australia and New Zealand. I was immediately invited to join U.S. Steel in Botswana.

I have already told this part of the "whole" story, slightly differently, in Story 19, "A Shower of Sparks", but it is important here for understanding my long, unfolding journey of inventing the Carr-B-Q.

****

So after nearly three years in South Africa, there I was driving a Land Cruiser I had previously sold to my new employers, driving along with the rest of the exploration party, as well as a Bedford 4X4, truck, West from Jo'burg, past Magaliesburg and Mafeking, the site of the famous "SIEGE OF MAFEKING", for which Lord Baden Powell (later founder of the Boy Scouts) achieved hero status, and across the border into BOTSWANA. Then on through Sir Seretse Khama's small, modern capital city, GABERONES, continuing past FRANCISTOWN and its large B.G.I. (Botswana Game Industries), WHERE MOST OF FRESHLY SLAIN AFRICA WAS CURRENTLY BEING STUFFED WHOLESALE by skilled taxidermists. Then North past Nata and its tenuous cattle ranching country – tenuous since lions and beef cattle are an unfortunate mix – and through the natural, still-untouched, unfenced, wild, open African bush, some of it jungle, to KASANE on the mighty Zambezi River, directly South of Zambia and about 100 miles upstream and West from the giant Victoria Falls in Rhodesia.

Butchering for meat a culled elephant in the Wankie game reserve

****

Kasane is the small Botswana town where the actress Elizabeth Taylor later remarried Richard Burton, promising a small medical facility for the use of the village in appreciation for African hospitality, for which, over 30 years later, as a point of general interest, THEY ARE STILL WAITING.

****

A few days were spent at Kasane, organising various things, where I met PAT CARR- HARTLEY (no relation), the local BIG GAME HUNTER, who held shooting concession rights over a few thousand square miles of the local area for international hunters wishing to shoot elephants, lions and the still-standing rest of living Africa.

We then ventured about 90 miles South, back down along the Nata track and about 30 miles West towards the Shinamba Hills, two little pointedly erect "tits" sticking up in the bush. We were an exploration party of about 30 persons, about 25 being Indigenous Africans, and had our very first brush with lions the very first night when, about midnight, I was interrupted having a "pee" outside my tent after tending the low-burning campfire. Standing in my birthday suit, unknowingly in front of a hidden and unseen lion, I had clearly offered a defenceless target. Having finished my pee, I stooped down, picked up and threw a large piece of wood into the still glowing embers of our campfire, sending up a GREAT SHOWER OF SPARKS which was accompanied by the GREAT SNORT OF A STARTLED LION as it sprang away back into the masking bushes, thankfully frightened by THE GODS OF FIRE, who at this time were fortunately on my side.

****

The next morning, the Africans quickly set to work digging six-inch diameter postholes, about a foot apart around the proposed building sites scratched loosely in the dirt, for building our 10 x 10 LION-

RESISTING ACCOMMODATION HUTS. This is when a series of "GUM POLES" were erected and tamped down firmly in their shallow, sandy holes, and YARDS OF GALVANISED BARBED WIRE were fastened, winding around and around the outside, about every foot of the rather odd small buildings being constructed, but leaving rudimentary space for a strong proper bolted door and small, square, glass-free, always-open, perpetually-clean windows.

At this time, additional two-inch wire chicken mesh was wrapped right around the horizontal barbed wire as further "Felis Leo" safety precautions. Then great bolts of hessian fabric were wrapped right around the outside of the building, and the barbed wire and the hessian were then tacked in place with u-shaped nails to the gum poles.

Then, OUT CAME THE WATERPROOF WHEELBARROW as a mobile liquids container, with A VERY THIN CEMENT AND SALTWATER MIX, which was painted on the outside of the hessian fabric using a soft broom as a giant paint brush. After less than an hour, the liquid cement-coated hessian was bone dry, wind and waterproof, and when flicked with a fingernail, sounded seemingly as hard as a rock. The purpose of the salt in the water was to attract and retain a little ambient moisture from the air in the otherwise dry mix to STOP DRY-WEATHER CEMENT FLAKING in the bone-dry Kalahari conditions.

At this time, the roofs were clad in sheets of new overlapping galvanised iron, brought up from Jo'burg in the Bedford 4 x 4, and the strong new doors were securely fitted. Then outward-looking window apertures on all four sides of the little building were completed so you could always see If lions were within 20 yards before ducking out for a quick pee in daylight. Night-time outside comfort excursions were, of course, obviously a definite NO, NO (we had to use a plastic bucket as a chamber pot!).

SO THERE WE WERE IN CUTE, LION-PROOF HOUSES in the African wilds. If a lion tried he simply couldn't get in, for underneath the flimsy canvas was a wall of barbed, galvanised fencing wire, then shape-holding chicken wire, and the gum poles were so close together – like the real bars of a lion cage – that a full-sized lion could not pass through the 12-inch gap between the vertical, parallel timbers.

****

Lions sorted, we had A MORE IMMEDIATE RISK FROM SNAKES. Our camp was around a large mopani tree (whose fermented fruit lying on the ground was, by the way, when in season, a favourite source of alcohol for the elephants). The mopani tree, with a lot of dead wood silhouetted against the sky, revealed a snake or two 80 feet up in the wood. It represented real and present DANGER. So I was asked to dispatch the threat with my .300 Winchester Magnum rifle.

The powerful bullet blew the eight-inch hollow log in the top of the tree to pieces, unexpectedly landing about A DOZEN VERY MUCH ALIVE "BLACK MAMBAS" in our midst! Our African workers set to work tooth and nail with crowbars, shovels and big lumps of wood, and quickly remedied the otherwise ever-present reptilian threat.

****

During the next few months I had a few other brief encounters with lions, two of which could have turned out badly but didn't, and several other episodes, usually after stopping for a pee when driving, only to discover lions close by, idly watching with a certain disquieting interest, as I innocently went about my pressing personal business.

I have told these stories earlier in more detail in "A SHOWER OF SPARKS", "THE SHINAMBA HILLS TRACK", "LIONS: IT HAPPENS",

"SIESTA INTERRUPTUS" and "CATTLE COUNTRY LIONS OF NATA". Each time I think about them I remember different details.

****

It was during this time at the SHINAMBA HILLS that I finally unearthed my Adelaide- sourced NATTY B.B.Q. from hidden storage in the bottom of my trunk for use in the Botswana bush. When put to use, its several inherent faults quickly became self- evident. By this time I had travelled down from Kasane, Botswana a few times via the sealed roads inside neighbouring Rhodesia to Johannesburg via Beit Bridge and back, and also travelled once a week to the small, neat, tourist township of VICTORIA FALLS, 90 miles across the Rhodesian border for groceries and mail, and I liked what I saw.

****

Finally, I had had enough of lions I sometimes couldn't see, the African bush and a lack of facilities such as running water, and I thought maybe I could plant roots in Rhodesia for a while and make a very much improved bush B.B.Q. loosely based on the original NATTY B.B.Q.. It was time to enjoy life in what seemed to be "Swinging

Rhodesia". I then promptly resigned from U.S. Steel and travelled to BULAWAYO in my Toyota Crown station wagon, took a small flat and rented a small workshop to fiddle with my long-latent BUSH B.B.Q. CONCEPT.

It was then I realised the horizontal support rod on the original NATTY B.B.Q. badly needed a handle in order to effectively raise or lower the cooking grill, and so I ADDED A CURVED HANDLE from near the central rod end of the B.B.Q. high up, then over, matching the outer extremity of the lower horizontal arm.

This VERY IMPORTANT MODIFICATION meant the entire handle, with its attached grill and food items, could easily be raised and/ or removed completely from the fire, and/ or lowered down anytime by a simple LIFTING AND TAKING THE LOCKING GRIP OFF THE UPRIGHT MOUNTING ROD; a simple and easy operation. The extra weight of the added handle also appreciably increased the off-set weight of the combined arm and handle, and meant the small, height-adjusting "thumbscrew"-fitted part of the NATTY B.B.Q. was NO LONGER NECESSARY, as the increased weight of the new concept enabled the moveable assembly to lock in place simply, held in position by its own offset weight.

****

At this point in time I had temporarily ceased fiddling with the now greatly modified B.B.Q. and was working for FIELD TECHNICAL SALES LTD as their Matebeleland sales representative. Field were agents for Norton abrasives and other light industrial equipment, and I travelled throughout the territory of Southern Rhodesia on sales business.

When in the ASBESTOS MINING TOWN OF SHABANI, I bought a ticket in the PLUMTREE LOTTO DRAW under the name J.C. Aussie, and a few days later was asked by our manager Bert Douglas if I had recently bought a ticket in a lottery.

Thinking hard, I realised I had, and had won the third prize of $3000, whereas the first prize was $10,000; not something to be sneezed at at that time.

As a result of my small winnings, I resigned from Field's and headed back to South Australia from Rhodesia for a visit to my elderly mother, caught up with all and sundry in Adelaide, flew up to Hong Kong with Johnno Johnson M.D. of Godfreys Vacuum Cleaners and a fellow member of the Game Fishing Club of South Australia, and carried on to London for a few weeks staying with my old English mate latterly from Johannesburg, RICHARD CHALMERS, at his mother's lovely country cottage at Holmbury St. Marys near Dorking in Surrey, then to Cairo, Nairobi and back to Rhodesia.

****

So, back in Bulawayo I joined the I.M.F. Machinery Company as their Matebeleland sales representative and commenced calling on industry and the mines of Southern Rhodesia. At this time I had re-pegged a number of old, Victorian-era gold mines (some of which had in the past been very rich), my best prospect being the "INGUBO", which had once yielded 3,000 ounces of gold from a single ton of rock, or 8,000 ounces overall from 12,000 tons of gold-bearing ore. I had produced a few ounces of mainly fine specimen gold while investigating the INGUBO and still working at I.M.F.

By about 1977, Rhodesia as a whole was in deep trouble, largely cut off from the outside world by international trade restrictions and embargoes. Petrol was severely rationed and the price of gold was still pegged at its 1934 price of U.S. $34 per ounce. The small nation was suffering as MR. MUGABE AND HIS FELLOW TERRORISTS SOUGHT TO TAKE OVER AT THE POINT OF A GUN. A NUMBER OF PEOPLE I KNEW HAD ALREADY BEEN MURDERED BY TERRORISTS.

Two African workers in my employ, when driving to the INGUBO early one morning, were blown up and killed. Clearly I had been the intended victim. Luckily for me I had changed my plans due to unexpected business matters in Bulawayo. The YOUNG RECENTLY MARRIED GEOLOGIST I knew at the Bulawayo Museum, who had loaned me the museum's "Woods Black Light" for finding the fluorescent Wolfram metal Scheelite in the dark, WAS LATER SHOT DEAD while on weekend army patrol in the rugged Zambezi escarpment opposite Zambia. And A LIKEABLE AUSTRALIAN NURSE, whom I had met a couple of times when she was working for Nestles, travelling in remote tribal areas to promote Lactogen to the local African nursing mothers, WAS HACKED TO PIECES with cane knives or "pangas" by terrorists hiding in an isolated African kraal.

IT WAS CLEARLY TIME TO GET OUT!

I left everything where it was – mining machinery, compressors, drills, Holman James' Tables, Gallagher Tables and a five-foot Ball Mill – all good working machinery. THERE WERE NO BUYERS. Virtually every non-Indigenous person in Rhodesia was a "seller" and wanted out.

****

And so I arrived back in Adelaide, South Australia, aged 43, with inside-out empty pockets. For a few weeks I sold Alfa Romeos for Pissano Motors, then Valiants, on their dying legs, for Southland Chrysler at Edwardstown, while seeking opportunity elsewhere.

Then prospects brightened up when I was employed by Mindrill Ltd. (a Victorian- based company manufacturing "Diamond" drilling equipment), Diamond Drill Bits and Associated Diamond Drillers (A.D.D.) – the Diamond Drilling Contractors – as their West Australian manager, based in the gold mining city of KALGOORLIE. A year later I was transferred to head office in WEST HEIDELBERG, VICTORIA, as the company was bought, then slowly strangled to death, by its new American owner, the rival Longyear company. Again I had to look elsewhere.

While still tenuously employed by Mindrill in Victoria, I saw a position advertised by a major U.S. Mining and Manufacturing Company, INGERSOL-RAND, for a Tasmanian manager, based in the offices of their Tasmanian-appointed agents, NOYES BROS, at Moonah in HOBART. I successfully applied for the position while Mindrill closed down behind me in Melbourne. It was then I started my employment with Ingersol-Rand in Tasmania.

****

It just happens my very favourite pastime was/ is trout fishing. In Tasmania I was in my absolute chosen element. TASMANIA REALLY WAS MY "OYSTER!"

****

I was in Tasmania at a very good time. The small natural Lake Pedder had recently been greatly enlarged by a number of small, high-level dam walls across several of the high-altitude outflowing rivers, enlarging the small original lake by about 100 times in area, which had been completed just a few years before my arrival. Trout fishing in these still blooming, almost virgin waters was fantastic; 15 to 20-pound catches guaranteed! TROUT PHOTOS were regularly in the "Mercury" or on T.V. My best was a 14-pound Brown Trout, while I was beaten by my old friend, ROBERT TEMME, who did better with a 17-pound monster.

I had purchased a small fiberglass, 10-foot catamaran-type, outboard motor-driven boat and fitted it with a 10 horsepower Evinrude motor for my weekend fishing enjoyment. At this time I ventured the full 20-mile length of the lake to the South end and was caught out suddenly by inclement weather. The temperature dropped, it rained, it hailed, it blew, icy water was somehow trickling down the small of my back under my ill-fitting waterproof rain jacket, and I was HUDDLED UP and SHIVERING LIKE BUGGERY when I saw a roaring, inviting CAMPFIRE, BLAZING HOT on a small island. Naturally I headed straight for it.

With cold and shaking hands I dragged my small boat up out of the water and asked the jovial "FIRE GODS" standing around the heat of the campfire if they would mind if I joined them in their invigorating huddle.

"NOT AT ALL. COME AND JOIN US".

That campfire was an absolute Godsend as they introduced me to "STONES DRY GINGER", a potent drop, which quickly stopped my incessant shivering, desensitised my mouth and somehow began to defrost my shaking "mits".[39] It was then I noticed my new-found saviours, ARTHUR WARD, owner of the Avon Court Holiday apartments in Hobart, and his young friends JUNE AND ROB from Adelaide, were trying to cook a good-sized trout, about a 10-pounder, suspended vertically from a long wooden skewer impaled sideways through its gills, the tail being RAPIDLY CREMATED in the mire of the fire, and the COOL TROUT'S HEAD GAZING DESPAIRINGLY SKYWARDS, ALMOST SHIVERING, INTO THE COLD, GREY, BLEAK, WINDSWEPT SKY.

I said, "I see you've got a bit of a problem. Just a moment, I've got a B.B.Q. here that should rectify matters", and produced one of my prototype barbecues, set it up in seconds, lay the partly-cooked trout on one side, then the other, and finished the cooking in a few short minutes.

"Wow! Where did you get that?", was the joint question on their united lips. "It's great, where did you get it?" I explained it was a PROTOTYPE I had been fiddling with for some time with the idea that I may make them for sale in the future. "FORGET THE FUTURE", said Arthur, "WE WANT TO BUY TWO. NOW! What's stopping you?"

This was when Rob said, "Well, if your name is CARR and you do make them commercially, WHY DON'T YOU CALL THEM 'CARR-B-Qs'?"

And since that high point moment in history, THANKS ROB, I have!

---

[39] "Mits" is a slang term for hands

Arthur Ward and Me at Lake Pedder Tasmania about 1980

Arthur Ward, John Carr, and Arthur's daughters at rear, and June and Rob, who actually named my B.B.Q. the CARR-B-Q. (I owe you one R ob)

Arthur Ward using a CARR-B-Q at Airlie Beach QLD in 1981

Back in Hobart about lunch time a couple of days later, I went into the local hardware shop at Kingston and enquired about various forms of inexpensive, RUST-PROOF COATINGS FOR PROTECTING BARBECUES FROM RUST. "What sort of barbecue?" asked the proprietor, quizzically, so I said, "Look, it's a bit hard to explain, but I've got one in the car. There's a strip of lawn outside your shop. I'll show you!"

Within a minute I had taken my prototype from the car and had it erected on the lawn to the amazement of the hardware shop proprietor. After deliberating for at least one second, he said, LET'S KNOW WHEN YOU'VE MADE THE FIRST TEN. SUBJECT TO PRICE, I'LL TAKE THEM". I went on to explain the many hoped-for attributes and advantages of the CARR-B-Q (or C.B.Q. for short). I was just about to dismantle the prototype C.B.Q and pack up when a gentleman who had been watching quietly and unobtrusively in the background said, "Before you put it away, my name is Richard Hunn, I'm the A.B.C. Channel 2 T.V. reporter for Hobart. Would you tell me first, IS IT NEW? IS IT YOUR IDEA? And if it is, would you mind showing me again?" "Well, yes", I said, "it is my concept, and I would have to say at this time I GUESS IT IS NEW". Richard said, "If it's OK with you, I'd like to have you on A.B.C. television tonight in the two-minute slot between the weather finishing at 6.58 and the nightly NEWS at 7:00 p.m.".

I went through the concept again and Richard said, "RIGHT, LET'S GET CRACKING. How about you getting your barbecue paraphernalia, tables and chairs, and we'll meet you on the lawns of the WATERWORKS RESERVE on the lower foothills of Mount Wellington at 3:00 p.m. for a B.B.Q. We'll supply the meat and drinks".

I was amazed at my good luck; it was like winning the lottery. Again. I went to my home in nearby Blackmans Bay, gathered my C.B.Q. bits and pieces, and then as an afterthought phoned the Hobart "Mercury" newspaper and told them the A.B.C. were about to film a

"NEW TASMANIAN INVENTION" – a very UNUSUAL BARBECUE APPARATUS – at the Waterworks Reserve, which would be on A.B.C. T.V. that night. I went on to suggest that the "Mercury" journalists and photographers arrive on site at 5:00 p.m., and perhaps bring some chops etc. and LIQUID REFRESHMENTS for the hereafter!

Mount Wellington behind Hobart, a view from my house at Blackmans Bay

Mount Wellington behind Hobart, a view from my house at Blackmans Bay They thanked me profusely in advance for my thoughtful information and accepted my invitation with heartfelt pleasure, and subsequently an impressive story and very good photo appeared in the Hobart Mercury the next morning. The A.B.C. and I came together on time at 3:00 p.m. and the "CARR-B-Q" demonstration went off without a hitch, except it was very detailed, thorough and overran it's time allocation so that the Mercury reporters arrived before the A.B.C. T.V. reporters had started to leave, which was slightly embarrassing.

The A.B.C. report at two minutes to seven on Channel 2 T.V. went very well indeed! I couldn't have done better if I was in fact actually paying for it! I was told a two-minute T.V. exposure at PRIME TIME WOULD OTHERWISE COST TENS OF THOUSANDS OF DOLLARS.

In hindsight, I REALLY WISH TO THANK MY LUCKY STARS.

Hobart Mercury photo of the Carr-B-Q and Me in 1979

I was still surprised when the next morning, Friday, at about 7:00 a.m., there was a very authoritative knock on my door at Blackman's Bay. A tall, greying gentleman with a voice from deepest Texas said, "My name is Richard Porter. I have here in my hand a cheque made out to you for $10,000, which I would be pleased for you to accept for a discussion about the American market for the 'Carr-B-Q'. Would you accept it?"

SO MUCH SO FAST. My feeble mind tried to think. "The Hobart Agricultural Show starts in two weeks, Ingersol-Rand are in the process of transferring me to their Tasmanian representatives, Noyes Bros, who pay a lower overall commission on sales…". This was tenuously pressing on my mind.

If I make a hundred "Carr-B-Qs" in two short weeks, take a stand at the show and sell them, it could be the start of something more to my liking. So I SHOOK HANDS WITH RICHARD PORTER, accepted his cheque, went to work, handed in my resignation that day and resigned forthwith. I then got busy and that same day bought a new Toyota Hi-Lux 4WD utility with a F.G. canopy, and went home for lunch. I also purchased a new "Brobo" cold-saw to "cleanly cut stainless steel without burring", an electric welder, etc., etc., and after lunch received a phone call from my bank that RICHARD PORTER'S CHEQUE HAD BEEN RETURNED MARKED "INSUFFICIENT FUNDS".

NOW WHAT???

Back on the phone to Mr. Porter. PANIC STATIONS. I had issued cheques that morning which were only partially covered. "Say John", said the Yankee drawl, "I didn't think you'd act so fast. Please re-present, I'm sure it will all be OK". And phew, at last, it was.

****

I arranged manufacture of the B.B.Q, ROUND WIRE GRILLS by A.R.C. Engineering in Hobart and instantly hired a young unemployed chap through "Centrelink" to give me a hand.[40] We then we set to work in my workshop at Blackmans Bay, cutting, bending, welding, grinding, turning on my lathe … and finished 100 mounting rods and shaped handles to complete my part of the NEW "Carr-B-Qs".

This was just in time for the chrome platers who did me a special favour and released the bright and shiny new chrome-plated C.B.Q, stock to me the last night before the Show was due to start. At this time, the A.B.C. "INVENTORS" was a popular, current, standalone inventors' program on National A.B.C. T.V., and the first remark I heard about the new "CARR-B-Q" from a passer-by at the Hobart Show was, "I saw it on the Inventors the other night!", which of course was not true. It had been just before the regular, nightly A.B.C. News, on Channel 2, while the actual Inventors show for me was still, hopefully, yet to come.

****

Instant success! I sold all my C.B.Q.s at the Hobart Show, after retaining a few for other "demo" and special client interests, including one I gave to the T.V. cooking talk-show host, Peter Russell Clark. I was very encouraged by my early success at the Show and did a quick run-around of outdoor stockists, hardware shops and the like in Hobart, and found Carr-B-Qs were easy to sell to retail shop proprietors, especially if interested customers, with curious open eyes and ears, were present in the store at the time I was demonstrating to the shopkeeper.

I made up several hundred more C.B.Q.s while living in Tasmania and sold them throughout the small Island State over a few months. I managed to catch a lot of trout at the same time!

****

---

[40] Centrelink is an Australian Government welfare service

IT WAS THEN I RECEIVED A VISIT TO MY HOME AT BLACKMANS BAY FROM BEVERLY GLEDHILL AND PAUL BELFANTI, THE ACTUAL PRODUCERS OF THE

A.B.C.'s "THE INVENTORS". After seeing the CARR-B-Q for the first time, they advised me they liked it and that I would shortly be on the program.

A few weeks went by and I eventually received a letter on an A.B.C. letterhead from Beverly Gledhill saying, "REGRETS, CANNOT USE YOUR INVENTION ON "THE INVENTORS" SHOW, signed Beverly Gledhill". I couldn't believe it. Beverly and Paul had both been very enthusiastic about my chances of success on the "Inventors" and now they had knocked me right out, with one punch; KO'd, kaput and finito. So be it!

MY HOPES WERE DASHED. I PHILOSOPHICALLY WITHDREW INTO THE CRAMPED, TIGHT CONFINES OF MY TINY SHELL FOR THE REST OF MY SAD AND SORRY NIGHT.

****

The next day I was very surprised to receive an impressive letter from T.V. Station Channel 9 about A BRAND-NEW INVENTORS PROGRAM to be entitled, "What'll They Think of Next", offering PRIZE MONEY of $2,000 to the winner of each weekly segment. "JOHN, LOVE TO HAVE YOU ON OUR NEW SHOW, signed Beverley Gledhill". WOW!

A couple of weeks later I received return air tickets from Hobart to Sydney for filming the third weekly edition of "What'll They Think of Next", and away I went to Channel 9 in Sydney. Two other contestants and I were exposed to the judging panel, which was in fact the entire transposed judging panel from the original A.B.C. "Inventors", who had all "jumped ship together", with one exception, Dianna Fisher, daughter of the Archbishop of Canterbury. Dianna is of course still fondly remembered for her trademark remarks at the original A.B.C. "Inventors" show; "IS IT SAFE?" "WHAT COLOURS DOES IT COME IN?" "WILL IT FIT IN MY MINI?".

Anyway, the judging commenced. A few nervous moments, various questions asked, then "the WINNER IS … JOHN CARR with his 'CARR-B-Q' barbecue". Elated and shaking hands, I was handed a framed A4 sized, GOLD-PLATED PLAQUE from the sponsors, the Beaurepaire Tyre and Rubber Company, and their very handy winner's cheque for $2,000.

****

Within days I started receiving various offers from industry and the public, but unfortunately none of marriage! I did have an offer from the Spring Division of the FORD MOTOR PLANT at Geelong, who had considerable spare light engineering, manufacturing capacity available, and one expression of interest from ROYTAL, the sheltered workshop division of the Royal Talbot Hospital in Kew. Roytal were also the main training centre for Guide Dogs in Melbourne, Victoria, and offered to manufacture and package Carr-B-Qs for me in "STRONG" cardboard cartons, as well as offering me an open monthly account; an offer too good to refuse. So I accepted and away I went, full steam ahead. I later crossed Bass Straight from Tasmania in the overnight ferry, collected NEW CARR-B-Q stock made by Roytal at Kew, loaded it into my new, fully-enclosed trailer towed behind my new Toyota Hi-Lux, and set forth with a silent "Whoopee" into the fray.

Calling on a camping goods shop or a hardware store, I would see the owner and without being able to hammer the Carr-B-Q rod into the floor, would as best I could show him how it worked. Sometimes the proprietor was only half interested but his eyes began to sparkle when various customers in the shop showed more obvious interest and were ready to buy direct from me if he was not interested. A single Carr- B-Q sale then usually became five or 10. I had a major problem though. I was selling just a one only, single product hand to mouth, and constantly driving ahead to new Carr-B-Q pastures. My CARR-B-Q was a brand-new product which was very difficult to stand up and display without drilling a special hole in the floor for the rod.

I had no spare money for any form of printed brochures or advertising, and certainly none at all for T.V., which was badly needed, as unfortunately one single T.V. exposure would use up my entire working capital in a single GULP! All I could do was demonstrate to the actual proprietor and very occasionally a member of their vital counter sales staff, if I was lucky. And even if the CARR-B-Q was fortunate enough to be mounted with the half-inch rod located in a specially drilled hole in the floor, in its correct operational attitude, IT WAS USUALLY LOADED UP WITH ALL SORTS OF OFF-PUTTING, NON-BARBECUE ITEMS, such as paint brochures etc., as being a foreign, integral stand; a part of their general non-barbecue-related display department and not a sales item.

Very, very occasionally the person behind the counter may be a RARE GEM; an instant and astute judge of a customer's potential. A young guy may come into the shop. The astute proprietor, identifying a likely prospect, quickly engages his brain and may say something like, "YOU LOOK LIKE YOU MIGHT DO A BIT OF HUNTING or FISHING?", and invariably the answer is, "WELL, YES I DO, AS A MATTER OF FACT", while the shopkeeper quickly re-engages his brain and responds, "SIT AROUND THE ODD CAMP-FIRE?" "OF COURSE!", was invariably the answer. "HAVE A LOOK AT THIS THEN", says the shopkeeper, and magically produces the strange, martian-looking CARR-B-Q for a first time ever glance. The shopkeeper shows how it works as the young guy's eyes light right up, he says he has never seen a B.B.Q, like it before, and if he is financial, a minute later he walks out with a

CARR- B-Q snuggled under his arm. I promise it has happened like this many times.

The only trouble is the scene described was not the usual sales scene. Generally counter staff may be on deck from 9 to 5, with an hour off for lunch. Sales staff have many odd items to sell, and morning and afternoon tea interrupts sales proceedings. They have absolutely NO INCENTIVE TO SELL any particular item, let alone a product without any detailed information, since they have thousands of dissimilar items to sell, and being counter staff without incentives, they usually couldn't care less. "IF NOT ASKED THEY WON'T OFFER".

Usually if the product is/ was an item such as the CARR-B-Q, without advertising material they didn't know how it worked, how it assembled, or what it's many practical advantages over any other B.B.Qs were. And in any case, why should they take sides?

****

I purchased over a hundred unsold Carr-B-Qs back from K-Mart in Sydney at their throw out price of $5 each, and PROMPTLY RE-SOLD THEM TO OTHER LOCAL SHOPS, "SPECIAL WHOLESALE", at $15 each within days! This was because K- Mart had absolutely no idea what the CARR-B-Q was! In their limp hands it was "effectively a dead duck!"

Fortunately, I did manage to get on local T.V. stations around Australia, "FREE", as a local News item a number of times, including in Mt Isa, Darwin, Alice Springs, Cairns, Townsville and Rockhampton. The trouble was I had left town the next morning before the previous night's T.V. exposure could have had any helpful effect, as I was desperately scrambling for cash and simply put, had to drive on to thin pastures in the South, or greener or distant outback pastures in established CARR-B-Q outback territory in the distant North, or inland North and West.

****

At that time, the original CARR-B-Q handle and grill was fabricated from cheaper chrome-plated, mild steel, while the half-inch rod was cadmium plated, which was a mistake. In prolonged use, the up/ down movement of the sliding joint handle quickly wore the soft cadmium plating off the rod and RUST easily set in if not continually cleaned, dried, and/ or kept oiled.

Likewise, A COUPLE OF CHROME-PLATED GRILLS STARTED BUBBLING AND FLAKING after being thoughtlessly left over a very hot campfire. This had SERIOUS LONG-TERM IMPLICATIONS WHICH HAD TO BE FIXED; that is, fixed the expensive way. Bite the bullet and make the entire Carr-B-Q from more expensive, but very much tougher, rustless stainless steel. UP WENT MY COST PRICE!

****

Sales in Southern Australia near the capital cities were seasonal and slow, but the further and further North or West I went across Australia, the better they were (while my expenses also increased disproportionally in the opposite direction!).

Seasonal bushfire restrictions meant Carr-B-Qs could rarely be used in summer near the major cities and not at all in national parks, but most purchasers were unaware of the law relating to fires just used for "COOKING". Sensible fire laws do allow use of Carr-B-Qs on days of undeclared fire risk, so long as PROPER WIDTH FIRE BREAKS are made about 30 feet in diameter (which only take minutes to clear with a rake) and a bucket of dousing water is on hand.

The CARR-B-Q REALLY COMES INTO ITS OWN when well away from cities, convention and civilisation IN THE ARID OUTBACK, THE BUSH, THE INLAND and NORTHERN AUSTRALIA, where 4WD drivers meeting on a little used bush track sometimes pull over for a yarn, maybe "boil a billy",[41] and perhaps grill a chop or two, or make a bit of toast before driving on.

The usually dry Australian climate and outback terrain is highly inducive to use of the CARR-B-Q. The bush is usually dry, long-dead fallen timber is everywhere, and tinder dry grass and leaves are usually right underfoot as instant, always ready-to-use, paper-free kindling.

In Broken Hill I made myself known to the celebrated BUSH ARTIST, JACK ABSALOM, who IMMEDIATELY FELL IN LOVE WITH THE CARR-B-Q CONCEPT and bought a number from me to give away as presents to friends and relations. He told me he was in the finishing stages of writing a book to be entitled "Cooking in the Camp Oven" and would include the CARR-B-Q in it, as he did, but WITHOUT A SINGLE WORD OR MENTION OF MY TRADEMARK NAME, THE "CARR-B-Q"!

Jack's book came out the next year and as far as I know is still in print. Just inside the front cover, Jack's brother Reg appears in a round photo using the CARR-B-Q.

I then sold over 600 chrome-plated model Carr-B-Qs over several weeks in Darwin in 1980, my best ever, followed up by a very healthy 222 in Alice Springs shortly after. I then ran completely out of stock.

****

I had to twiddle my toes in the Alice for six weeks while awaiting new stock to arrive on pallets by rail from far off Melbourne, and when they arrived on open, unprotected pallets, nearly all THE SO-CALLED "STRONG" CARDBOARD CARTONS WERE SQUASHED FLAT, useless and totally UNSALEABLE, unless offered for sale at give-away prices. I was now operating very frugally, day-to-day, hand-to-mouth.

---

[41] Make a can full of tea over a fire

Failed Times and Twisted Follies

Whereas I had earlier been staying in hotels and motels, operating money was becoming a major problem and now I had to endure three more weeks waiting for new, replacement cartons to arrive in Alice Springs for labour-intensive re-packing by me. To fill in tons of empty time while waiting, I borrowed a Whites metal detector from Bruce Chalmers, owner of the Stuart Arms Hotel, and collected a number of small, nickel-iron meteorites from the Henbury craters about 70 miles south of the Alice. I was now living in back-packer level accommodation, and disastrously, on reflection, looking back 30 years later, "All was not peaches and cream".

****

Squashed flat Carr-B-Qs on arrival in Alice Springs, 1981

I HAVE NOT BEEN BACK TO THE TERRITORY SINCE 1981 TO SHOW THE ALL NEW, ALL STAINLESS CARR-B-Q. I HAVE NEVER TRIED THE INTERNET OR E-BAY, but am just about to explore those rather obvious avenues using my one finger computer typing expertise.

I have in the past visited most of the 4WD clubs in Sydney, with considerable success. The large Toyota Club was highly successful about 20 years ago, where I made about 60 sales to a very large gathering of over 600 members. The smaller Range Rover Club was also good, about five years ago, with about 15 sales to about 80 members – a better strike rate – while I still remember the smaller Suzuki, Subaru, Land-Rover etc. and other similar clubs with affection. I have not paid a visit to clubs outside the Sydney basin, let alone interstate, and I am now 80.

****

In order to show I am not quite dead, I have made and provisionally patented a smaller B.B.Q. which shares some of the original CARR-B-Q features, but not others. Importantly, it is VERY COMPACT, fits in a flat A 4 sized pack, and is intended for use by hikers, cyclists, balloonists, canoeists, horsemen, etc. In particular, it is intended for sale to foreign tourists, who may be looking for a compact, TRULY UNIQUE AUSTRALIAN-INVENTED AND MANUFACTURED SOUVENIR of Australia, since it really is unique!

The new barbecue concept is very interesting. It involves almost, but not quite endless, perpetual motion in its routine operation, and really should be seen in action over a campfire to be appreciated. It is truly an absolute pleasure to use. It will be called a "BOOMERANG BARBECUE" for reasons that become readily apparent when you see it!

I guess I should get off my backside and show it to the Boy Scouts at Prince Alfred's, my old school in Adelaide, and/ or return to the 4WD clubs in the city, and/ or AT LAST, FINALLY TRAVEL INTERSTATE FOR THE FIRST TIME IN 30 YEARS.

****

So this, then, is the up-to-date, lowly status of the CARR-B-Q and the new infant, as yet still commercially undisclosed "BOOMERANG BARBECUE", in my 80th year.

Dr Dallas Clark, of Norwood using the original model CARR-B-Q at his holiday shack somewhere near the Murray River

The Absolute End!

Well, not quite …

79.
MEMORIES OF MY FATHER, JOHN EDWIN CARR

My name is Francis Louis Carr, "Frank" to my friends. I am John Carr's son living in New Zealand.

I was born at the Mater Hospital in Epsom, Auckland, New Zealand, on the 14th of January 1966 and brought up in Takapuna, Auckland, by my mother and her parents, Lou & Ween Metcalfe.

What I knew of my father, when I was young, was that my parents were separated. My mother had stayed in touch with John's mother Dorothy (who secretly forwarded my cards & photos to John).

In 1978 my gran had bought her ticket and was looking forward to meeting us in New Zealand. Sadly, my gran died before the trip.

I had no contact with John until I first spoke with him on the phone at my 21st Birthday party (1987). My mother had been in touch with Aunt Pam and organised it. My mother and I travelled to Sydney and visited with John not long after and John escorted us on some excursions to places of interest (Blue mountains/ Coffs Harbour/ Mossman/ Double Bay).

Following that I visited Australia numerous times, getting to know him a little better each time.

On one occasion John had organised a trip for us from Sydney to Adelaide in his Toyota Landcruiser. We lurched into the journey on his somewhat square 'off-road' tyres from his place in Beaconsfield and found ourselves in heavy Sydney traffic. We approached a roundabout intersection and waited for quite some time behind a car driven by a very hesitant driver. Opportunities to enter the intersection came and went, and still the driver hesitated. I said to my Dad, "This guy is never going to go, give him a toot on the horn!" For some reason, best known to John, the Landcruiser was equipped with a mighty truck horn below the bonnet.

Anyway, John gave him a polite toot, whereupon the startled driver leaped into the intersection and promptly had a collision with traffic already on the roundabout. Now that the way was clear we went on our way, raising an eyebrow at the curiosity as we passed. How inconvenient…

I soon came to learn that John Carr was an enigma and had lived an extraordinary life already.

The first place we visited in Adelaide was a pub in Waterfall Gully where he went straight up behind someone playing at the pool table and smacked the back of his cue just as he was about to make the shot. When the bloke swung around I thought he was going to swing for John – then he recognised him, and we sat down and had a beer together. John was like that.

If you knew him, then nothing he did could really surprise you. His affairs were in chaos; however, that was just normal. I came to accept that.

So when John started to enter dementia the transition was subtle. If he did something, or made a radical decision, it was impossible to draw a line between whether it was a reasoned and crazy decision in a way John of old would make, or the illness taking over. He called me a couple of times in recent years (before hospitalisation), distressed that he had realised he might have made some bad decisions. It was then that I realised that he was losing control of his destiny. I think he had realised that too. He fought it, but reluctantly accepted help. He was a little like the Sulphur Crested Cockatoo with a broken beak that we found on the side of the road from Narrabri to Wee Waa. The poor bird would never have let us near it otherwise, but it trusted us and knew we were trying to help.

We got it to the vet clinic – I never did know what happened to that bird, but it would have been better than starving at the roadside. He had a real empathy for animals, especially cats, and hated the fact that in the past he had done the "great white hunter" thing and shot the "top five" animals in Africa. A pyrrhic victory. It didn't bring any sense of achievement – just sadness and regret.

John was proudly independent, and so it must have really gone against the grain to accept help. His was a free spirit, so it was sad for the need for him to be in secure care in his final years.

He led a remarkable life which would surprise many and be the envy of others. He was always "the cat who walked by himself", never meant to be contained. He is free once more.

To that end I must really thank Pam & Paul Kelly for the care they have shown him, and Tim & Janet Kelly for the tower of strength and support they have provided for my Dad. I cannot thank you enough.

In 2010 I married Brigid Slykerman in Auckland. John came over for our wedding and impressed everyone with his charm and stories. Always witty, he got on well and made friends with Brigid's relatives, especially her eldest uncle Bill Slykerman. Brigid and I have a daughter, John's granddaughter, Caitlin Carr. She is 8 now and does ballet, plays piano, is learning guitar and doing swimming lessons every week. She still loves the Xmas teddy she received from John.

She is clever and creative, and I think her grandad would be proud of her.

Frank.

80.
JOHN CARR: EULOGY

We are here today to celebrate the marvelous life of John Edwin Carr. John was born at Quambi Nursing Home in Adelaide on the 8th March 1934, son of Dorothy and Terry Carr and little brother of Pam. He passed away peacefully at Glenview Homes, Gumeracha on 22nd August 2021. He was aged 87.

John was married twice. He married Eireen 'Faye' Metcalfe in Blenheim New Zealand around 1964. Their son Francis, 'Frank', was born in 1966 but John and Faye's marriage did not last. While Frank only connected with his father when he was 21, he came to know and understand John better than most, showing a keen inte rest in John's life and history. Grandchild, Caitlin Louise Faye Carr arrived to Frank and his wife Brigid in 2013. Frank made sure Caitlin had chances to meet her grandfather.

Unfortunately, Frank lives in New Zealand and could not be here today because of Covid-19 restrictions.

John's second wife Joy was 'the Rhodesian wife' and while this marriage didn't last either, John maintained that he, Joy and her subsequent husband John Brook always remained friends.

During his life, John's circle of friends and acquaintances was huge. He was kind, caring, always seeking recognition and approval, and socially oblivious at times. He had a wealth of stories about his life, explorations and adventures. Towards the end of his life, John had gathered anecdotes and stories of his life in South Africa, Botswana, Rhodesia, the NT, WA and New Zealand in a book *Failed Times and Twisted Follies* – a wealth of tales about encounters with lions, smuggling gold out of Rhodesia and rubbing shoulders with the rich, famous and interesting. One of the best of these stories was of John and his group camping in Botswana. In the middle of the night he was 'busting' to go to the toilet. He emerged from the tent naked, did the deed and as he returned to the tent decided to throw a log on the fire. A shower of sparks lit up the eyes of a pack of lions watching him at the edge of the camp. Fortunately, the shower of sparks probably saved John from becoming a midnight snack!

As a boy, John was raised to begin with on the family farm at Lipson near Tumby Bay and then Greenhill Road, Burnside with his mother, sister, extended family and others. Pam tells the story of preschool aged John hiding in the bush at the farm on Eyre Peninsula when he didn't want to come when called. His mother would pretend to be going into town and start the car and John would emerge from the scrub, afraid of missing out on the trip. In middle childhood, staying at the family beach house in Port Noarlunga, Pam and John would take off for the day unsupervised, sometimes going up the Onkaparinga River in a dingy, perhaps a foretaste of adventures to come.

Growing up at the house on Greenhill Road, John would frequently have the policeman knocking on the door to advise that John's pet kangaroo had boxed someone in the street. Towards the end of the war the family had 6 men billeted with them at Greenhill Road. Sitting on the veranda one day, one of the men saw that someone had a rifle trained on them. He took off at a low crouch and disabled the potential sniper. It was John with a rifle.

In his own words John,

'… grew up in an all-female household without the benefit of any experienced male advice or guidance readily at hand relating to my forthcoming irresponsible life and times ahead.

Failed Times and Twisted Follies

When I was halfway through my Intermediate year in 1950 I was enticed to leave school by Gary Wight P.A.C. and join NEWS LTD as a Copy Boy at TWO POUNDS A WEEK. This was the year before young Rupert Murdoch about a year or two older than me was installed by his father at the News to begin clawing his way up the long ladder to success. Rupert I am sure would have been paid a bit more than TWO POUNDS A WEEK.'

John was curious, adventurous, creative, artistic, an animal lover, driven, focussed and yet chaotic. He was a likeable strong character with natural leadership ability, poor logic and dubious priorities, often resulting in bad outcomes. Using a shotgun as a can opener was probably not such a good idea.

Some of John's achievements included being part of the team which discovered the El Sherana Uranium Mine in the Northern Territory in 1954, owning and riding two extremely fast 'Black Shadow' motor bikes, meeting the NT Indigenous couple who had disappeared for 30 years because they were the wrong skin group, and helping to reintroduce them to their people, working as a mineralogist on the construction of the Manapouri hydro station in New Zealand, winning the TV 'Inventors' competition, 'What will they think of next?' with his Carr- B-Q, goldmining in Rhodesia, managing Ingersol-Rand (Tasmanian mining company) and driving limos and buses for Murrays in Sydney. John hunted wild animals in Africa and came to regret this in later years.

Towards the end of his life, John's sister Pam Kelly persuaded, cajoled and organised for John to move to South Australia close to her and the family because his dementia was becoming worse. Tim and particularly Janet Kelly looked after John in recent years, ensured he was well cared for at Glenview Homes Gumeracha, and took him on outings and to family gatherings. As a free and adventurous spirit John often found it hard to understand that he was suffering from dementia and why he couldn't just hop into his car, hitch on the caravan and take off. He passed away peacefully with Pam and Janet close by, a nurse holding his hand, soft music and stars on the ceiling.

Susanna Jose (John's niece)

81.
Roger Klobe

(by Frank Carr)

On 17 OCTOBER 2021 my fathers little secret, Roger Klobe – my half brother, made his presence known via 'Ancestry'.

In 1951 John had an dalliance with girl a year or two older than him. She fell pregnant and apparently there was hell to pay. The girls boyfriend of the time was allegedly implicated with blame being apportioned with associated howling and gnashing of teeth. The child 'Anthony' was born on 26 June 1951 in Victoria and passed over to the Klobe family 6 days later along with a suitcase of expensive children's clothes. I knew 'of' Roger's existence for twenty years, or so, thanks to my Aunt Pam whispering in my ear – so not a surprise when his DNA match appeared on 'Ancestry'.

Roger wrote the following note to me,

'Thanks for your lovely response Frank. It's been a big life mate , lots to tell.

You have lots of relations. I have just celebrated my 50th wedding anniversary with Jenny [nee Fyfe]. We have 2 sons, David and Mark, and in between a daughter Karina. We have 16 grand children [1 in QLD, 1 in Texas] the rest in Victoria. We also have 4.5 great grandchildren.

One thing that intrigues me is why I was born in Coleraine, and of course I now live only 30K away. I lived in Nhill for 7 years, moved to a farm at Yulecart [near Hamilton] and then into town when I was 12. I had a Tech. school education, did an apprenticeship, and was an electrician for 6 years. I then joined the PMG in '73 and was a telecom tech. until 1990 when I formed a company called Sheds Galore [now run by Mark]. [check out on internet].

I have built 4 houses in and around Hamilton over the last 50 years. We currently live in the last one 3K out of town on 20 acres, overlooking the Grampians Mountains. Over the years my interests have been playing guitar [in a band in the 70's] stage lighting, SES volunteer, and British motorcycles. I restore and ride old Nortons [6] and one Triumph. I am a life member of the BSA owners club, and am looking forward to my 38th consecutive All British Rally which I ran for several years.

I was in Rotary for 20 years and am a past President and PHF. I have been living with prostate cancer for 11 years, but still have a pretty good quality of life. My adoptive family had 1 natural son who died this year aged 78. I also have a sister also adopted aged 63 in Melbourne. I was the white haired boy, and always well accepted by the extended Klobe family, so never really thought of looking for my biological parents. My mum died in1990 and dad in1994. Have travelled to UK, Ireland and of course Isle of Man, and was over your way 3 years ago. Only did the South Island and of course a week at Invercargill for the Burt Monroe festival.'

Unknown to John, it appears he was already an great great grandfather, which makes me an half 'great granduncle'. Caitlin has gained all sorts of cousins. Being adept with 'Ancestry' and over 30 years doing genealogy it did not take me long to locate Roger's mother's family. Some searching questions with my dad's remaining contemporary friends eventually yielded an name, and then more information fell out of the records. Roger's birth mother (Scottish/German descent) married a year or two later to a son of an Adelaide family of German descent. She had a daughter and two boys that I know of. We do not know if Roger's mother has passed on or not.

Roger is currently waiting on an official reply from the adoption agency to confirm his birth parent's names.

www.ingramcontent.com/pod-product-compliance
Lightning Source LLC
Chambersburg PA
CBHW051542010526
44118CB00022B/2549